MENTAL ILLNESSES AND TREATMENTS

PSYCHOPATHOLOGY

SYMPTOMS, CHALLENGES AND CURRENT CONCEPTS

Mental Illnesses and Treatments

Additional books in this series can be found on Nova's website under the Series tab.

Additional e-books in this series can be found on Nova's website under the e-books tab.

MENTAL ILLNESSES AND TREATMENTS

PSYCHOPATHOLOGY

SYMPTOMS, CHALLENGES AND CURRENT CONCEPTS

JEREMY WILLIAMS
EDITOR

New York

Library of Congress Cataloging-in-Publication Data

Library of Congress Control Number: 2016945952
ISBN: 978-1-63485-745-1

Published by Nova Science Publishers, Inc. † New York

CONTENTS

PREFACE

This book provides new research on the symptoms, challenges and current concepts of psychopathology. Chapter One reviews the stipulative definitions of poor and protective prognostic factors as applied in the field of clinical mental health. Chapter Two discusses the categorical and dimensional models of personality pathology and highlights the advantages and disadvantages associated with each perspective. Chapter Three investigates the association between the Dark Triad (DT) and early maladaptive schema domains. Chapter Four reviews the main instruments for assessing avoidance as well as treatment suggestions. Chapter Five addresses the intergenerational transmission of trauma (ITT). Chapter Six presents mental health intervention concepts on pre- and postnatal mental health. Chapter Seven focuses on the advances in the study of male psychopathy. Chapter Eight presents a relatively recent approach to help individuals deal with stress and achieve relaxation, and describes its application on two specific clinical conditions, i.e., perinatal mood disorders and eating disorders.

Chapter 1 – This chapter reviews the stipulative definitions of poor and protective prognostic factors as applied in the field of clinical mental health. In this regard, prognostic factors refer to features that positively and/or negatively influence a person's symptom presentation. Examples of these factors include, but are not limited to, education and social support. In clinical practice, these factors may be reviewed generically as either protective or guarded prognostic factors. However, the influences of these factors require contextual review if psychopathologists are to appropriately gauge the impact on the presentation. This chapter aims to illustrate the ways in which typical prognostic factors range on a continuum of positive and negative influences. Although the approach to describing these factors will be rooted in practical knowledge of everyday clinical practice, the authors review current events that may (re-)shape the influence of a given prognostic factor. Contemporary examples are cited and academic sources are used to explore the psychological impact of these events. The purpose of this approach is to engage the reader in critical thinking and petition the clinician to place emphasis on contextualizing influential features. For example, literature describes the psychological defense mechanism of 'altruism' as a probably mature functional pattern of developing self-satisfaction by serving the needs of others. Arguably, present social phenomena has pathoelaborating prowess, and suggests that the seemingly mature defense 'altruism' may have the potential to become pathological. By way of example, suicide bombers have been described as carrying out an extreme form of terrorism (on one end of the continuum), and a last plight of altruistic servitude (on the other end of the continuum). As such, a protective prognostic factor from one perspective (e.g., the patient's community) could be regarded as a poor prognostic factor from another perspective (e.g., the health care practitioner's). The question then becomes: how can we conceptualize discrepant prognostic factors? To respond to this, a critical analysis of this antithetical dynamic is offered, concluding with recommendations of a new prognostic category. The chapter does not aim to provide conclusions on the positive or negative influences of these factors, but to offer a platform for psychopathologists to evaluate (or re-revaluate) how they think about these influential features.

Chapter 2 – There has been considerable controversy during recent years regarding the conceptualization of personality pathology. An important aspect of this controversy has involved whether personality pathology should continue to be viewed according to the traditional categorical model or modified to include a dimensional perspective. The debate concerning these perspectives resulted in the most recent version of the Diagnostic and Statistical Manual of Mental Disorders (DSM-5; American Psychiatric Association, 2013) retaining the categorical model, but introducing the Alternative DSM-5 Model for Personality Disorders in Section III ("Emerging Measures and Models" in need of further study). This alternative model led to the development of the Personality Inventory for DSM-5 (PID-5; Krueger, Derringer, Markon, Watson, & Skodol, 2012) which captures the following pathological personality traits: negative affectivity, detachment, antagonism, disinhibition, and psychoticism. In this chapter, the authors will discuss the categorical and dimensional models of personality pathology and highlight the advantages and disadvantages associated with each perspective. They will also provide an overview of recent research that has utilized the PID-5 and offer potential directions for future research.

Chapter 3 – Study of the Dark Triad (DT) has been attracting researchers from several fields of psychology. Although personality traits and behaviors of Machiavellians, narcissists, and psychopaths are well-studied, little has been known about underlying cognitive constructs yet. In this study, the authors investigated the association between the DT and early maladaptive schema domains, i.e, underlying cognitive constructs. 503 adolescents (357 girls; 16.03 ± .93 years of age on average) completed self-report measures of the DT and early maladaptive schemas. Results showed Impaired Limits schema domain as the common schema domain of DT traits. Analyses were also able to differentiate between the Dark Dyad (i.e., psychopathy and Machiavellianism) and narcissism and to reveal schema domain patterns specifically related to psychopathy. Results are discussed in the context of contemporary theorizing about dark personality traits. The authors conclude that the theory of early maladaptive schemas can be a useful approach to the better understanding of the DT.

Chapter 4 – The concept of avoidance is central to the conceptualization and diagnostic criteria of the Axis I anxiety disorders described by the *Diagnostic and Statistical Manual of Mental Disorders* (4th ed., text rev., DSM-IV-TR; American Psychiatric Association, 2000). Its study has been expanded from motor behaviors in the presence of phobic stimuli to other areas. In the short term, avoidance reduces distress, but in the long term contributes to the maintenance of anxiety. With regard to depression, Ferster (1973) postulated a central role for avoidance in his depression theory. For this author, depressed people escape from aversive internal and external stimuli and frequently avoid related situations. Depression would be characterized by passivity as opposed to action. In this sense, Behavioral Activation as a treatment for depression (Jacobson, Martell, & Dimidjian, 2001; Martell et al., 2001) represents a renewed interest in the concept of avoidance. The relevance of avoidance study is also expanding into other areas of psychopathology, such as psychotic disorders (Vilardaga, Hayes, Atkins, Bresee, & Kambiz, 2013). In this case, some authors propose that avoiding feelings of low self-worth can contribute to paranoid thinking (Udachina, Varese, Myin-Germeys, & Bentall, 2014).

Three main types of avoidance can be distinguished: behavioral avoidance, which includes putting off decisions, turning down opportunities, isolating oneself, and giving up on tasks before they are completed; cognitive avoidance, which refers to a wide variety of coping strategies such as rumination, intentionally trying to suppress thoughts, and attempting to dissociate from negative experiences; and, experiential avoidance, which includes according to Hayes, Wilson, Gifford, Follette, & Strosahl (1996) both avoidance and escape in all of their forms, as long as they are used as methods of altering the form or frequency of experiences and the contexts that occasion them.

The present chapter also reviews the main instruments for assessing avoidance as well as treatment suggestions.

Chapter 5 – The intergenerational transmission (IT) of trauma can be defined as the influence of a disruptive experience perpetuated from a generation to another. Disruptive experiences can promote the onset psychopathological symptoms, compromising both the individual and the interpersonal functioning. Thus, literature (Kaitz et al., 2009; Pat-Horenczyk et al., 2014) has highlighted that the presence of this psychopathological pattern affect the way the parent respond to the emotional and physical needs of the child, which in turn may lead toward emerging difficulties of the child itself. Despite these evidences, only a few studies (Schwerdtfeger et al., 2013; Starr et al., 2014) have investigated the presence of different trajectories for the transmission of traumatic symptoms suggesting that the intergenerational transmission of traumatic symptoms can follow two different routes: direct and indirect transmission. Direct transmission is represented by specific effects of the parents' symptomatic behaviors, while the indirect transmission is described as the overall parental difficulty shown because of his/her own traumatic history.

Aim of the current review is to report those studies where the intergenerational transmission (IT) of the trauma has been taken into account according to three main perspectives: 1) the IT impact on the individual functioning; 2) the family dynamics involved in the IT of trauma; and 3) the community/social implications related to the IT.

Chapter 6 – In order to prevent the development of psychopathology symptoms in individuals psychiatry, psychoanalysis, and infant mental health research have conceptualized early intervention approaches. Since especially the postnatal relationship between baby and mother/father has been examined extensively in the last decades, some progress has been accomplished as to how parents-to-be can be prepared for parenthood. Parental competencies have also been well-examined; e.g., intuitive parental competencies which are processed within a time frame of 200 to 600 milliseconds are supposed to be universal, potentially existing in any person, and in the relational objects the baby has. Personal factors such as psychopathology can compromise the expression of intuitive parental competencies, however societal factors seem to be underestimated as to psychic functioning. Apart from intrapsychic and interpersonal factors, societal superstructure might influence the level of psychic functioning and of developing of psychopathology symptoms in general. While structured interventions preparing for parenthood cannot make up for societal shortcomings they can give parents-to-be hands-on advice as well as give them access to their emotional experiences. In Germany, a few intervention programs for parents-to-be exist, focusing on bonding, on relational issues, and on educational practices. For pre-schoolers there are structured interventions for kindergartens, including the involvement of parents.

In the chapter, the above mentioned interventions are presented along with aspects of developmental psychopathology, especially of violence in its different facets. Also, an insight into personal factors' influences on intuitive parental competencies is given. Prenatal and postnatal educational tasks especially for secondary school education can be derived from the intervention concepts outlined, most of which should be viable for extenuating the development of psychopathology symptoms.

Chapter 7 – This article reviewed three of most important advances that have been made in the understanding of psychopathy in the past half century since the landmark 1966 study of Lee Robins. This study had a major influence on the subsequent study of psychopathy which is arguably the most important construct in the study of violence. The advances occurred in identifying the basic personality traits of psychopathy, its earlier developmental manifestations, and its neural underpinnings. The review concluded with a recommendation that next 50 years of research on psychopathy should have prevention as its paramount focus.

Chapter 8 – Biofeedback application is an evidence-based technique to induce relaxation. Literature highlighted the efficacy of this technique in helping selected patients modify specific responses or response patterns associated with a mental disorder. For example, a "*relaxed*" Autonomic Nervous System (ANS) pattern include slow, regular heart rate, increased heart rate variability, dominance of EEG frequencies in the theta to low alpha bandwidth range, and warm skin temperature due to increased vasodilatation. Vice versa, an "*hyperactivation*" is reflected by increased heart rate and decreased heart rate variability, high electrodermal activity, along with higher frequency EEG bandwidth ranges in high-alpha or beta, often reflecting anxiety and/or panic states (Putman 2000). Thus, biofeedback which targets maladaptive physiology may help enable patients to recognize and change problematic physical symptoms (Pal Singh and Kaur 2007) that may be promoting and/or perpetuating the associated psychological problem.

The clinical efficacy of biofeedback has been investigated in a range of psychiatric disorders, such as anxiety and depressive disorders, and through different approaches such as the EEG neurofeedback and the heart rate variability biofeedback (HRVB).

Aim of the current review is to report the state of the art of the literature about the use of the biofeedback as a tool to reduce psychopathological symptoms, and to improve mental health condition. In detail, the authors' goal is to describe the efficacy of biofeedback on two major health diseases, namely perinatal mood disorders and eating disorders.

In: Psychopathology
Editor: Jeremy Williams
ISBN: 978-1-63485-745-1

Chapter 1

PROGNOSIS IN CONTEXT

Nicole Schluep [*] ***and Junaid Hassim***
Department of Psychiatry, Faculty of Health Sciences,
University of Pretoria, Pretoria, South Africa
Department of Clinical Psychology, Weskoppies Hospital,
Pretoria, South Africa

ABSTRACT

This chapter reviews the stipulative definitions of poor and protective prognostic factors as applied in the field of clinical mental health. In this regard, prognostic factors refer to features that positively and/or negatively influence a person's symptom presentation. Examples of these factors include, but are not limited to, education and social support. In clinical practice, these factors may be reviewed generically as either protective or guarded prognostic factors. However, the influences of these factors require contextual review if psychopathologists are to appropriately gauge the impact on the presentation. This chapter aims to illustrate the ways in which typical prognostic factors range on a continuum of positive and negative influences. Although the approach to describing these factors will be rooted in practical knowledge of everyday clinical practice, the authors review current events that may (re-)shape the influence of a given prognostic factor. Contemporary examples are cited and academic sources are used to explore the psychological impact of these events. The purpose of this approach is to engage the reader in

[*] Corresponding author: nicoleschluep@gmail.com.

critical thinking and petition the clinician to place emphasis on contextualizing influential features. For example, literature describes the psychological defense mechanism of 'altruism' as a probably mature functional pattern of developing self-satisfaction by serving the needs of others. Arguably, present social phenomena has pathoelaborating prowess, and suggests that the seemingly mature defense 'altruism' may have the potential to become pathological. By way of example, suicide bombers have been described as carrying out an extreme form of terrorism (on one end of the continuum), and a last plight of altruistic servitude (on the other end of the continuum). As such, a protective prognostic factor from one perspective (e.g., the patient's community) could be regarded as a poor prognostic factor from another perspective (e.g., the health care practitioner's). The question then becomes: how can we conceptualize discrepant prognostic factors? To respond to this, a critical analysis of this antithetical dynamic is offered, concluding with recommendations of a new prognostic category. The chapter does not aim to provide conclusions on the positive or negative influences of these factors, but to offer a platform for psychopathologists to evaluate (or re-revaluate) how they think about these influential features.

CASE VIGNETTE

The words *suicide bomber* elicit provocative images, thoughts and feelings, most of which are potentially negative from the perspective of a psychopathologist. Words such as irrational, uneducated, antisocial, acts of desperation and terrorist may come to the fore. With regards to being irrational and uneducated, the converse seems to be true, namely that suicide bombers may in fact be fairly educated individuals, who actually are (or need to be) in full control of their mental ability to succeed in their endeavours (Wintrobe, 2009). As a suicide bomber, being able to complete one's task probably requires the following emotional and social strengths: poise, emotional regulation, motivation, ego strength, stress management, team work, and average to above-average executive functioning. Although some may deem suicide bombers as being antisocial, systems theorists may commend a suicide bomber's interconnectedness with his or her group.

Suicide bombers seem to demonstrate high levels of social cohesion and belonging, and fight in the best interests of their people. They may be perceived to be giving up their autonomy for solidarity; behavior which reflects selflessness and altruism.

It can also be argued that belonging to a terrorist group fosters feelings of attachment, and may provide additional benefits not necessarily attainable if the individual were not part of the group. Examples of benefits could include housing, financial resources, and social support; all of which as previously explained are positive prognostic factors.

Compliance, as a trait of group cohesion, could easily be regarded as a good prognostic factor. Can one then not compliment suicide bombers on their compliance and allegiance to their group/leader? Apart from personalised views or social constructions on the matter, compliance as a trait of the group member suggests a competency to engage in complementary group dynamics. In the case of 'terrorist'/militant groups in the present era, individuals seem to be rejected for missions if they are married, have family responsibilities and are the sole wage earners of their families. These exclusion criteria may reflect the group's compassionate and mindful traits, as does the idea that sponsors of the suicide-bombing missions may pay some money to the deceased bombers' families. Payment for family members suggests that suicide bombing may actually be an inter-generational investment (Azam, 2005), as the monies paid out can be invested in education and medical resources, both of which contribute towards generational longevity.

Usually, groups associated with carrying out suicide bombing missions are labelled as cruel extremists; however, other organizations or groups with more positive labels (such as a national defense force) may not receive a negative labelling even though they do not necessarily provide monetary compensation for the families of the deceased. Inasmuch as a suicide bomber may be able to save some lives, the suicide bomber also places the lives of others in grave danger. Regarded as an act of terrorism, suicide bombing is likely to encourage counter-acts of terrorism which potentially increases the mortality rate. While a suicide bomber claims to fight for civil liberty, his or her actions impinge on the civil rights of others.

INTRODUCTION

The case vignette illustrates the multidimensional and sometimes contradictory nature of a manifestation, whether it is an action, behaviour, or emotion. Admittedly, the vignette intentionally emphasizes a provocative issue. Enjoying wide-ranging media coverage and social attention, the topic of suicide bombing is likely to elicit subjective views on the matter. Ranging from incense to endorsement, various media forums appear to consistently report diverse views on recent acts of suicide bombing. While we do not condone personal or social harm, the topic appears to be nothing short of peaking social attention, and it is for this reason that such an opinionated issue is offered at the outset of this chapter. As an overture to the text, the case vignette presents the reader with an opportunity to reflect on the dynamic influences of an opinionated view and a view that is conceivably noncommittal.

This inquiring approach paves way to the central approach of the chapter, namely highlighting the need for critical thinking skills in clinical assessment practices. However, attending to all areas concentrated on in mental health assessment would be impractical. The chapter is therefore focused on prognostic factors, an area that has arguably received limited research attention. To supplement the present body of literature, this chapter provides a conceptualization on the core tenet ‘prognosis’. Good prognostic factors are then introduced as one of the two commonly-assessed prognosis categories. This section of the chapter addresses important subcategories, including emotional prognostic factors among others. As such, the chapter provides a developmental approach to understanding the concept of ‘prognosis’, and the ways in which prognostic factors are typically reviewed in practice.

Subsequent to this conceptually-grounded foundation, the chapter logically introduces the need for contextual review of prognostic factors. While one may consider a contextual review to be an obvious approach, this section underscores the complexity of facilitating such an approach. By way of illustration, conditions that may alter the prognostic domains are presented. Ease of reference to the content is facilitated by structuring these conditions according to the good prognostic factors described earlier in the chapter. The section concludes with cautionary content, introducing a judicious review on appropriate contextual assessment.

This review serves as justification for the authors’ recommendation to introduce an additional prognostic category. This category is formulated in terms of its definitional qualities, and is followed by brief examination of the category in applied practice. This section is supplemented by practical recommendations for prognostic evaluation. As a point of departure, important concepts that underpin the content of this chapter are outlined.

1. CONCEPTS

Psychopathology refers to the difficulties, manifestations, impairments and mal-adaptations in mental health that are not age or culturally appropriate. Thus psychopathology has a negative impact on a person's functional capacities. In light of this effect, the work of a psychopathologist centers around four key domains: *assessment*, *diagnosis*, *treatment* and *prognosis* of mental illness or distress. This chapter essentially focuses on prognosis, and aims to critically review the defining elements of what constitutes poor and protective prognostic factors.

Professionals within the field of mental health regularly make judgments regarding an individual's mental health prognosis (McMahon, 2014). In the training context, for example, specialized (or tertiary) training facilities require that trainees review a patient's prognosis and provide evidence thereof. Some may question the need to even make a prognostic evaluation or wonder about the role of prognosis in treatment. McMahon (2014) is of the opinion that improved prediction of treatment responses may have numerous benefits, one of which is reducing the health care costs accrued from suboptimal treatments. Prognosis as it applies to certain psychopathologies is well documented in the research domain, as is the case with schizophrenia (Tsuang & Farone, 1997). The large body of literature on schizophrenia evidences a great deal of surrounding factors that have the potential to impair or improve a person's functional capacities. In other words, the research regards factors which affect the prognosis.

Interestingly, however, is the lack of research sources that describe all the elements, factors and variables that have a probable bearing on prognosis. As such, there is limited opportunity to access a central resource that accounts for wide-ranging and cohesive information in this area. At present, the available sources appear to lack interaction with other data, focusing primarily on isolated constructs and localized research samples. While these studies are essential to progressing clinical practice, the restricted research focus often fails to accommodate the extensive tapestry of factors associated with judging an individual's mental health prognosis. The academic domain is likely to appreciate that the involution of scores of influences which affect the metamorphosis of a given factor has the aptitude to discombobulate research processes. However, it is a reality which academics and clinicians alike lament due to the dynamic nature of human psychological processes.

Apart from formal research limitations, various mediums such as the news and professional council reports suggest that some psychopathologists generically review the context in which prognostic factors unravel. That is, the reality that prognostic evaluations are often made without a) considering the unique intricacies of each individual and/or b) critically evaluating the prognostic factors themselves. The chapter aims to address both these shortcomings and, in doing so, provide psychopathologists with a critical lens by which to view prognosis. The supplementary aim of the chapter is to highlight the prudence required to make appropriate prognostic determinations.

2. Prognosis Conceptualized

A prognosis refers to the likely outcome of a condition or is a future prediction of the duration, course and severity of a condition. Psychopathologists speak about either a good or guarded (poor) prognosis, and base such claims on either the absence or presence of certain factors, hereafter referred to as prognostic factors. Prognosis is the only method currently available by which professionals are able to identify which individuals are likely to either a) return to their baseline functioning, b) deteriorate, or c) remain at their new baseline functioning. The term 'baseline functioning' refers to the functioning of the individual prior to the onset of psychopathology. New baseline functioning refers to the functioning of an individual who has some residual symptoms but has stabilized on medication. An individual with a fairly good prognosis is likely to return to baseline functioning, or the person remains at his/her new baseline functioning. An individual deemed to have a poor or guarded prognosis is projected to deteriorate or relapse.

Now that we have explored what constitute a prognosis, let us consider the qualities of good prognostic factors.

3. Good Prognostic Factors

There are various variables which have a bearing on whether or not an individual will experience good mental health in the future. Good prognostic factors may also be referred to as protective factors, that is, those factors which render an individual less vulnerable to either developing mental illness, or which may protect an individual from experiencing repeated episodes of debilitating symptoms (Sadock & Sadock, 2007). In this regard, while protective factors may not preclude the manifestation of symptoms, they may be able to delimit the degree of severity of repeated episodes.

a) Emotional

An individual who has effective coping mechanisms is deemed less likely to suffer from psychopathology and is also perceived to be at lower risk of developing symptomatology in the future. Essentially, this would be the reason for defining the mechanism as 'effective'. Healthy, effective coping mechanisms include an ability to manage one's emotions, mediate appropriate emotional regulation processes, appropriately access stress reduction faculties, facilitate healthy mobilization of resources, and sustain effective communication skills. Being motivated is also deemed to be a positive prognostic factor. In other words, health-seeking behaviors and a willingness to 'do what it takes' with regards to treatment are perceived to be good prognostic factors. Professionals related to the discipline of psychology often speak about individuals with a high Emotional Quotient (EQ) as being more protected against psychopathology, or as being better able to deal with psychopathology. Individuals with a high EQ are said to have a high degree of self-awareness, tend to be more emotionally resilient, and are not dominated by negative emotions. Having a strong and well defined ego structure is also deemed to be a good prognostic factor; these individuals are described as being able to make decisions or voice opinions based on sound independent judgement, rather than influence or coercion by others. An individual's exposure and response to trauma also loads onto the quality of the prognosis. For example, an individual with minimal trauma, or an individual who has appropriately dealt with his or her trauma, is less susceptible to developing psychopathology and/or more likely to access adaptive coping skills to deal with symptoms of psychopathology.

Professionals employing a psychodynamic lens to assess prognosis take note of the degree to which an individual mobilizes defense mechanisms. The assessor would evaluate whether the person initiates a mature adaptive coping strategy or a maladaptive coping strategy. Both strategies aim to facilitate adaptation, but mature defenses (e.g., humor) are likely to preserve a person's reality testing, while maladaptive defenses (e.g., projective identification) have the potential to significantly compromise the person's perception of reality. A defense mechanism is an unconscious attempt to deal with pain and can be mature or less mature. The latter specifier ranges in degree, and can be classified from immature to pathological, among others. An individual who competently uses mature defense mechanisms is often viewed as having a better prognosis than an individual who reverts to using immature defense mechanisms. Altruism serves as an example. Altruism is a form of sublimation whereby an individual manages his or her own anxiety by focusing on meeting the needs of others. In the psychosocial domain, altruism could emerge in the form of an activist group that voluntarily protects the needs of the community. Altruism is mutually beneficial in that altruistic behaviors also contribute towards the emotional wellbeing of the altruist. More commonly, the altruist feels self-fulfilled that s/he makes a charitable contribution to the benefit of others. Additionally, the altruist may experience increased social recognition and support which are important variables in sustaining good mental health.

b) Interpersonal

Social support is regarded as a significant positive prognostic factor. An individual who has a network of family and friends that are able to offer nurturance, guidance and support during challenging periods, is better able to deal with some of the adversities of psychopathology. Social support does not only refer to supportive resources from individuals, but also to organizations within the immediate environment and broader community. Having the support of a religious community is considered to be an important buffer against psychopathology. This is because such structures provide individuals with a sense of belonging, offer hope when hope disappears, and allows individuals to feel that there is a greater force (or greater forces) assisting them on their unique journey through life. An important aspect in evaluating the influences of social support include a considered review on the individual's capacity to proactively utilize such support optimally. Social support, by and of itself, does not necessarily imply a good prognostic factor. Being in an intimate relationship is regarded to be another good prognostic factor, as research has shown that single individuals often have a higher incidence rate of psychopathology, and/or take longer to recover after being diagnosed. The active involvement of parental figures is yet another factor that is considered to be a good prognostic factor. Individuals who have at least one parental figure that is emotionally available and able to provide the necessary psychological, physical and spiritual support, fair better with regards to the management and treatment of psychopathology.

c) Cognitive

In terms of the cognitive domain, a higher intellect is regarded to be a good prognostic factor in that it suggests that an individual will demonstrate good insight and judgement. An individual whose intellectual functioning is deemed fair is more likely to explore evidence for or against a problem or challenge, will have better resources to seek out appropriate channels of support, and will use intellectual decision-making (instead of compromised emotional decision-making) to carry out activities of daily living or self-care. Higher cognitive-functioning individuals also have an enhanced ability to think abstractly which makes them more amenable to psychotherapy. The reason being that these individuals are able to *join the dots* (generalize from events and experience and connect them to others) and in doing so, are more able to recognize repeating patterns in their lives and how they are influenced by (and influence) significant others.

d) Biological

A discussion on prognostic factors necessitates mention of biological and physiological factors, as these play a crucial role in the acquisition and development of certain forms of psychopathology. Firstly, an individual without a familial history of psychopathology is said to fair better with regards to his/her susceptibility to developing certain types of psychopathology. The age of onset is also an important prognostic factor and research indicates that the later the onset of psychopathology, the better the prognosis. The duration of the specific illness also has a bearing on prognosis and a shorter duration most often implies a better prognosis. In addition, the type of psychopathology an individual is diagnosed with has a bearing on whether the prognosis is viewed more favorably or not. For example, an individual diagnosed with schizophrenia is considered to have a poorer prognosis than an individual diagnosed with major depression. Of importance, too, is whether or not an individual has a co-morbid (i.e., a co-occurring) diagnosis. It is suggested that individuals without co-occurring disorders have better outcomes as regards the impact of the psychopathology on their lives.

e) Educational

Formal education and training are considered to be good prognostic factors. Psychopathologists place positive emphasis on a person achieving undergraduate and postgraduate qualifications, not only because education implies enhanced intellect, but because education implies the potential to receive a higher income and certain benefits associated thereto, for example, finances to pay for treatment.

f) Compliance

Compliance, also referred to as adherence, speaks about the degree to which an individual follows advice given by a professional within the health sciences. Patients with a subjective positive regard for the treating professional and who emphasize the importance of the doctor-patient relationship seem to have better treatment outcomes (McMahon, 2014). Additionally, a patient who has demonstrated compliance in the past is said to have a better prognosis as it is believed that the medical advice or treatment provided will ensure alleviation or management of symptoms. This means that non-compliance is perceived negatively and that individual deviations from the proposed treatment plan are viewed skeptically. A willingness to engage in treatment is also deemed to be a good prognostic factor as the individual is likely to follow-up and keep a 'pulse' on his or her treatment management.

g) Lifestyle

An individual's lifestyle is determined by numerous variables, each of which have consequences in their own right. However, either separately or when coupled together, they have a bearing on prognosis. Arguably, the most important variable is occupation. The more revered the occupation, the higher the income and increased likelihood of good mental health. Firstly, an individual who is employed and experiences financial freedom is likely to be able to afford quality medical services and can access these services timeously (i.e., proactive and preventative mental illness intervention, rather than reactive treatment). Secondly, a higher economic status suggests that an individual can reside within a vicinity that is fairly close to all amenities, thereby having fairly convenient access to facilities that assist stress-reduction.

This may contribute towards improved mental health. Thirdly, not having to worry about finances, or struggling to live above the bread-line, suggests reduced depression and anxiety as has been widely suggested in the research domain. Indirectly, as is also widely reported in research, an absence of difficulties relating to these basic needs may reduce the incidences of maladaptive coping mechanisms such as substance abuse, as there could be less need to self-medicate (i.e., to use a potentially unhealthy process to 'escape' the experience of distress).

Another important variable is an individual's living conditions, as denoted by the type and condition of one's home, as well as the area in which one lives. A better prognosis is very often afforded to individuals who experience their physical living premises as comfortable, pleasant, hygienic, and safe. In addition, living in an area void of extreme social deprivation and social instability (e.g., crime and drug trafficking) is likely to contribute towards improved psychological wellbeing. As discussed before, another noteworthy variable is access to quality education. Being afforded quality education suggests that an individual has increased potential to demonstrate appropriate health-seeking behaviors, and subsequently minimize exposure to dangerous physical illness and medical conditions, for example, contracting HIV through unprotected sexual intercourse.

The discussion thus far has concentrated on elucidating those variables which contribute towards a good prognosis. These variables appear to hold significant predictive power as their presence in an individual's life suggests better global mental health or enhanced immunity against psychopathology. Additional observations also suggest that the power of these variables lie in how they contribute towards a good prognosis, which is seldom questioned. That is, a number of practitioners seem to accept a generic or superficial understanding of prognostic factors, without necessarily delving into the finer subtleties of each one. The authors maintain that the finer subtleties have influence and unfold when the variables are unveiled within different contexts. For this reason, the discussion now considers contextualizing each of the prognostic factors discussed.

4. Contextualising Prognosis

The question that remains is whether the prognostic factors previously discussed meet the requirements of protective factors? We argue that this is not inherently the case. While adequate housing, good social support, education and the like, reflect a good prognosis; the context within which these factors occur loads onto whether the factor is protective or restrictive in nature. The determination of this is dependent on the influence it has on the person. The good prognostic factors that were identified earlier in the text will be now be re-reviewed within context, thereby facilitating a review of the restrictive dynamics within certain protective factors.

a) The Restrictive Aspects of Emotional Functioning

Refer to the previous discussion on how mature defenses contribute towards an individual having a good prognosis. Although this holds true in many instances, there are also situations in which mature defenses are imbued with negative aspects that may be more pathological than healthy. The defensive operation of altruism could serve as case example. Firstly, normal, healthy altruism may lead to enhanced self-esteem; but pathological forms of altruistic behavior often have a narcissistic component (Holmes & Miller, 2002; Seelig & Rosof, 2001). Even when an individual believes himself/herself to be acting selflessly, she or he may be serving his or her own interests. Hence, an unselfish act may not be as selfless if it is inherently motivated by self-interests or a need to avoid something else. Consider the example of a wealthy business man who sponsors the building of a school in a rural village. While this could be regarded as a wholly prosocial act, what if the gesture is made in an attempt to "undo" social denigration after having been arrested for driving under the influences of alcohol? Essentially, this reflects an egoistic process rather than a selfless one, as the businessman commits a good act in order to overshadow a negative one. Secondly, altruism may exacerbate a problem instead of alleviating it. A case in point refers to the subtle nuances between two constructs: empowerment and enabling. An individual may think that they are empowering a drug addict by paying off their debts (altruistic act), however the altruist may be encouraging the individual's drug habit as there are less consequences for behavior or accountability of actions.

Altruism is widely documented as being a mature defense mechanism as it may assist in affect regulation, and involves a feeling of self-fulfillment as a result of helping someone or something. Altruism, however, may also result in affect dysregulation or create negative affective states for the individual. For example, an individual might rescue animals from euthanasia by housing them at her home. She may feel self-assured in the knowledge that her actions are humane and therefore rewarding. However, a potential inability to set boundaries may result in her over-extending and over-committing herself to the cause. The logistical result may be that she has to provide shelter for far too many animals, lacking sufficient space and funds. The emotional result may be that she experiences an escalation in anxiety. Hence, the more altruistic she is, the more anxiety she experiences. This example also demonstrates how altruism is often at a cost to self, and that neglecting ones' own needs for those of others is likely to result in manifestations of depression and anxiety. An altruistic act may be labelled as a mature defense mechanism in various influential academic sources but, upon closer scrutiny, an altruistic act may better reflect an immature defense mechanism (e.g., reaction formation). Reaction formation involves the process whereby anxiety-provoking or unacceptable emotions and impulses are mastered by exaggeration of the directly opposing tendency (Baumeister et al., 1998). In the case of our example, solicitude (a seemingly altruistic act) may be a reaction formation against cruelty. In a similar psychological process, a husband who is physically and sexually abusive towards his wife may donate large sums of money to a rape crisis center. In this example, the husband's seeming concern for victims of sexual abuse is probably not authentic, but defensive and maladaptive.

In a similar vein, the benefits of having a high emotional quotient (EQ) are widely documented in research and are considered to contribute to a good prognosis . However, there are also significant research results that highlight the 'dark side of emotional intelligence' (Austin et al., 2007). Some researchers are of the opinion that individuals with increased ability to hone in on their emotional skills are better at manipulating the emotions of others. They may also be more equipped to disguise their authentic emotions. This has the potential for numerous ramifications. By way of example, consider the patient who disguises his or her depression, subsequently gets discharged from hospital, and commits suicide upon returning home. As another example, consider the high EQ manager who, during a speech, informs employees of their retrenchment. He or she may inject the speech with emotionally-laden content in an attempt to divert the employees' attention from their retrenchment onto the positive contributions of the company over the years.

Being able to control one's emotions may also assist with follow-through on criminal activities. Having the ability to remain poised and calm are beneficial when, for example, distracting a cashier allows an accomplice to successfully carry out a theft. Having a high EQ can also render one vulnerable to exploitation and manipulation. An empathic person's decision-making can be more easily influenced if the appeal has positive outcomes. As an illustration, picture an empathic person's potential tendency to be seduced by an impassioned sales pitch to support a worthy charity. Regardless of his/her suspicion that fraudulent goods are being sold, the potential benefit of the sale might be regarded more earnestly due to his or her increased capacity for empathy.

b) Potential Difficulties in Interpersonal Elements

In some instances, a patient's prognosis is deemed to be good by mere acknowledgment that they have a caring, involved support network comprising individuals and organizations. However, social support is not necessarily without problems, and may contribute towards a poorer prognosis in some instances. Social support in the form of family involvement may reflect enmeshed dynamics, enabling potentially problematic relational patterns such as the patient being silenced to award major decision-making responsibilities to other family members. The active involvement of family members may also be counter-productive if it results in conflict in belief systems, adherence to non-evidence based treatment, and patients feeling pressurized. In South Africa, professionals are often confronted with the scenario whereby the patient wishes to comply with modern Western treatment prescribed by a mainstream psychological practitioner, but family members exert interpersonal pressure on the patient to rather follow treatment prescribed by a traditional healer. This dilemma may result in increased symptoms of psychopathology whilst the patient attempts to resolve the conundrum. Not only do the family members' religious/spiritual affiliations serve as potential barriers, but so too does the patient's own choice thereof. A patient's choice of religion or spiritual affiliation may serve two sides of the same coin. On the one side of the coin, religious/spiritual support can assist patients during times of vulnerability, relapse or crisis (Koenig, 2009). However, on the other side of the coin, it can also increase vulnerability, relapse and crisis. Take the example of a patient whose religious/spiritual affiliation precludes psychiatric services. He or she is likely to refuse evidence-based psychiatric medication and potentially increases his or her vulnerability to relapse or encounter serious psychiatric symptoms in the future.

There are certain attitudes which bode well for an individual's interpersonal mental health, as these attitudes suggest perceptions and beliefs which are humanitarian in nature, and generate interpersonal cohesiveness.

Psychopathologists are likely to view an individual more positively should he or she demonstrate loyalty to their country, uphold a national identity and exude solidarity. However, the same positive attributes may not apply when evaluated within a different context. Consider the case of national identity and xenophobia. Xenophobia involves the dislike or prejudice against people from other countries, and may involve a group of individuals enforcing physical violence against foreigners. We could ask: Are the group of individuals not showing camaraderie, unity and allegiance to their country? Should they not be praised for their need to protect their heritage? Perhaps these attitudes deserve criticism and suggest tendencies towards asocial traits and inciting violence? How one chooses to view such individuals will depend on which side of the fence a psychopathologist finds him or herself, and whether he or she is able to deepen the degree of rapport with the patient. This would allow the clinician to assess the legitimacy of the attitude. Historic events can be conceptualized along similar parameters. The example of the creation and eventual collapse the Berlin Wall in Germany is probably one such event, which could either symbolize protection or division.

The values of the collective culture in which an individual finds him or herself should also be taken into consideration. In some cultures, getting divorced is frowned upon and deemed a poor prognostic factor as the individual will no longer have the support of a partner. However, divorce may actually result in being a good prognostic factor, especially if the individual evades negative experiences, such as escaping spousal abuse. Earlier in the chapter, having a partner or living with a partner was described as contributing towards mental health, as it implies increased support. However, the context in which living together unfolds is vitally important. Consider the example of a couple who live together in a community that frowns upon cohabitation out of wedlock. Individuals in this dyad are likely to be ostracized and disrespected, suggesting poorer interpersonal satisfaction and potentially poorer mental health prognosis in the long term.

c) Cognitive Functioning as Poor Prognostic Factor

In terms of therapy, a higher level of cognitive functioning is viewed positively as it suggests that an individual may be more therapy-fit, more amenable to sophisticated forms of therapy and will have better insight into their psychopathology. Although this may be true in some case, the opposite may also be true in other cases. In this regard, an individual may demonstrate extraordinary intellectual insight, but this may suggest that his or her understanding is superficial. This could result in unsuccessful efforts at cognitive, emotional and behavioral change. Essentially, true insight would allow for the positive interplay of qualities from these dimensions.

Symptoms may not be so apparent within individuals with higher intellectual functioning. Whether this is as a result of the individual being better able to mask symptoms or because others are ‘fooled’ by his or her stronger verbal skills, the individual is likely to suffer certain consequences. Masking symptoms may preclude the individual’s opportunities to elicit necessary medical, social and emotional support. Furthermore, the individual may be more aware of, and influenced by, societal stereotypes and norms. Hence, he or she may not admit to experienced symptoms for fear of being labelled as ‘crazy’ or of being viewed as weak, sick or incompetent.

Defiance, rebellion and resistance may feature more prominently in individuals with higher intellectual functioning, as they are able to reflect on, research, and access information pertaining to treatment plans, regimens and the effects of treatment. However, patients with higher intellectual functioning may resist treatment due to knowledge on certain side effects, or may question one type of psychotherapy if they perceive another type of therapy as more effective treatment for his or her symptoms. In light of this dynamic influence, intellectual functioning may have both positive and negative outcomes depending on the context.

d) Biological Elements Negatively Impacting Prognosis

A number of biological and medical variables can negatively impact an individual’s prognosis. Without intending to typecast gender, several research sources suggest that being a young male with a co-morbid diagnosis and having a family history of mental health difficulties seems to reflect a negative biological vulnerability. Mention was made earlier on in the chapter that a shorter illness duration bodes well for prognosis. Although a shorter duration implies more vigorous and potentially effective treatment, a duration of the first episode may be problematic for the following reasons. Firstly, as a result of a shorter duration, some mental illness symptoms may go undetected, as in the case of different forms of depression; or may not be deemed severe enough to warrant treatment, as in the case of negative symptoms in some types of schizophrenia. Secondly, a shorter duration may result in the individual and family not adequately preparing for relapse or putting into place the most effective treatment strategies to delimit relapse. Another aspect to consider is if an individual is optimized fairly quickly on pharmacological treatment, he or she may be less inclined to commence psychotherapy or make lifestyle adjustments as there may appear to be no need to do so. Alternatively, individuals who have had a longer duration of mental illness symptoms are more likely to have 'contingency plans' and optimized treatment strategies in place (e.g., outpatient group psychotherapy, individual psychotherapy), thus potentially enhancing their prognostic capacity.

Additionally, one ought to be mindful of the diverse ways in which pharmacological treatments may be metabolized/absorbed by different individuals. If a person has a tendency to metabolize pharmaceuticals more slowly, and little significance is ascribed to this metabolic process, there is increased risk of medication being over-prescribed due to the seemingly ineffective influence of the medication. This could place an individual at increased risk of overdosing, or experiencing severe side-effects. That medication is dependent on prescription is reflective of the potential dangers associated with its misuse. Take Metadate, a form of Ritalin, as an example. It has been known to cause tics/Tourette's Syndrome and there is some evidence that Ritalin could lead to psychotic episodes, violent behavior and disorganized behavior ("The side effects of common psychiatric drugs", n.d., pp7).

Finally, clinically diagnosed syndromes are not necessarily dependent on traditional medical investigations, such as blood analysis. The risk that a patient may misuse psychiatric medications to deal with an unrelated physiological/biological problem increases. For example, dissatisfaction with one's metabolic rate might prompt an individual to depend on stimulants (e.g., methylphenidate) even if the drug does not positively influence the psychiatric symptoms for which the medication was prescribed (e.g., attention). Therefore seemingly appropriate mediums (e.g., healthy eating, exercise) are not used to regulate the physiological/biological processes and, in the long term, a perceived positive prognostic factor would probably be appreciated as a guarded prognostic factor.

e) Education as a Poor Prognostic Factor

The chapter previously suggested that the higher the education, the seemingly better the prognosis. By default, then, psychopathology ought to be less prevalent or less severe among university students. This notion is inherently flawed, which can be illustrated by a practical example. If one looks at the "fees must fall" campaign in South Africa, the central premise underpinning this campaign is the belief that education should be completely free. The campaign resulted in thousands of university students protesting, disrupting university activities, damaging university and personal property, and assaulting fellow students, security and university staff. The students sanctioned their actions by reiterating the campaign's lobby for equal access to education for all, regardless of socio-economic status. Various deductions can be made. Firstly, educated individuals may not necessarily act pro-socially. Secondly, violence and the transgression of rules may be more easily justified by people with relatively high intelligence. Thirdly, educated individuals may display dysfunctional or irrational decision-making as a result of groupthink (a process whereby an individual abandons his or her own opinion/position for the sake of a group's). This example would contradict the stereotype that educated people certainly exercise independent decision-making and have more control in regulating their emotions. Lastly, one could argue that the actions of the students were admirable as the students demonstrated an awakened social duty and fervent social obligation to fight for the rights of others. What becomes apparent from the last deduction is that the same action can be praised or rejected depending on the context.

In a similar example, the media's disapproval of online communities that encourage self-mutilation is probably more opinionated than noncommittal, perhaps reflective of the greater social construction on self-harming behaviors. One could argue that such communities provide an individual with a sense of community, fostering understanding and support; but one could simultaneously argue that such an online community fosters self-deprecation, depressive thinking and defiance.

Just as psychopathology has intrigued practitioners and researchers for eras, so has very talented individuals. Society in fact, seems to be encouraging the 'production' of geniuses, with many parents striving for their child to become the top achiever, the most successful, or the most beautiful. The general stereotype seems to be that those who are gifted, intelligent, talented or 'super smart' are less likely to suffer from psychopathology. The contrary may be true, whereby poor mental health may be more prevalent among individuals who have a sizeable share of good prognostic factors, such as adequate housing and ample financial resources. A more recently introduced term, 'tortured genius', has become more entrenched in certain academic circles. This term highlights the position that geniuses often struggle with psychopathology, have poor interpersonal relationships, experience adjustment problems and a propensity towards substance abuse; all whilst simultaneously excelling in another achievement-based area. One can also not ignore the idea that the expectation to excel may, in itself, be a stressor for the 'gifted' person.

Another undesirable consequence of receiving a superior education is the influence and role of technology. In the present time, many esteemed schools make use of computers and technology in the classroom and encourage scholars to become more computer savvy. Social media, screen time and the web are fast becoming the norm and deemed to be important in shaping intellect, character, and moral values. Although technology is beneficial, there are strong opinions in media and research that this may be primarily negative in terms of prognostic value. The internet, screen time and computer work may:

- Impair healthy interpersonal development
- Restrict healthy emotional expression and development
- Encourage psychopathology, e.g., narcissism, paedophilia, agoraphobia
- Encourage addictive behavior, e.g., gambling, pornography

Another negative aspect related to the domain of education is the likelihood that certain schools, usually those with more financial affluence and social prestige, afford individuals the opportunity to receive specialized tuition, as could be the case with a girl's only school or a Christian-based school. Although such schools hold social value and are appealing to a great deal of society, they may foster a) disconnection; b) rigid, narrow-minded thinking, c) discrimination, d) stereotyping, and e) fundamentalism. All of these attributes are likely to infringe on an individual's healthy intra- and interpersonal functioning; subsequently having a negative impact on mental health.

f) The Dark Side of Compliance

For many years, psychopathologists have equated treatment compliance with a better prognosis. This is based on the belief that if individuals follow medical advice, their risk of relapse is significantly reduced. However, the context in which an individual finds him or herself may prove the reverse, with treatment compliance evidencing a negative impact on mental health and overall prognosis. This is likely the case with individuals who reside within a community where mental illness is still stigmatized. Such individuals are more likely to default treatment for fear of being ostracized and rejected. Psychopathologists should be mindful of this reality in various community settings: enforcing treatment compliance may render individuals susceptible to anxiety (poorer mental health); especially if it is mandatory to receive medication in a public environment/setting.

The next point is also relevant to the emotional functioning, interpersonal functioning and lifestyle subsections introduced thus far. Guardedness, which has an interpersonal withholding quality to it, is regarded to be an aspect of non-compliance. Mental health practitioners would probably not be considered as being peculiar if they express concern regarding an individual's deliberate secrecy or misrepresentation of information. Nevertheless, lying or deceitfulness falls within personality psychopathology and such misrepresentation does not bode well in terms of the clinical picture and estimating the individual's prognosis. Upon further investigation, a psychopathologist my come to realize that guardedness in context may actually be a protective factor, as is the example of a Muslim boy who is homosexual. According to Islam, homosexuality is technically punishable by death and hence, the boy not disclosing his sexuality is a means of extending his life (good prognostic factor) rather than ending it. While this may be something of an extreme example which may not hold much utility in modern times, our experience has suggested that there is probably a similar negative consequence in Westernised Muslim societies, albeit less threatening to one's mortality. In contemporary times, disclosure of homosexuality may be met with exposure to social ostracism or forms of interpersonal and spiritual damnation. This example reiterates the point that inferences made about compliance should always be viewed within the broader context and practitioners should exercise greater sensitivity to influential factors before reaching conclusions.

A less obvious consequence of encouraging compliance is that it has the potential to foster dependency. The difficulty with compliance is that some individuals, like those with personality pathology, may struggle to negotiate the boundaries of compliance, and come to rely too heavily on health care professionals. Take for example the patient who continues taking medication as prescribed even though he or she experiences severe side effects or is developing a metabolic syndrome. Over-reliance and dependence on the mental health care system may also encourage institutionalization, as is evident in some patients who have sufficient ego strength to live independently, but remain in in the institutional context as this environment is perceived to be safer, less threatening and a more familiar option.

g) The Restrictive Nature of Life-Style as a Prognosis

Psychopathologists are more likely to award an individual with a good prognosis if the individual lives in a house, with ample living space for each family member and the family unit as a whole. Less often than expected, a fair share of psychopathologists enquire about the dynamic milieu of the individual's living arrangements. Indeed, having a house may be quite stressful on an individual and may serve as a poor prognostic factor, rather than a positive one. Not being able to sell one's house at a profit; losing value on a house as a result of declines in the property market; having accumulated arrears on loan repayments; and living in a high-crime area all contribute towards poorer mental health.

The town or city in which one lives also has a bearing on mental health prognosis. Certain areas are typecast in a specific way, and incorrect assumptions may be made accordingly. For example, assuming an individual is more prone to substance abuse if they live in an area perforated with drugs, or assuming that an individual will make use of mental health care services because they live in an urban area, may actually manifest differently in real-world contexts. One needs to appreciate the nuances of each area, made up of different classes and subgroups. The classes and subgroups experience further group differentiation, facilitating the creation of smaller class differentiations and subgroups. Hence, prognostic evaluations should not only be area-specific, but also person-specific, where subtle individual differences are accommodated for. In addition, any area-specific inferences should be appreciated as inference; conclusions ought to be reached only after thorough investigation.

Earlier, the chapter described how employment and its associated monetary benefits may improve a person's global mental health and impact positively on the prognosis. Money can, however, be a double-edged sword. Inasmuch as it maintains or can contribute towards improving mental health, so can it compromise mental health. An individual who has an abundance of financial resources is at higher risk of being lured into dangerous psychosocial territories, such as substance abuse, gambling or using money for emotional fulfilment. In such instances, money or financial freedom impinges on healthy mental functioning rather than contributes towards it. Employment conditions themselves may also contribute towards problematic intra and interpersonal functioning. Long working hours, having to work away from home, or having to work regularly for six or seven days a week, all contribute towards an unbalanced lifestyle. These individuals are likely to expend less energy on personal growth/introspection, family time and social engagements – these domains are vital components of good mental health and enhance mental health prognosis.

Many esteemed occupations, such as being a diplomat, may require individuals to relocate regularly. One needs to consider the implications that frequent relocation may have on the individual's mental health. Relocation may result in adjustment difficulties, sometimes even clinically-significant disorders, and may place significant pressure on the individual's financial, emotional, and social functioning.

Having a chronic physical illness or being diagnosed with any life-long medical condition is yet another factor regarded as having a negative impact on mental health. The type of medical illness, however, plays a significant role in how psychopathologists view an individual's mental health, and the assumptions made about certain aspects of the individual's psychological functioning. An individual who has contracted HIV (e.g., through unprotected sex or the sharing of contaminated needles) is vulnerable to be labelled as having poor insight, being at high risk, and regarded to have a poor prognosis. However, the same individual may become a role model in society, by acts such as social advocacy for living positively with HIV. In such a situation, the labels become very different. These may include terms such as 'resilient', 'good insight', 'good coping mechanisms', and 'better prognosis'. The only condition that has changed is the context in which the individual is perceived, and the resulting implication is a revision of prognostic factors that are alarmingly different to the expected prognosis.

5. Be Careful What We Wish for

Much of the discussion in the chapter thus far has focused on defending the notion that not all positive prognostic factors are necessarily constructive; some may turn out to be negative prognostic factors in another context. Since psychopathologists study and treat mental disorders, much of the research focuses on the elimination of clinically-significant symptoms in an individual's life. Since this chapter is aimed at revealing the dualism of prognostic factors (e.g., 'the good in the bad'), the authors propagate the paradoxical notion that not all psychopathology is necessarily bad – some symptoms may actually be beneficial to an individual, particularly if the symptoms do not impair all domains of functioning. In reality, psychopathology may underpin the processes of self-actualization, transformation, and success. In such a situation, the functional significance of the symptoms could be commended instead of being disparaged.

To elucidate, consider the following situations. First, certain types of psychopathological symptoms may be useful for certain occupations. Individuals with obsessional tendencies that manifest as perfectionism may excel at very structured occupations, they may succeed in jobs that require high levels of conscientiousness, and they may perform exceptionally well in tasks that demand attention to detail. The anxiety associated with an obsessional tendency can be a useful condition to have as it is usually coupled with sensitivity, vigilance and attentiveness; all of which are useful traits in professions involving working with people. Certainly if the obsessional intensity impairs functioning, this would be counterproductive to sustaining appropriate mental wellbeing. Similarly, manic symptoms may also benefit individuals in occupations that demand high output levels, such as data capturers. Secondly, mental illness may cultivate creativity, and generate refreshing ideas, as is evident in the social knowledge statement 'great art comes from great pain'. To attest to this statement, many well-known artists (such as Sylvia Plath) have achieved fame as a result of work produced during the midst of a depressive episode. Thirdly, mental illness symptoms may inspire an individual's spiritual or religious journey – one which may have been deficient prior to the onset of symptoms. This journey may serve to encourage a greater sense of contentment, create a framework to understand culturally-sanctioned explanations for his or her symptoms, or perhaps even prevent the person from engaging in self-harm behaviors. If the person's spiritual awakening increases his or her capacity to facilitate inner peace then the liable symptoms probably serve as a positive prognostic factor.

6. A New Prognostic Category: Adaptive Prognosis

Classic prognostic review strategies require transformation when double-edged aspects are presented during assessment. The transformation demands a qualitative analysis of a) social norming (that is society's expectations) and other social influences on the patient as well as, b) the patients evolving context. The degree of consistency between (a) and (b) may serve to enhance the predictive utility of the person's intra- and interpersonal experiences. Indeed, social norming may differ considerably between different groups of people, as well as from local and mainstream opinions. In this regard, assessment of the impact of the differences (or similarities) on micro-, meso-, and macro- environments becomes imperative to projecting prognosis. Apart from mainstream social expectations, the intricate tapestry of influential factors is extensive enough to convolute clinical practice.

A routine review of prognostic factors as was outlined earlier on in the chapter is not uncommon in clinical practice. The chapter illuminates the dichotomous nature of prognostic factors, and one would therefore be hard-pressed to make a more fairly reliable prognostic judgement given the vast range of influences on each factor. This serves as additional justification for the need for transformation in prognostic assessment practices. Our contribution to this transformation reflects a revision of mainstream clinical assessment practices, which we term *analytical functional assessment.* Defined, analytical functional assessment is the systematic use of explorative inquiry to develop explanative conclusions. In other words, instead of reducing the field of inquiry, the aim is to amplify the field of inquiry so that prognostic factors are evaluated more thoroughly. Thorough evaluation of influential variables on the prognosis has the capacity to harness a more reasonable prognostic judgment. The assessor would therefore aim to use exploratory analyses with the intention to facilitate abductive reasoning.

Unlike the term abductive inference in research methodology, we recommend the use of the term *abductive reasoning* for clinical assessment. This conceptual revision punctuates information provided by the patient and is not simply an inference or presumption made by the clinician. For example, instead of asking questions that have limited responses, e.g., "Do you have access to education"; one would rather ask exploratory or open ended questions, e.g., "What are some of the negatives of the education environment? Which factors outside of the education environment affect your experience of your education?" Comprehensive consideration of probable influences on prognosis is therefore central to analytical functional assessment. Irrespective of the practitioner's use of subaudition (unconfirmed hypotheses) or the patient's spontaneous description, candid appraisal (see Impey & Heun, 2012) of dichotomous factors provides for improved reasonability in information gathering, and may support equitability in the patient-clinician dyad.

From our definition, analytical functional assessment has the capacity to unravel divergent influences on prognostic factors. Indeed, experience in the field and the research domain abounds with examples of multiple influences (e.g., positive and counteractive) on a single prognostic factor (e.g., access to housing).

While we concur that the two mainstream prognostic categories (that is good and guarded) are both identifiable and indispensable to the clinical field, we contend that using these two categories alone restricts diagnostic prudence by decaying the manifold influences on certain factors. From this perspective, we propose a third essential prognostic category for routine clinical assessment procedures. This category aims to transcribe those factors which possess seemingly incongruous prognostic properties but have been reasonably assimilated into the patient's context (e.g., as a coping strategy); the term *adaptive* prognosis therefore appears to be an appropriate category title. Multiple communication strategies may be better equipped to facilitate this process and include, but are not limited to, abstraction, abstract reasoning, co-regulation, and systems analysis. The category of adaptive prognosis thus depends on synthesis of information gathered during the analytical functional assessment and accommodates critical enquiry into potentially multifaceted prognostic factors.

7. Recommendations for Clinicians

Based on this exposition of prognostic evaluation, the following guidelines may expand assessment potential:

1. Consider your present approach to evaluation, and assess the degree to which your interviewing style can be amended.
2. Critically question the central domains and ask the opposite of what is expected, e.g., how does having a high-paying job work against you?
3. Regard the person in context. Context includes a broad situational range and may include areas like gender, age and sexuality. We will use the case of culture to illustrate the dynamic nature of one type of context. Every culture has different nuances, even those cultures which share a great degree of similarity. Within each culture, subcultural nuances are likely to develop; transforming the qualities of the overarching culture. Furthermore, an individual may incorporate views from other cultures, essentially facilitating a personalized

perspective. Consideration of these subtle nuances ought to add significant to the prognostic determination.

4. Be an ecological detective. Use an enquiring approach to intensify rapport, which ought to assist in meticulously probing potentially influential factors.
5. Extend your range of reporting prognostic factors. Make a concerted effort to present the information that belongs to the third prognostic category (introduced in the chapter). This should be presented alongside the good and guarded prognostic categories to demonstrate the legitimacy of the clinical picture. Question whether potentially negative factors have potentially positive effects, and vice versa. For each domain that you assess, scale the estimated average effect of positive and negative influences before deciding on the appropriate prognostic category.
6. Embrace collaborative empiricism in your questioning style. As an example of the many skills used within this framework, person-centered theory uses relationship-building strategies to support comprehensive enquiry. These strategies include, but are not limited to, displaying empathy and having unconditional positive regard. As part of your evolving assessment repertoire, one could actively practice using open ended questions, Socratic questioning, and motivational interviewing to assess the person's actual relational approach. Bear in mind that collaborative empiricism, here, also suggests that collateral sources are consulted to corroborate information. Besides document sources of information, people in the patient's life could be consulted. As social beings, significant others may contribute meaningfully to the clinical decision making process. These collaborative options are certainly feasible without transgressing ethical practices.
7. Ascertain the reliability of your prognostic judgments. Prognostic judgment is vulnerable to merely being an impressionistic estimation of the clinician's assessment. Instead of automatically leaning towards making prophetic conclusions, review your hypotheses in consultation with the patient. This method of substantiation ought to supplement the assessment processes used in mainstream practice. Consider that psychological tests, for example, are at best able to create an estimation of cognitive prognosis rather than forecast the actual outcome. Interrogation of the person's cognitive functioning in everyday living could yield unpredicted results.

8. Practice a qualitative approach to the assessment process so as to maximize the capacity for accuracy in collecting and interpreting the information. This may imply extending the time-frame of evaluation, but has the capacity to yield exceptional clinical findings.

Conclusion

This chapter commenced with a provocative case vignette to encourage the reader to reflect on the dynamic influences of opinionated views and noncommittal views. The central feature of the chapter regarded the multidimensional influences on prognostic factors. This included conceptual and applied reviews on good prognostic factors, as well as various factors that may influence the clinician's prognostic judgment. Throughout the chapter, the authors employed compelling literary strategies to encourage critical thinking skills in clinical assessment practices. Using a developmental approach to presenting the content, the chapter reads as both practical and comprehensible, presenting a systematic approach to the need for contextual analysis.

'Contextual analysis' was examined, suggesting open-ended analysis of prognostic factors. This section emphasized the complexity of such an analysis, and considered instrumental influences such as intersubjective spaces (e.g., patient-clinician, person-community, local-global). In light of the conditions that may alter prognostic domains, cautionary content was introduced as part of a judicious review on topic.

This review prompted the authors' to conceptualize an additional prognostic category, which was defined and described to supplement academic and applied erudition. This chapter gradually reaches its conclusion by offering practical recommendations for prognostic evaluation.

References

Austin, E. J., Farrelly, D., Black, C. & Moore, H. (2007). Emotional intelligence, Machiavellianism and emotional manipulation: Does EI have a dark side? *Journal of personality and individual differences*, *43*(1), 179-189.

Azam, J. (2005). Suicide-bombings as inter-generational investment. *Public Choice*, *122*, 177-198.

Baumeister, R. F., Dale, K. & Sommer, K. L. (1998). Freudian defense mechanisms and empirical findings in modern social psychology: reaction formation, projection, displacement, undoing, isolation, sublimation and denial. *Journal of Personality*, *66*(6), 1081-1124.

Holmes, J. G. & Miller, D. T. (2002). Committing altruism under the cloak of self-interest: The exchange fiction. *Journal of experimental social psychology*, *38*(2), 144-151.

Impey, M. & Heun, R. (2012). Completed suicide, ideation and attempt in attention deficit hyperactivity disorder. *Acta psychiatrica Scandinavica*, *125*(2), 93-102.

Koenig, H. G. (2009). Research on religion, spirituality, and mental health: A Review. *The Canadian Journal of psychiatry*, *54*(5), 283-291.

McMahon, F. J. (2014). Prediction of treatment outcomes in psychiatry – where do we stand? *Dialogues in Clinical Neuroscience*, *16*(4), 455-464.

Sadock, B. J. & Sadock, V. A. (Eds.) (2007). Kaplan and Sadock's Synopsis of psychiatry. Behavioural Sciences/Clinical Psychiatry. (10th ed). Philidelphia: Lippinocot Williams & Wilkins.

Seelig, B. J. & Rosof, L. S. (2001). Normal and pathological altruism. *Journal of the American Psychoanalytic Association*, *49*(3), 933-959.

The side effects of common psychiatric drugs. A report by the citizens commission on human rights international. Retrieved from http:// www. cchr.org/sites.

Tsuang, M. T., & Faraone, S. V. & Johnson, P. D. D. (1997). *Schizophrenia: the facts.* New York: Oxford University Press

Wintrobe, R. (2009). Can suicide bombers be rational? In Wintrobe, R. (Ed). *Rational Extremism. The political economy of radicalism.* Cambridge, Cambridge University Press, 108-143.

In: Psychopathology
Editor: Jeremy Williams
ISBN: 978-1-63485-745-1

Chapter 2

PATHOLOGICAL PERSONALITY TRAITS: THE DARKER ASPECTS OF PERSONALITY

Gillian A. McCabe, Jennifer K. Vrabel and Virgil Zeigler-Hill[*]
Department of Psychology, Oakland University, Rochester, Michigan, US

ABSTRACT

There has been considerable controversy during recent years regarding the conceptualization of personality pathology. An important aspect of this controversy has involved whether personality pathology should continue to be viewed according to the traditional categorical model or modified to include a dimensional perspective. The debate concerning these perspectives resulted in the most recent version of the Diagnostic and Statistical Manual of Mental Disorders (DSM-5; American Psychiatric Association, 2013) retaining the categorical model, but introducing the Alternative DSM-5 Model for Personality Disorders in Section III ("Emerging Measures and Models" in need of further study). This alternative model led to the development of the Personality Inventory for DSM-5 (PID-5; Krueger, Derringer, Markon, Watson, & Skodol, 2012) which captures the following pathological personality traits: negative affectivity, detachment, antagonism, disinhibition, and psychoticism. In this chapter, we will discuss the categorical and

[*] Virgil Zeigler-Hill e-mail: zeiglerh@oakland.edu.

dimensional models of personality pathology and highlight the advantages and disadvantages associated with each perspective. We will also provide an overview of recent research that has utilized the PID-5 and offer potential directions for future research.

Keywords: PID-5, pathology, personality, personality disorder, DSM-5

INTRODUCTION

The categorical model for personality disorder (PD) diagnosis was introduced in the third edition of the Diagnostic and Statistical Manual of Mental Disorders (DSM-III; American Psychiatric Association [APA], 1980) and maintained that PDs are maladaptive constellations of personality traits that cause significant distress and/or functional impairments because of their stability across time and situations. Since its introduction, considerable effort has been dedicated to refining the representation of PDs in the DSM because of the important role the DSM has in shaping the way mental health issues are conceptualized. For example, the categorical model creates a universal language (e.g., diagnostic labels) that can easily convey a great deal of information (Trull & Durrett, 2005). The model also allows for easy decision making regarding whether or not to provide treatment to a particular client (Trull & Durrett, 2005) and it simplifies the choice of appropriate treatment by orienting the clinicians approach to a primary psychopathology (Gunderson, 1992).

Although the categorical model has some positive aspects, it is important to note that this sort of classification system also presents a number of challenges. The categorical model is a hierarchical taxonomic system in which the PDs are given discrete boundaries defined by approximately seven to nine criteria, of which a subset (approximately five) must be met in order to reach the diagnostic threshold for the PD (APA, 2013). There are several ways in which an individual can meet a diagnostic threshold which means that this system allows for a tremendous amount of heterogeneity within each PD. For example, according to Trull and Durrett (2005), there are 126 different combinations of criteria that can result in a borderline personality disorder diagnosis which adds an aspect of ambiguity to the information conveyed through the categorical model's universal language. In addition, there are relatively narrow boundaries placed around each PD which often makes it difficult for individuals to meet the criteria for a traditional PD diagnosis

(Trull & Durrett, 2005). As a result, the PD symptoms reported by individuals often span multiple PDs which may perpetuate an overreliance on Not-Otherwise-Specified (NOS) diagnoses (e.g., APA, 2013). Further, it is unlikely that the choice of appropriate treatment is simplified when patients receive NOS diagnoses because this type of diagnosis does not necessarily orient the clinician toward a primary psychopathology. The categorical model also perpetuates the high rates of comorbidity that are frequently observed (e.g., APS, 2013; Krueger, 2013; Trull & Durrett, 2005) which suggests that, contrary to the categorical model's conceptualization, PDs are not mutually exclusive (e.g., APS, 2013; Trull & Durrett, 2005). Therefore, it is not surprising that researchers have suggested that the categorical model should be abandoned in favor of a dimensional classification model that would better represent the variations in personality (e.g., Krueger, 2013; Widiger & Clark, 2000).

PERSONALITY INVENTORY FOR DSM-5 (PID-5)

In an effort to ameliorate the challenges of the categorical model, an alternative hybrid model of classification was added to the DSM-5 in Section III ("Emerging Measures and Models" in need of further study). This alternative model characterizes PDs by the level of impairment in personality functioning and the presence of pathological personality traits (APA, 2013). By assessing the severity and duration of functional impairments – rather than merely determining whether impairments are present – the alternative model provides clearer boundaries between diagnoses (e.g., Few et al., 2013; James, Anders, et al., 2015).

By assessing the presence of pathological personality traits, the alternative model better accommodates the variations in individual personality (e.g., Krueger, 2013). The DSM-5 Personality and Personality Disorder Work Group proposed five pathological personality traits as well as 25 underlying facets relevant to PD diagnosis (Krueger et al., 2012). Pathological personality traits are assessed within the alternative model using the Personality Inventory for DSM-5 (PID-5; Kruger et al., 2012) which captures the following pathological personality traits: negative affectivity (i.e., the tendency to experience an array of negative emotions), detachment (i.e., characterized by introversion, social isolation, and anhedonia), antagonism (i.e., aggressive tendencies accompanied by assertions of dominance and grandiosity), disinhibition (i.e., impulsivity and sensation seeking), and psychoticism (i.e., a disconnection from reality and a tendency to experience illogical thought patterns).

The PID-5 consists of 220 items that measure 25 facets across five pathological personality traits: negative affectivity facets (e.g., emotional lability, anxiousness, separation insecurity), detachment facets (e.g., withdrawal, anhedonia, intimacy avoidance), antagonism facets (e.g., manipulativeness, deceitfulness, grandiosity), disinhibition facets (e.g., irresponsibility, impulsivity, distractibility), and psychoticism facets (e.g., unusual beliefs and experiences, eccentricity, perceptual dysregulation; APA, 2013). Pathological personality traits can also be assessed using the Personality Inventory for DSM-5 – Brief Form (PID-5-BF; Krueger et al., 2012) which is a 25-item inventory that only measures the five pathological personality traits. Since the development of the PID-5, researchers have constructed an informant-report form (PID-5IRF; Markon, Quilty, Bagby, & Krueger, 2013) and have examined the PID-5 in a range of samples including adolescents (De Clercq et al., 2014) and older adults (Van den Broeck et al., 2014).

Psychometric Properties of the PID-5

During its initial construction, the PID-5 demonstrated strong internal validity at the trait level (Krueger et al., 2012) and has continuously demonstrated at least adequate internal validity in subsequent studies (e.g., Bastiaens et al., 2016; De Fruyt et al., 2013; Few et al., 2013; Gutiérrez et al., in press). However, certain facets have not demonstrated such strong internal validity (e.g., grandiosity; Al-Dajani, Gralnick, & Bagby, 2016). Using a clinical sample, Wright et al. (2015) found that after a period of approximately a year and a half, participants' reported levels of pathological personality traits were relatively unchanged. However, Wright et al. (2015) found that small individual changes in PID-5 scores from Time 1 to Time 2 were associated with patient-reported psychosocial functioning. That is, clinician assessment of pathological personality traits at Time 1 predicted self-reported psychosocial functioning at Time 2.

The PID-5 traits can be conceptualized as maladaptive variants of normal personality domains from the Five-Factor Model (Thomas et al., 2013). That is, negative affectivity, detachment, antagonism, disinhibition, and psychoticism converge with neuroticism, (low) extraversion, (low) agreeableness, (low) conscientiousness, and openness to experience, respectively. Several studies have shown that negative affectivity, detachment, antagonism, and disinhibition correlate strongly with their Five-Factor Model counterparts (e.g., Few et al., 2013; Quilty, Ayearst, Chimielewski, Pollock, & Bagby, 2013; Thomas et al., 2013). However, the association between PID-5 psychoticism and openness to experience is less consistent and one of the most notable weaknesses of the PID-5. Some previous studies have found overlap between psychoticism and openness to experience (e.g., De Fruyt et al., 2013; Gore & Widiger, 2013), whereas others have not (e.g., Few et al., 2013; Watson, Stasik, Ro, & Clark, 2013).

In relation to the HEXACO (Lee & Ashton, 2004), a six-factor model of personality, Ashton, Lee, de Vries, Hendricks, and Born (2012) found that the PID-5 traits of detachment and disinhibition had strong associations with their HEXACO counterparts (i.e., extraversion and conscientiousness, respectively). However, antagonism was found to overlap with the HEXACO's sixth domain of honesty-humility, whereas negative affectivity was associated with multiple HEXACO domains (i.e., emotionality, extraversion, and agreeableness) and psychoticism was not associated with any of the HEXACO domains.

The PID-5 been shown to overlap with other models of maladaptive personality traits. Anderson et al. (2013) found that negative affectivity, detachment, antagonism, disinhibition, and psychoticism were moderately correlated with the Personality Psychopathology Five (PSY-5; Harkness, McNulty, & Ben-Porath, 1995) domains of negative emotionality, introversion, aggressiveness, disconstraint, and psychoticism, respectively. Southard, Noser, Pollock, Mercer, and Zeigler-Hill (2015) found that the PID-5 traits were correlated with the Dark Triad personality traits (i.e., narcissism, Machiavellianism, psychopathy). Specifically, Southard et al (2015) found that the PID-5 traits were positively associated with the exploitative/entitlement subscale of Narcissistic Personality Inventory (NPI; Ackerman et al., 2011), the vulnerability subscale of the Pathological Narcissism Inventory (PNI; Pincus et al., 2009), the callous affect and antisocial lifestyle subscales of the Self-Report Psychopathy Scale (SRP-III; Mahmut, Menictas, Stevenson, & Homewood, 2011), and Machiavellianism (MACH-IV; Christie & Geis, 1970). Additionally, Southard et al. (2015) found that the PID-5 traits had strong positive associations with sadistic impulses (SSIS; O'Meara, Davies, & Hammond, 2011) and spitefulness (SS; Marcus, Zeigler-Hill, Mercer, & Norris, 2014).

Clinical Utility of the PID-5

The clinical value of the PID-5 as a diagnostic tool has been investigated with promising results. Hopwood, Thomas, Markon, Wright, and Krueger (2012) found that the PID-5 traits accounted for a moderate amount of the variance in scores on the Personality Diagnostic Questionnaire in a nonclinical sample. In a sample of treatment-seeking adults, Few et al. (2013) found that the PID-5 contributed to the prediction of personality disorders. James, Anders, et al. (2015) found that veterans diagnosed with posttraumatic stress disorder (PTSD) reported higher levels of detachment and psychoticism than did veterans without PTSD diagnoses. Further, James, Anders, et al. (2015) found that veterans with PTSD diagnoses reported significantly higher levels of PID-5 facets related to internalizing psychopathology than veterans without PTSD diagnoses. In a Spanish speaking sample, Gutiérrez et al. (in press) found that participants in an outpatient sample scored significantly higher on the PID-5 than did participants in a community sample. Similarly, in an inpatient Finnish sample, Bastiaens et al. (2016) found that individuals with a PD diagnosis scored significantly higher on negative affectivity, antagonism, and disinhibition than did those without a formal PD diagnosis.

Past research has also looked at the associations between alcohol use disorders and categorical personality disorders (e.g., Sher, Trull, Bartholow, & Vieth, 1999). For example, Morgenstern, Langenbucher, Labouvie, and Miller (1997) found that individuals suffering from alcohol use disorders may be more likely to meet the diagnostic threshold for antisocial personality disorder, borderline personality disorder, and paranoid personality disorder. Relatively little is known in regard to the connections between the alternative model of PD diagnosis (i.e., Section III of the Diagnosis and Statistical Manual of Mental Disorders) and alcohol use disorders. However, recent research into this connection has revealed that the PID-5 traits of antagonism and disinhibition were related to problematic alcohol use (i.e., hazardous drinking; Creswell, Bachrach, Wright, Pinto, & Ansell, 2016). More specifically, high levels of antagonism predicted greater alcohol use in older individuals but not younger individuals. In contrast, disinhibition predicted alcohol use in younger individuals rather than older individuals. Taken together, these results provide early evidence that the PID-5 is an effective prognostic tool for predicting alcohol misuse.

In addition to its potential as a useful assessment and prognostic tool (e.g., Few et al., 2013; Wright et al., 2015), the PID-5 may serve an added function of improving – and expanding – the ways personality disorders are characterized within the DSM (Al-Dajani et al., 2016). For example, the DSM-5's classification of narcissistic personality disorder outlines elements of grandiosity but does not officially recognize its vulnerable characteristics (APA, 2013). Yet, the PID-5 has been shown to account for a moderate portion of the variance in both grandiose and vulnerable narcissism (Miller, Gentile, Wilson, & Campbell, 2013; Wright et al., 2013).

The DSM has also been criticized for its narrow conceptualization of antisocial personality disorder because of the PD's similarity to psychopathy. Critics have argued that the primary distinction between antisocial personality disorder and psychopathy is that antisocial personality disorder lacks the affective and interpersonal breadth provided by the construct of psychopathy (e.g., Strickland, Drislane, Lucy, Krueger, & Patrick, 2013). Although unrecognized by the DSM, psychopathy's affective and interpersonal components are of clinical and empirical importance. For example, Drislane, Vaidyanathan, and Patrick (2013) used electroencephalography (EEG) imaging to measure sensitivity to aversive stimuli in a sample of incarcerated men and found that those with high levels of psychopathy experienced less physiological arousal in response to threatening stimuli compared to individuals who met the criteria for antisocial personality disorder. This physiological response deficit was accounted for by the affective and interpersonal features of psychopathy (Drislane et al., 2013), which suggests that there may be clinically relevant physiological differences that are unidentifiable through the narrow boundaries of antisocial personality disorder. Additionally, all but three of the men with high levels of psychopathy met the criteria for antisocial personality disorder (Drislane et al., 2013). Further, Strickland et al. (2013) found that the PID-5 was able to adequately capture antisocial personality disorder in addition to both the affective and interpersonal features of psychopathy.

Adaptive Costs and Benefits

Personality exists on a continuum. Therefore, it is likely that equally strong selection pressure is placed on both extremes of a personality trait such that each extreme is favored under different conditions (Penke, Denissen, & Miller, 2007). In other words, specific levels of a personality trait may increase fitness in one environment but decrease fitness in another. Neuroticism, for example, is positively associated with physiological stress (e.g., Neeleman, Sytema, & Wadsworth, 2002) but under conditions where novel people and situations are commonplace, these physiological costs may be outweighed by the benefits associated with the form of hypervigilance to threat that characterizes individuals with high levels of neuroticism (Penley & Tomaka, 2002). Findings such as these indicate that personality traits come with trade-offs with regard to fitness costs and benefits (e.g., Nettle, 2006).

PID-5 traits – as with normal personality traits – likely have adaptive costs and benefits (e.g., Nettle, 2006). Harkness, Reynolds, and Lilienfeld (2014) propose five adaptive systems that are reflected in the pathological personality traits of the PID-5: short-term danger detection system (i.e., increased sensitivity to danger and cues of potential threat), resource acquisition system (i.e., enhanced or inhibited arousal in response to resources acquisition opportunities), agenda protection system (i.e., balancing the goals of others with the goals of the self), long-term danger and benefit projection system (i.e., behavioral constraint or disconstraint in response to predictions of future conditions), and the reality modeling system (i.e., maintaining mental models of external environments).

Negative affectivity – characterized by a tendency to experience negative emotions (e.g., anxiety, depressivity; Krueger et al., 2012) – is reflected in the short-term danger detection system (Harkness et al., 2014). This system consists of mechanisms designed to detect immediate danger as well as signals of potential threats (Harkness et al., 2014) and likely evolved in response to the numerous dangers our ancestors encountered (e.g., predators, rivals). High levels of negative affectivity may therefore increase one's chances of survival. The short-term danger detection system elicits physiological responses characteristic of anxiety (e.g., increased heart rate and blood pressure; Harkness et al., 2014).

Detachment – characterized by social withdrawal and anhedonia (Krueger et al., 2012) – is reflected in the resource acquisition system, which can be characterized as either extraverted/high positive emotionality or introverted/low positive emotionality (Harkness et al., 2014). Individuals in the former group actively seek out opportunities to acquire resources and experience joy when resources are consumed, whereas those in the latter group have difficulty experiencing joy (i.e., anhedonia) when consuming resources and therefore opportunities for resource acquisition are met with ambivalence (Harkness et al., 2014).

Antagonism – characterized by aggression and dominance (Krueger et al., 2012) – is reflected in the agenda protection system, which is a process for balancing the drives and desires of the self with those of the group (Harkness et al., 2014). When one's goals are threatened, the agenda protection system triggers irritation and/or aggression to intensify focus on overcoming the obstacles that are preventing goal attainment (Harkness et al., 2014). High levels of antagonism may therefore increase one's fitness – although potentially at the expense of other individuals in the social environment.

Disinhibition – characterized by irresponsibility and sensation seeking (Krueger et al., 2012) – is reflected in the long-term danger and benefit projection system (Harkness et al., 2014). This system functions as a means of weighing the consequences of one's behavior (Harkness et al., 2014). Because individuals are able to predict future circumstances, some will constrain certain behaviors in the present in order to obtain benefits or avoid dangers in the future. However, present circumstances are more certain than those predicted for the future and therefore other individuals may instead choose not to restrict their present behavior (Harkness et al., 2014).

Psychoticism – characterized by a disconnection from reality and patterns of illogical thoughts (Krueger et al., 2012) – is reflected in the reality modeling system, which maintains mental models through assimilation or accommodation such that accommodation modifies old schemas to fit new information whereas assimilation manipulates new information to fit preexisting schemas (Harkness et al., 2014). Individuals with high levels of psychoticism have a tendency to assimilate rather than accommodate which may explain the paranoia and disconnect from reality observed in those with psychotic disorders (Harkness et al., 2014).

CURRENT APPLICATIONS

In the years since its introduction, researchers have begun examining the associations that the PID-5 traits have with various constructs. Below we outline much of the research that has employed the PID-5. It is important to note that, despite the relative breadth of the research that has used the PID-5, additional research is still needed in order to more fully understand the following associations (e.g., causal pathways).

Emotions

Emotions are subjective feeling responses, expressive displays, and physiological activations that likely evolved in order to motivate individuals to engage in survival-promoting behaviors (Tooby & Cosmides, 1990). Emotions play a significant role in one's personality and psychopathology (Vachon & Krueger, 2015). For example, emotion regulation difficulties have been found to be relevant to certain pathological personality features (Pollock, McCabe, Southard, & Zeigler-Hill, 2016). Emotion regulation can be defined as the ability to monitor, evaluate, understand, and modify emotional reactions in a way that is beneficial (e.g., Tooby & Cosmides, 1990). In contrast, unsuccessful emotion regulation (i.e., emotion dysregulation) occurs when an individual reacts in a way that is problematic (e.g., failing to accept an emotion; Gratz & Roemer, 2004). An individual suffering from emotion dysregulation may face more negative interpersonal outcomes than others because emotional experiences provide crucial information about one's social environment (e.g., Frijda & Mesquita, 1994).

Pollock et al. (2016) found that the PID-5 traits were associated with each of the six aspects of emotion dysregulation outlined by Gratz and Roemer (2004): non-acceptance of emotional responses (i.e., lack of acceptance of one's distress), difficulties engaging in goal-directed behavior (i.e., experiencing negative emotions prevents focus), impulse control difficulties (i.e., an individual is unable to control his or her behavior while experiencing negative emotions), lack of emotional awareness (i.e., an individual is unware of his or her emotional responses), limited access to emotion regulation strategies (i.e., the belief that negative emotions cannot be changed), and lack of emotional clarity (i.e., individual does not understand his or her emotions). More specifically, Pollock et al. (2016) found that negative affectivity was positively associated with all aspects of emotion dysregulation except for emotional awareness, which suggests that individuals with high levels of negative affectivity lack the ability to monitor, evaluate, understand, and modify their emotions in a beneficial way. Detachment had positive associations will all aspects of emotion regulation strategies – with the exception of goal-directed behavior. Antagonism was positively related to impulse control difficulties and limited access to emotion regulation strategies. These findings suggest that individuals with high levels of detachment and antagonism have difficulty evaluating and modifying negative emotions and lack behavioral control during negative emotional experiences (Pollock et al., 2016). Disinhibition had positive relationships with all aspects of emotional dysregulation except for non-acceptance of emotional responses, which suggests that disinhibited individuals are unable to adequately evaluate or understand their emotional experiences or control their behavior while experiencing negative emotions (Pollock et al., 2016). Lastly, psychoticism was positively related to non-acceptance of emotional responses, impulse control difficulties, and lack of emotional clarity (Pollock et al., 2016). This finding is not surprising given that individuals with high levels of psychoticism have difficultly accommodating their existing mental models of reality to fit new information (Harkness et al., 2014), which may impact their ability to control their emotional experiences (Pollock et al., 2016).

The PID-5 traits have also been found to be associated with emotional reactivity to daily events. For example, results suggest that people with high levels of negative affectivity experience greater emotional reactivity to negative interpersonal events (Pollock et al., 2016). Further, regardless of whether or not a negative interpersonal event had been experienced, individuals with high levels of detachment and antagonism reported high levels of negative affect, whereas individuals with low levels of detachment and antagonism only reported high levels of negative affect after experiencing a negative interpersonal event (Pollock et al., 2016). These findings are consistent with previous research showing that the adaptive variants of detachment (i.e., extraversion) and antagonism (i.e., agreeableness) are positively associated with heightened reactivity following negative events (e.g., Jensen-Campbell, Knack, Waldrip & Campbell, 2007). Taken together, these findings demonstrate that each of the PID-5 traits are associated with a lack of behavioral control during negative emotional experiences, which may, at least partially, explain some of the negative intrapersonal and interpersonal outcomes linked to pathological personality traits.

Moral Values

Recent advancements in the theory of morality (e.g., Haidt & Graham, 2007) have led researchers to consider individual differences in moral judgment and moral reasoning. These differences have been examined in connection to an array of outcomes including political ideology (Graham et al., 2011) and pathological personality features (Noser et al., 2015). Moral Foundations Theory (Graham et al., 2011) captures these individual differences via two higher order domains of moral values: individualizing values and binding values. Individualizing values are based on issues concerning the rights and welfare of individuals, whereby harm/care and fairness/cheating are its core foundations (Graham et al., 2011). In contrast, binding values capture issues regarding group cohesion, social order, and sustaining respect towards authority (Graham et al., 2011). Consequently, the binding value system consists of three main foundations: authority/disrespect, in-group/betrayal, and purity/degradation (Graham et al., 2011).

Pathological personality features have been found to be linked with the two higher-order domains of the Moral Foundations Theory (i.e., individualizing and binding values). Noser et al. (2015) found that both antagonism and disinhibition were negatively associated with individualizing values, which suggests that individuals who have high levels of either antagonism or disinhibition are less concerned with the rights and welfare of others when making moral decisions. These findings may be, at least partially, explained by the frequent deceptive and manipulative behaviors antagonistic individuals engage in (e.g., Holden, Roof, McCabe, & Zeigler-Hill, 2015) and the tendency for individuals with high levels of disinhibition to be self-destructive and impulsive (APA, 2013). Noser et al. (2015) also found that negative affectivity was positively associated with both binding and individualizing values, which suggests that individuals with high levels of negative affectivity are less likely to deviate from social norms and more likely to place importance on the welfare of themselves and others. These findings may not be surprising given that negative affectivity has been found to be associated with anxiousness (Krueger et al., 2012) and increased negative affect after experiencing negative interpersonal events (Pollock et al., 2016). Lastly, individuals with high levels of psychoticism are less concerned with binding values, which may be, at least partially, explained by the abnormal behaviors (e.g., eccentricity, perceptual dysregulation) that characterize psychoticism, as binding values place a great deal of importance on following social norms (Noser et al., 2015). Taken together, these findings suggest that, compared to others, individuals with high levels of negative affectivity are concerned with the welfare of others and the maintenance of social order, those with high levels of antagonism and disinhibition are less concerned with the welfare of others, and individuals with high levels of psychoticism are less concerned about maintaining social order.

Age Differences in PID-5 Traits

Personality pathology for younger age groups is a contentious topic (De Clercq et al., 2014). This is partially due to the fact that PD symptomology in adolescence is unlikely to persist into adulthood (APA, 2000). As a result, there has been a general lack of research on the vulnerabilities and consequences of personality pathology in younger age groups (e.g., Cohen,

2008). However, with the introduction of the DSM-5's alternative model, researchers have begun to examine personality pathology in adolescence (De Clercq et al., 2014) as well as in older age groups (Van den Broeck, Bastiaansen, Rossi, Dierckx, & De Clercq, 2013). Investigating pathological personality traits in adolescent samples may have important implications for personality pathology (De Clercq et al., 2014). For instance, some research has found that personality pathology can be traced back to adolescence or even childhood (e.g., Cicchetti & Crick, 2009; Cohen, 2008). Therefore, the PID-5 may be able to provide insight into effective treatments for younger populations without the stigma that often comes with PD labels.

Relatedly, researchers have investigated whether the PID-5 is an accurate age-neutral personality assessment (Van den Broeck et al., 2013). For instance, results from an item-response theory analysis showed that DSM-IV Axis II criteria did not meet adequate face validity in an older age sample (Balsis, Gleason, Woods, & Oltmanns, 2007), which could influence the diagnosis of personality pathology in older adult populations (Van den Broeck et al., 2013). Further, one criticism of the PID-5 is that an older adult population was not examined during its construction (Van den Broeck et al., 2013). Using a Dutch sample, Van den Broeck et al. (2013) found that four PID-5 facets (i.e., withdrawal, attention seeking, rigid perfectionism, and unusual beliefs) had large Differential Item Functioning (DIF) – which occurs when both younger and older adults report similar levels of a trait but do not have the same probability of adopting that trait (Edwards & Edelen, 2009). When DIF occurs it can result in flawed interpretations of significant results and between-group differences (Millsap, 2011).

Van den Broeck et al. (2013) found that younger adults endorsed certain items that measure withdrawal (e.g., "I'm not interested in making friends") as opposed to older adults (e.g., "I keep my distance from people"). This may be explained, at least in part, by the fact that as people age they have a tendency to be more selective concerning their social interactions (Carstensen, 1991) and experience a decline in the number of the social interactions they encounter (Van den Broeck et al., 2013). Differences also occurred between the responses of younger and older adults on the attention seeking facet. For example, younger adults endorsed the item "I love getting attention", whereas older adults adopted the "I crave attention" item (Van den Broeck et al., 2013). Older adults may favor craving attention because they are more likely to be lonely (e.g., Holmen & Furukawa, 2002). In addition, younger adults scored higher on the item "I focus too much on minor details," which captures the rigid perfectionism facet. This finding may be, at least partially, explained by the fact that younger adults more likely have an occupation, whereas older adults may be retired (Van den Broeck et al., 2013). Lastly, younger adults were more likely to endorse the items assessing unusual beliefs (e.g., "I see unusual connections between things," "People can move things in their minds"). This may be explained by younger adults' desire to embrace individualism and deviate from traditional norms, whereas older adults are more likely to embrace traditional norms (Reed & Carstensen, 2012). Taken together, these findings suggest that research using the PID-5 facets should be interpreted with caution. In particular, the age of participants should be taken into consideration when interpreting results using the PID-5. From this perspective, future research may consider items that are written particularly for younger adults and older adults (Van den Broeck et al., 2013). For example, the pathological personality facet "suspiciousness" has been found to have poor reliability in older age groups (Van den Broeck et al., 2013). In addition, future research should look at the possibility of making the particular items that load on to this facet more efficient. However, despite these age differences the PID-5 has been found to be an accurate and reliable measurement tool for pathological personality traits across a large section of the life span (De Clercq et al., 2014).

Humor Styles

Humor has many different functions (Zeigler-Hill, McCabe, & Vrabel, in press) and can provide insight into how an individual feels about the self (Besser & Zeigler-Hill, 2011). For example, humor has been conceptualized as a defense mechanism (Freud, 1928) as well as an intrapsychic (e.g., stress management; Martin, Puhlik-Doris, Larsen, Gray, & Weir, 2003) and interpersonal regulator (e.g., relationship maintenance; Martin, 2007). Humor can be understood through two underlying dimensions – the first dimension defines humor as either being benign or injurious, and the second dimension of humor is designed to either enhance relationships with others or enhance the self (Martin, 2007). These two underlying dimensions of humor combine to make four specific styles of humor: affiliative humor (benign humor that enhances relationships with others), self-enhancing humor (benign humor that enhances the self), self-defeating humor (injurious humor that enhances relationships with others), and aggressive humor (injurious humor that enhances the self; Martin, 2007).

Basic personality features have been found to be associated with humor styles (Veselka, Schermer, Martin, & Vernon, 2010). For example, past research has shown that individuals with high levels of extraversion adopt positive humor styles (Veselka et al., 2010). Recent research has extended such findings by focusing on the connections between PID-5 traits and humor. For example, Zeigler-Hill et al. (in press) found that the PID-5 traits are related to humor styles. Specifically, Zeigler-Hill et al. (in press) found that negative affectivity and detachment were found to be negatively associated with self-enhancing and affiliative humor styles. Given that individuals with high levels of negative affectivity are prone to negative emotional experiences (e.g., Krueger et al., 2012) and those high in detachment are cold, avoidant (Wright, Pincus et al., 2012), and do not engage in expressions of warmth (Ackerman & Corretti, 2015), these findings are consistent with previous work showing a positive association between self-enhancing and affiliative humor styles and positive moods and emotions (Martin et al., 2003) These findings suggest that individuals with high levels of negative affectivity and detachment lack the ability to engage in humor that strengthens their relationships (i.e., affiliative humor) or humor that is used as a coping mechanism for the self (i.e., self-enhancing humor).

Disinhibition was found to have a positive relationship with self-defeating and aggressive humor styles (Zeigler-Hill et al., in press). One possible explanation for this is that disinhibited individuals are more likely to engage in behaviors that are impulsive and destructive to themselves and others (APA, 2013). Psychoticism was found to have a positive relationship with a self-defeating humor style (Zeigler-Hill et al., in press), which may have developed because individuals with high levels of psychoticism tend to engage in behaviors related to physical self-harm (Hopwood et al., 2013). Antagonism was found to be positively associated with an aggressive humor style and negatively associated with a self-enhancing humor style (Zeigler-Hill et al., in press), which is consistent with the interpersonal features of antagonism (e.g., cold, callous, manipulative; Wright, Pincus, et al., 2012). Therefore, antagonistic individuals may be inclined to avoid affiliative humor in favor of aggressive humor as a means of self-enhancement. For example, individuals with high levels of antagonism are concerned with fulfilling their own needs even if it negatively impacts others (e.g., Harkness et al., 2014). Taken together, these findings suggest that individuals with high levels of negative affectivity and detachment may be less likely to employ benign humor styles whereas individuals with high levels of antagonism, disinhibition, and psychoticism may be more likely to employ injurious humor styles. Therefore, the PID-5 traits are an important tool for understanding individual differences in humor styles.

Interpersonal Functioning

Interpersonal dysfunction is one of the impairments at the heart of personality pathology (APA, 2013). Associations have been found between pathological personality traits and diminished interpersonal functioning (e.g., Williams & Simms, 2015). A common means of empirically assessing interpersonal functioning is with the interpersonal circumplex, a conceptual representation of an orthogonal two-dimensional model of interpersonal behaviors (i.e., agency and communion; Wiggins, Phillips, & Trapnell, 1989). For example, negative affectivity has been positioned within the Unassured-Submissive octant (Southard et al., 2015) and the Warm-Agreeable octant (Wright, Pincus, et al., 2012), which would suggest that individuals with high levels of negative affectivity have fearful and passive interpersonal styles (Wiggins et al., 1989). Southard et al., (2015) found that detachment fell within the Aloof-Introverted octant, whereas Wright, Pincus, et al. (2012) found that the trait fell between the octants of Aloof-Introverted and Unassured-Submissive, which suggests that introverted anhedonic individuals have interpersonal styles characterized by avoidance and restricted affect (Wiggins et al., 1989). Antagonism was found to fall within the Cold-hearted octant (Southard et al., 2015) and within the Assured-Dominant octant (Wright, Pincus, et al., 2012), which suggests that individuals with the tendency to be aggressive and domineering have manipulative, uncooperative, and unsympathetic interpersonal styles (Wiggins et al., 1989). Disinhibition was found to map onto the Cold-hearted octant (Southard et al., 2015) and the Arrogant-Calculating octant (Wright, Pincus, et al., 2012), suggesting that impulsive and sensation seeking individuals have relatively callous, irresponsible, and unkind interpersonal styles (Wiggins et al., 1989). Psychoticism has been positioned within the octant representing Aloof-Introverted (Southard et al., 2015) and Arrogant-Calculating (Wright, Pincus, et al., 2012), suggesting that individuals with the tendency to experience illogical thought patterns have callous and avoidant interpersonal styles (Wiggins et al., 1989). Taken together, these findings suggest that all PID-5 traits – with the possible exception of negative affectivity (Wright, Pincus, et al., 2012) – have interpersonal styles marked by varying degrees of hostility (Southard et al., 2015) and lack communion (Wright, Pincus, et al., 2012).

Importantly, these findings have been mirrored using a clinical sample (e.g., Williams & Simms, 2015).

Romantic Relationship Behaviors

The interpersonal dysfunction associated with pathological personality traits may also have an impact on romantic relationship functioning. Basic personality traits have been shown to be associated with the strategies employed in relationship maintenance (e.g., Holden, Zeigler-Hill, Pham, & Shackelford, 2014). Using an adult community sample, Holden et al. (2015) found that certain pathological personality traits were associated with the ways in which individuals retain their romantic partners. More specifically, negative affectivity and antagonism were positively associated with benefit-provisioning (i.e., engaging in behaviors that highlight the positive aspects of maintaining one's current romantic relationship) and cost-inflicting mate retention behaviors (i.e., engaging in behaviors that generate costs to the partner if he or she decides to leave the relationship or behave unfaithfully), whereas detachment was negatively associated with both forms of mate retention behaviors (Holden et al., 2015). In other words, individuals prone to experiencing negative emotions (i.e., negative affectivity) and those prone to aggression (i.e., antagonism) were more likely to provide benefits and inflict costs on their romantic partners – as well as potential romantic rivals – as a means of maintaining their relationships (Holden et al., 2015). In contrast, introverted and anhedonic individuals (i.e., individuals high in detachment) were less likely to provide benefits or inflict costs on their romantic partners – or romantic rivals – in order to prevent the dissolution of their romantic relationships (Holden et al., 2015). Certain pathological personality traits have also been shown to predict various motives for remaining close with former romantic partners. Mogilski and Welling (in press) found that negative affectivity positively predicted sentimental motives for remaining friends with a former romantic partner, whereas negative affectivity and antagonism both positively predicted pragmatic motives for remaining friends with a former romantic partner. Taken together, these findings suggest that individuals with high levels of negative affectivity and antagonism may be more inclined to retain their mates as well as more motivated to remain close to them after the relationship ends, whereas those high in detachment may be relatively disinterested in retaining or remaining close with their romantic partners.

Neurobiology

A substantial body of research has been focused on the neurobiological bases for personality (e.g., DeYoung et al., 2010). For example, previous work has shown that positive emotionality is connected to greater mass in the left amygdala, whereas negative emotionality is linked to thickness of the medial orbitofrontal cortex (Lewis et al., 2014). Wright et al., (2006) found that extraversion and neuroticism are negatively associated with the thickness of the right medial inferior frontal cortex and the left orbitofrontal cortex, respectively. Previous work has also linked extraversion to the volume of the medial orbitofrontal cortex, neuroticism to the mid-cingulate cortex, the cingulate gyrus, the cingulate cortex, the cerebellum, the right dorsomedial prefrontal cortex, and the left medial temporal lobe, agreeableness to the posterior cingulate cortex, the superior temporal sulcus and gyrus, and conscientiousness to the volume of the lateral prefrontal cortex and the posterior fusiform gyrus (DeYoung et al., 2010).

In the first attempt to understand the connections between neurobiology and the PID-5 traits, James, Engdahl, Leuthold, Krueger, and Georgopoulos (2015) used magnetoencephalography (MEG) imaging to compare the resting-state neural communication patterns of healthy veterans to those of veterans formally diagnosed with PDs. James, Engdahl, et al., (2015) found that lower levels of PID-5 traits were associated with decorrelated neural network activity (i.e., weakened neural signals that are observed in healthy brain function and associated with an increased capacity for information processing; e.g., Kohn, 2007). In contrast, high levels of PID-5 traits were associated with hypercorrelation of neural network activity (i.e., overactive neural signals; James, Engdahl, et al., 2015). Importantly, veterans in the PD group scored significantly higher on all PID-5 traits – with the exception of antagonism – than veterans in the healthy control group.

Future Directions

Despite the inherent disadvantages of a categorical diagnostic system and the growing evidence supporting a dimensional framework for diagnosis, the transition to a dimensional system remains strongly opposed (APA, 2013). More research is needed to support the implementation of the alternative model as the primary classification system for future versions of the DSM.

Longitudinal

Past research has found significant longitudinal results regarding the Big Five personality traits (Soldz & Vaillant, 1999). For example, conscientiousness in younger adulthood has been found to predict functioning in older adulthood (Soldz & Vaillant, 1999). In addition, neuroticism in younger adulthood has been found to predict depression and alcoholism in older adulthood (Soldz & Vaillant, 1999). Future research should investigate the maladaptive variates of these domains and whether pathological personality features predict certain life outcomes. Longitudinal studies could possibly clear up the complexity of age and personality disorders. For example, whether pathological personality features change over the course of one's lifespan or remain stable. To our knowledge, the only longitudinal research on the PID-5 (i.e., Wright et al., 2015) found that pathological personality traits remained relatively unchanged over the course of approximately a year and a half. Further research should assess the stability of the PID-5 traits over a greater length of time.

Cross-Cultural

Rounsaville et al. (2002) argue that culture needs to be taken into consideration when investigating diagnostic criteria. In particular, previous research has found that collectivism and individualism vary with regard to cognition, motivation, emotion, well-being, and social behaviors (see Triandis & Suh, 2002 for a review). Additionally, the Big Five personality traits have been found to be universal in some studies (Goldberg, 1981). However, some criticize these findings because the sample cultures were too similar (Triandis & Suh, 2002). In respect to these findings, future research should be conducted regarding whether the PID-5 dimensions are relevant across cultures. Cross-cultural findings could help improve the PID-5 and make pathological personality assessment applicable to other cultures.

Self-Esteem

Self-esteem has been found to be associated with an array of issues (e.g., life satisfaction; Myers & Diener, 1995). Recently, self-esteem has been found to be more complex than simply whether it is high or low (e.g., Zeigler-Hill,

2013). For example, self-esteem can be either secure (e.g., well-anchored, realistic feelings of self-worth) or fragile (e.g., vulnerable, unrealistic feelings of self-worth; Jordan & Zeigler-Hill, 2013). One potential component of fragile self-esteem is whether an individual's self-esteem is unstable (i.e., fluctuations in one's state self-esteem around his or her self-esteem level; e.g., Jordan & Zeigler-Hill, 2013; Kernis, 2005). There is a lack of research concerning the associations that the PID-5 traits may have with these aspects of self-esteem and future research should address this gap in the existing literature.

Other Pathological Traits and Domains

Future research should consider the possibility that other pathological personality traits and facets may exist (e.g., Krueger et al., 2012). For example, the 25 personality facets that make up the PID-5 are not exhaustive and more research is needed to identify other potential maladaptive facets. Further, 10 out of the 25 PID-5 facets (i.e., attention seeking, callousness, despressivity, hostility, preservation, restricted affectivity, rigid perfectionism, risk taking, submissiveness, and suspiciousness) load on more than one PID-5 trait. It is possible that additional pathological personality features that have yet to be uncovered.

Unifying Normal and Maladaptive Personality

Normal and abnormal personality traits exist on the same continuum (Thomas et al., 2013). Previous work has attempted to identify a means of measuring both the normal and pathological aspects of personality simultaneously (e.g., DeYoung, Carey, Krueger, & Ross, 2016; Watson et al., 2013). However, research should be focused on capturing both poles of abnormality. In other words, the PID-5 measures pathological personality traits on one end of the continuum but does not measure the abnormality that exists on the other end of the continuum (Pettersson et al., 2014). For example, pathological vigilance may exist on the same continuum as conscientiousness and disinhibition (Nettle, 2006). Future research should continue to focus on capturing the pathological ends of the personality continua.

Conclusion

The PID-5 is an empirically driven method of identifying pathological personality traits in clinical and nonclinical samples (e.g., James, Engdahl, et al., 2015) and deserves further research. To date, researchers have found associations between PID-5 traits and an array of outcomes including morality (Noser et al., 2015), mate retention (Holden et al., 2015), humor (Zeigler-Hill et al., in press), and emotion dysregulation (Pollok et al., 2016), yet research concerning the PID-5 is still in its nascent stages. Additional research concerning the PID-5 traits may offer significant clinical advantages. In particular, the possibility of identifying other pathological personality features may provide a better understating for personality impairments, as well as more effective treatment options for certain disorders (e.g., alcohol use disorder).

References

Ackerman, R. A., & Corretti, C. A. (2015). Pathological personality traits and intimacy processes within roommate relationships. *European Journal of Personality*, *29*, 152-172.

Ackerman, R. A., Witt, E. A., Donnellan, M., Trzesniewski, K. H., Robins, R. W., & Kashy, D. A. (2011). What does the Narcissistic Personality Inventory really measure? *Assessment*, *18*, 67-87.

Al-Dajani, N., Gralnick, T. M., & Bagby, R. M. (2016). A psychometric review of the Personality Inventory for DSM–5 (PID–5): Current status and future directions. *Journal of Personality Assessment*, *98*, 62-81.

American Psychiatric Association. (1980). *Diagnostic and statistical manual of mental disorders* (3rd ed.). Washington, DC: American Psychiatric Publishing.

American Psychiatric Association. (2000). *Diagnostic and Statistical Manual of Mental Disorders* (4th ed., text revision). Washington, DC: American Psychiatric Publishing.

American Psychiatric Association. (2013). *Diagnostic and statistical manual of mental disorders* (5th ed.). Washington, DC: American Psychiatric Publishing.

Anderson, J. L., Sellbom, M., Bagby, R. M., Quilty, L. C., Veltri, C. O., Markon, K. E., & Krueger, R. F. (2013). On the convergence between

PSY-5 domains and PID-5 domains and facets implications for assessment of DSM-5 personality traits. *Assessment*, *20*, 286-294.

Ashton, M. C., Lee, K., de Vries, R. E., Hendrickse, J., & Born, M. P. (2012). The maladaptive personality traits of the personality inventory for DSM-5 (PID-5) in relation to the HEXACO personality factors and schizotypy/dissociation. *Journal of Personality Disorders*, *26*, 641-659.

Balsis, S., Gleason, M. E., Woods, C. M., & Oltmanns, T. F. (2007). An item response theory analysis of DSM-IV personality disorder criteria across younger and older age groups. *Psychology and Aging*, *22*, 171-185.

Bastiaens, T., Claes, L., Smits, D., De Clercq, B., De Fruyt, F., Rossi, G., & De Hert, M. (2016). The construct validity of the Dutch Personality Inventory for DSM-5 Personality Disorders (PID-5) in a clinical sample. *Assessment*, *23*, 42-51.

Besser, A., & Zeigler-Hill, V. (2011). Pathological forms of narcissism and perceived stress during the transition to the university: The mediating role of humor styles. *International Journal of Stress Management*, *18*, 197-221.

Carstensen, L. L. (1991). Selectivity theory: Social activity in life-span context. *Annual Review of Gerontology and Geriatrics*, *11*, 195-217.

Christie, R., & Geis, F. (1970). *Studies in Machiavellianism*. New York, NY: Academic Press.

Cicchetti, D., & Crick, N. R. (2009). Precursors and diverse pathways to personality disorder in children and adolescents. *Development and Psychopathology*, *21*, 683–685.

Cohen, P. (2008). Child development and personality disorder. *Psychiatric Clinics of North America*, *31*, 477-493.

Creswell, K. G., Bachrach, R. L., Wright, A. G., Pinto, A., & Ansell, E. (2016). Predicting problematic alcohol use with the DSM-5 alternative model of personality pathology. *Personality Disorders: Theory, Research, and Treatment*, *7*, 103-111.

De Clercq, B., De Fruyt, F., De Bolle, M., Van Hiel, A., Markon, K. E., & Krueger, R. F. (2014). The hierarchical structure and construct validity of the PID-5 trait measure in adolescence. *Journal of Personality*, *82*, 158-169.

De Fruyt, F., De Clercq, B., De Bolle, M., Wille, B., Markon, K., & Krueger, R. F. (2013). General and maladaptive traits in a five-factor framework for DSM-5 in a university student sample. *Assessment, 20*, 295-307.

DeYoung, C. G., Carey, B. E., Krueger, R. F., & Ross, S. R. (2016). Ten aspects of the Big Five in the Personality Inventory for DSM-5. *Personality Disorders: Theory, Research, and Treatment, 7*, 113-123.

DeYoung, C. G., Hirsh, J. B., Shane, M. S., Papademetris, X., Rajeevan, N., & Gray, J. R. (2010). Testing predictions from personality neuroscience: Brain structure and the Big Five. *Psychological Science, 21*, 820-828.

Drislane, L. E., Vaidyanathan, U., & Patrick, C. J. (2013). Reduced cortical call to arms differentiates psychopathy from antisocial personality disorder. *Psychological Medicine, 43*, 825-835.

Edwards, M. C., & Edelen, M. O. (2009). Special topics in item response theory. In R. E. Millsap & A. Maydu-Olivares (Eds.), *The SAGE handbook of quantitative methods in psychology*. (pp. 178-198). Thousand Oaks, CA: SAGE.

Few, L. R., Miller, J. D., Rothbaum, A. O., Meller, S., Maples, J., Terry, D. P., & MacKillop, J. (2013). Examination of the Section III DSM-5 diagnostic system for personality disorders in an outpatient clinical sample. *Journal of Abnormal Psychology, 122*, 1057-1086.

Freud, S. (1928). Humour. *International Journal of Psychoanalysis, 9*, 1-6.

Frijda, N. H., & Mesquita, B. (1994). The social roles and functions of emotions. In S. Kitayama & H. R. Markus (Eds.), *Emotion and culture: Empirical studies of mutual influence*. (pp. 51-87) Washington, DC: American Psychological Association.

Goldberg, L. R. (1981). Language and individual differences: The search for universals in personality lexicons. *Review of Personality and Social Psychology, 2*, 141-165.

Gore, W. L., & Widiger, T. A. (2013). The DSM-5 dimensional trait model and Five-Factor models of general personality. *Journal of Abnormal Psychology, 122*, 816-821.

Graham, J., Nosek, B., Haidt, J., Iyer, R., Koleva, S., & Ditto. (2011). Mapping the moral domain. *Journal of Personality and Social Psychology, 2*, 366-385.

Gratz, K. L., & Roemer, L. (2004). Multidimensional assessment of emotion regulation and dysregulation: Development, factor structure, and initial validation of the difficulties in emotion regulation scale. *Journal of Psychopathology and Behavioral Assessment, 26*, 41-54.

Gunderson, J. G. (1992). Diagnostic controversies. *American Psychiatric Press Review of Psychiatry, 11*, 9-24.

Gutiérrez, F., Aluja, A., Peri, J. M., Calvo, N., Ferrer, M., Baillés, E., & Krueger, R. F. (in press). Psychometric properties of the Spanish PID-5 in a clinical and a community sample. *Assessment.*

Haidt, J., & Graham, J. (2007). When morality opposes justice: Conservatives have moral intuitions that liberals may not recognize. *Social Justice Research*, *20*, 98-116.

Harkness, A. R., McNulty, J. L., & Ben-Porath, Y. (1995). The personality psychopathology five (PSY-5): Constructs and MMPI-2 scales. *Psychological Assessment, 7*, 104-114.

Harkness, A. R., Reynolds, S. M., & Lilienfeld, S. O. (2014). A review of systems for psychology and psychiatry: adaptive systems, personality psychopathology five (PSY-5), and the DSM–5. *Journal of Personality Assessment*, *96*, 121-139.

Holden, C. J., Roof, C. H., McCabe, G., & Zeigler-Hill, V. (2015). Detached and antagonistic: Pathological personality features and mate retention behaviors. *Personality and Individual Differences*, *83*, 77-84.

Holden, C. J., Zeigler-Hill, V., Pham, M. N., & Shackelford, T. K. (2014). Personality features and mate retention strategies: Honesty-humility and the willingness to manipulate, deceive, and exploit romantic partners. *Personality and Individual Differences*, *57*, 31-36.

Holmén, K., & Furukawa, H. (2002). Loneliness, health and social network among elderly people—a follow-up study. *Archives of Gerontology and Geriatrics*, *35*, 261-274.

Hopwood, C. J., Thomas, K. M., Markon, K. E., Wright, A. G., & Krueger, R. F. (2012). DSM-5 personality traits and DSM-IV personality disorders. *Journal of Abnormal Psychology*, *121*, 424-432.

Hopwood, C. J., Wright, A. G. C., Krueger, R. F., Schade, N., Markon, K. E., & Morey, L. C. (2013). DSM-5 pathological personality traits and the personality assessment inventory. *Assessment, 20*, 269-285.

James, L. M., Anders, S. L., Peterson, C. K., Engdahl, B. E., Krueger, R. F., & Georgopoulos, A. P. (2015). DSM-5 personality traits discriminate between posttraumatic stress disorder and control groups. *Experimental Brain Research*, *233*, 2021-2028.

James, L. M., Engdahl, B. E., Leuthold, A. C., Krueger, R. F., & Georgopoulos, A. P. (2015). Pathological personality traits modulate neural interactions. *Experimental Brain Research*, *233*, 3543-3552.

Jensen-Campbell, L. A., Knack, J. M., Waldrip, A. M., & Campbell, S. D. (2007). Do Big Five personality traits associated with self-control influence the regulation of anger and aggression? *Journal of Research in Personality*, *41*, 403-424.

Jordan, C. H., & Zeigler-Hill, V. (2013). Fragile self-esteem: The perils and pitfalls of (some) high self-esteem. In V. Zeigler-Hill (Ed.), *Self-esteem* (pp. 80-98). London: Psychology Press.

Kernis, M. H. (2005). Measuring self-esteem in context: The importance of stability of self-esteem in psychological functioning. *Journal of Personality*, *73*, 1569-1605.

Kohn, A. (2007). Visual adaptation: physiology, mechanisms, and functional benefits. *Journal of Neurophysiology*, *97*, 3155-3164.

Krueger, R. F. (2013). Personality disorders are the vanguard of the post-DSM-5.0 era. *Personality Disorders: Theory, Research, and Treatment, 4*, 355-362

Krueger, R. F., Derringer, J., Markon, K. E., Watson, D., & Skodol, A. E. (2012). Initial construction of a maladaptive personality trait model and inventory for DSM-5. *Psychological Medicine*, *42*, 1879-1890.

Lee, K., & Ashton, M. C. (2004). Psychometric properties of the HEXACO personality inventory. *Multivariate Behavioral Research, 39*, 329-358.

Lewis, G. J., Panizzon, M. S., Eyler, L., Fennema-Notestine, C., Chen, C. H., Neale, M. C., & Franz, C. E. (2014). Heritable influences on amygdala and orbitofrontal cortex contribute to genetic variation in core dimensions of personality. *Neuroimage*, *103*, 309-315.

Mahmut, M. K., Menictas, C., Stevenson, R. J., & Homewood, J. (2011). Validating the factor structure of the Self-Report Psychopathy Scale in a community sample. *Psychological Assessment*, *23*, 670–678.

Marcus, D. K., Zeigler-Hill, V., Mercer, S. H., & Norris, A. L. (2014). The psychology of spite and the measurement of spitefulness. *Psychological Assessment*, *26*, 563–574.

Markon, K. E., Quilty, L. C., Bagby, R. M., & Krueger, R. F. (2013). The development and psychometric properties of an informant-report form of the personality inventory for DSM-5 (PID-5). *Assessment, 20*, 370-383.

Martin, R. A. (2007). *The psychology of humor: An integrative approach.* Burlington, MA: Elsevier.

Martin, R. A., Puhlik-Doris, P., Larsen, G., Gray, J., & Weir, K. (2003). Individual differences in uses of humor and their relation to psychological well-being: Development of the Humor Styles Questionnaire. *Journal of Research in Personality*, *37*, 48-75.

Miller, J. D., Gentile, B., Wilson, L., & Campbell, W. K. (2013). Grandiose and vulnerable narcissism and the DSM-5 pathological personality trait model. *Journal of Personality Assessment, 95*, 284-290.

Millsap, R. E. (2011). *Statistical approaches to measurement invariance*. New York, NY: Routledge.

Mogilski, J. K., & Welling, L. L. (in press). Staying friends with an ex: Sex and dark personality traits predict motivations for post-relationship friendship. *Personality and Individual Differences*.

Morgenstern, J., Langenbucher, J., Labouvie, E., & Miller, K. J. (1997). The comorbidity of alcoholism and personality disorders in a clinical population: Prevalence and relation to alcohol typology variables. *Journal of Abnormal Psychology, 106*, 74-84.

Myers, D. G., & Diener, E. (1995). Who is happy? *Psychological Science, 6*, 10-19.

Neeleman, J., Sytema, S., & Wadsworth, M. (2002). Propensity to psychiatric and somatic ill-health: evidence from a birth cohort. *Psychological Medicine, 32*, 793-803.

Nettle, D. (2006). The evolution of personality variation in humans and other animals. *American Psychologist, 61*, 622-631.

Noser, A. E., Zeigler-Hill, V., Vrabel, J. K., Besser, A., Ewing, T. D., & Southard, A. C. (2015). Dark and immoral: The links between pathological personality features and moral values. *Personality and Individual Differences, 75*, 30-35.

O'Meara, A., Davies, J., & Hammond, S. (2011). The psychometric properties and utility of the short sadistic impulse scale (SSIS). *Psychological Assessment, 23*, 523–531.

Penke, L., Denissen, J. J., & Miller, G. F. (2007). The evolutionary genetics of personality. *European Journal of Personality, 21*, 549-587.

Penley, J. A., & Tomaka, J. (2002). Associations among the big five, emotional responses and coping with acute stress. *Personality and Individual Differences, 32*, 1215-1128.

Pettersson, E., Mendle, J., Turkheimer, E., Horn, E. E., Ford, D. C., Simms, L. J., & Clark, L. A. (2014). Do maladaptive behaviors exist at one or both ends of personality traits? *Psychological Assessment, 26*, 433-446.

Pincus, A. L., Ansell, E. B., Pimentel, C. A., Cain, N. M., Wright, A., & Levy, K. N. (2009). Initial construction and validation of the pathological narcissism inventory. Psychological *Assessment, 21*, 365-379.

Pollock, N. C., McCabe, G. A., Southard, A. C., & Zeigler-Hill, V. (2016). Pathological personality traits and emotion regulation difficulties. *Personality and Individual Differences*, *95*, 168-177.

Quilty, L. C., Ayearst, L., Chimielewski, M., Pollock, B. G., & Bagby, R. M. (2013). The psychometric properties of the personality inventory for DSM-5 in an APA DSM-5 field trial sample. *Assessment, 20*, 362-369.

Reed, A. E., & Carstensen, L. L. (2012). The theory behind the age-related positivity effect. *Frontiers in Psychology, 3*, 1-9.

Rounsaville, B. J., Alarcón, R. D., Andrews, G., Jackson, J. S., Kendell, R. E., & Kendler, K. (2002). Basic nomenclature issues for DSM-V. In. D. J. Kupfer, M. B. First, & D. A. Regier (Eds.), *A research agenda for DSM-V.* (pp. 1-29). Arlington, VA: American Psychiatric Association.

Sher, K. J., Trull, T. J., Bartholow, B. D., & Vieth, A. (1999). Personality and alcoholism: Issues, methods, and etiological processes. In K. E. Leonard & H. T. Blane (Eds.) *Psychological theories of drinking and alcoholism (*2nd ed., pp. 55-105). New York, NY: Plenum Press.

Soldz, S., & Vaillant, G. E. (1999). The Big Five personality traits and the life course: A 45-year longitudinal study. *Journal of Research in Personality*, *33*, 208-232.

Southard, A. C., Noser, A. E., Pollock, N. C., Mercer, S. H., & Zeigler-Hill, V. (2015). The interpersonal nature of dark personality features. *Journal of Social and Clinical Psychology*, *34*, 555-586.

Strickland, C. M., Drislane, L. E., Lucy, M., Krueger, R. F., & Patrick, C. J. (2013). Characterizing psychopathy using DSM-5 personality traits. *Assessment, 20*, 327-338.

Thomas, K. M., Yalch, M. M., Krueger, R. F., Wright, A. G. C., Markon, K. E., & Hopwood, C. J. (2013). The convergent structure of DSM-5 personality trait facets and Five-Factor model trait domains. *Assessment, 20*, 308-311.

Tooby, J., & Cosmides, L. (1990). The past explains the present: Emotional adaptations and the structure of ancestral environments. *Ethology and Sociobiology*, *11*, 375-424.

Triandis, H. C., & Suh, E. M. (2002). Cultural influences on personality. *Annual Review of Psychology*, *53*, 133-160.

Trull, T. J., & Durrett, C. A. (2005). Categorical and dimensional models of personality disorder. *Annual Review of Clinical Psychology*, *1*, 355-380.

Vachon, D. D., & Krueger, R. F. (2015). Emotion and the joint structure of personality and psychopathology. *Emotion Review*, *7*, 265-271.

Van den Broeck, J., Bastiaansen, L., Rossi, G., Dierckx, E., & De Clercq, B. (2013). Age-neutrality of the trait facets proposed for personality disorders in DSM-5: a DIFAS analysis of the PID-5. *Journal of Psychopathology and Behavioral Assessment, 35*, 487-494.

Van den Broeck, J., Bastiaansen, L., Rossi, G., Dierckx, E., De Clercq, B., & Hofmans, J. (2014). Hierarchical structure of maladaptive personality traits in older adults: Joint factor analysis of the PID-5 and the DAPP-BQ. *Journal of Personality Disorders, 28*, 198-211.

Veselka, L., Schermer, J. A., Martin, R. A., & Vernon, P. A. (2010). Relations between humor styles and the Dark Triad traits of personality. *Personality and Individual Differences, 48*, 772-774.

Watson, D., Stasik, S. M., Ro, E., & Clark, L. A. (2013). Integrating normal and pathological personality: Relating the DSM-5 trait-dimensional model to general traits of personality. *Assessment, 20*, 312-326.

Widiger, T. A., & Clark, L. A. (2000). Toward DSM-V and the classification of psychopathology. *Psychological Bulletin, 126*, 946-963.

Wiggins, J. S., Phillips, N., & Trapnell, P. (1989). Circular reasoning about interpersonal behavior: Evidence concerning some untested assumptions underlying diagnostic classification. *Journal of Personality and Social Psychology, 56*, 296-305.

Williams, T. F., & Simms, L. J. (2015). Personality disorder models and their coverage of interpersonal problems. *Personality Disorders: Theory, Research, and Treatment, 7*, 15-27.

Wright, A. G., Calabrese, W. R., Rudick, M. M., Yam, W. H., Zelazny, K., Williams, T. F., & Simms, L. J. (2015). Stability of the DSM-5 Section III pathological personality traits and their longitudinal associations with psychosocial functioning in personality disordered individuals. *Journal of Abnormal Psychology, 124*, 199-219.

Wright, A. G., Pincus, A. L., Hopwood, C. J., Thomas, K. M., Markon, K. E., & Krueger, R. F. (2012). An interpersonal analysis of pathological personality traits in DSM-5. *Assessment, 19*, 263-275.

Wright, A. G., Pincus, A. L., Thomas, K. M., Hopwood, C. J., Markon, K. E., & Krueger, R. F. (2013). Conceptions of narcissism and the DSM-5 pathological personality traits. *Assessment, 20*, 339-352.

Wright, A. G., Thomas, K. M., Hopwood, C. J., Markon, K. E., Pincus, A. L., & Krueger, R. F. (2012). The hierarchical structure of DSM-5 pathological personality traits. *Journal of Abnormal Psychology, 121*, 951-963.

Wright, C. I., Williams, D., Feczko, E., Barrett, L. F., Dickerson, B. C., Schwartz, C. E., & Wedig, M. M. (2006). Neuroanatomical correlates of extraversion and neuroticism. *Cerebral Cortex, 16*, 1809-1819.

Zeigler-Hill, V. (2013). The importance of self-esteem. In V. Zeigler-Hill (Ed.), *Self-esteem* (pp. 1-20). London: Psychology Press.

Zeigler-Hill, V., McCabe, G. A., & Vrabel, J. K., (in press). The dark side of humor: DSM-5 pathological personality traits and humor styles. *Europe's Journal of Psychology*.

In: Psychopathology
Editor: Jeremy Williams

ISBN: 978-1-63485-745-1

Chapter 3

EARLY MALADAPTIVE SCHEMA DOMAINS AND THE DARK TRIAD: CORE BELIEFS SHOW WHAT IS COMMON AND WHAT IS DISTINCT IN DARK PERSONALITIES

András Láng*

Institute of Psychology, University of Pécs,
Pécs, Hungary

ABSTRACT

Study of the Dark Triad (DT) has been attracting researchers from several fields of psychology. Although personality traits and behaviors of Machiavellians, narcissists, and psychopaths are well-studied, little has been known about underlying cognitive constructs yet. In this study, we investigated the association between the DT and early maladaptive schema domains, i.e, underlying cognitive constructs. 503 adolescents (357 girls; 16.03 ± .93 years of age on average) completed self-report measures of the DT and early maladaptive schemas. Results showed Impaired Limits schema domain as the common schema domain of DT traits. Analyses were also able to differentiate between the Dark Dyad (i.e., psychopathy and Machiavellianism) and narcissism and to reveal schema domain patterns specifically related to psychopathy. Results are discussed in the context of contemporary theorizing about dark

* E-mail: andraslang@hotmail.com, Phone: + 36 30 2686322.

personality traits. We conclude that the theory of early maladaptive schemas can be a useful approach to the better understanding of the DT.

Keywords: Dark Triad, Machiavellianism, narcissism, psychopathy, early maladaptive schema domains, Impaired Limits

1. Introduction

The Dark Triad (DT) – including subclinical psychopathy, subclinical narcissism, and Machiavellianism – has been a widely studies construct since its introduction (Paulhus and Williams 2002). Nevertheless, underlying cognitive constructs (e.g., core beliefs) have not been systematically investigated yet. The schema-approach (Young 1999) might be a promising framework to further extend our knowledge about the DT with respect to core beliefs.

Since its introduction by Paulhus and Williams (2002), there has been intensive research to reveal the common core of the DT – i.e., characteristics shared by all three components – and the distinctive characteristics of each component. Disagreeableness (Paulhus and Williams 2002), pursuit of a fast life strategy (Jonason and Webster 2010), manipulative behavior and callousness (Baron-Cohen 2011; Jones and Figueredo 2013), and the lack of honesty and humility (Book, Visser and Volk 2015; Lee and Ashton 2014) are all common characteristics of DT traits. Psychopaths are distinctively characterized by stimulation-seeking, impaired behavioral control, and several forms of antisocial, delinquent behavior (Neumann and Hare 2008). Narcissists have an unrealistic positive image of the self; they feel entitled and long for permanent social affirmation (Rhodewalt and Peterson 2011). Machiavellianism can be considered as a strategic variant of the Dark Triad; Machiavellian individuals are best characterized by calculated social manipulation (Jones and Paulhus 2011a).

Schema theory (Young, Klosko and Weishaar 2003) represents a contemporary and promising approach to the understanding of chronic mental diseases and personality pathology. Given the relationship between personality dysfunction and the DT (Paulhus and Williams 2002), schema theory might be a potentially fruitful theoretical framework in understanding the core beliefs underlying the DT. Although the term schema itself has a long history in the field of psychology (Young et al. 2003), it was Beck (1967) who suggested a broader use of the term. In his opinion schemas are general organizing principles that help people understand and make meaning of life experiences. Young (1999) labeled a subset of these schemas as early maladaptive schemas (EMSs). EMSs are "self-defeating emotional and cognitive patterns that begin early in our development and repeat throughout life" (Young et al. 2003, p. 7.). EMSs are emotional and cognitive patterns, so behaviors are not part of them. Rather behaviors emerge as defensive responses to uncomfortable emotions evoked by the activation of EMSs. Besides EMSs, five overarching categories of EMS domains (see Table 1 for list and descriptions) were also introduced.

Table 1. List and descriptions of early maladaptive schema domains

Schema domain	Description
Disconnection and Rejection	The expectation that one's needs for security, safety, stability, nurturance, empathy, sharing of feelings, acceptance, and respect will not be met in a predictable manner.
Impaired Autonomy and Performance	Expectations about oneself and the environment that interfere with one's perceived ability to separate, survive, function independently, or perform successfully.
Impaired Limits	Deficiency in internal limits, responsibility to others, or long-term goal orientation. Leads to difficulty respecting the rights of others, cooperating with others, making commitments, or setting and meeting realistic personal goals.
Other-Directedness	An excessive focus on the desires, feelings, and responses of others, at the expense of one's own needs in order to gain love and approval, maintain one's sense of connection, or avoid retaliation. Usually involves suppression and lack of awareness regarding one's own anger and natural inclinations.
Overvigilance and Inhibition	Excessive emphasis on suppressing one's spontaneous feelings, impulses, and choices or on meeting rigid, internalized rules and expectations about performance and ethical behavior, often at the expense of happiness, self-expression, relaxation, close relationships, or health.

Young et al. 2003, pp. 14-17.

Although temperamental effects are also emphasized, Young and colleagues (2003) suggest that EMSs develop from experience with toxic childhood environments, i.e. environments with caregivers who are unable to meet the core developmental needs of their offspring. Using the polarity theory, Elliott and Lassen (1997) argue that there is an adaptive schema vis a vis each EMS. Thus, adaptive and maladaptive schemas can be considered as successful and unsuccessful resolutions of Erikson's psychosocial crises, respectively (Young et al. 2003).

Two components of the DT with explicit clinical relevance, namely narcissism and psychopathy (with narcissistic personality disorder and antisocial personality disorder as their clinical analogues), have been already investigated in relation with EMSs. Young and his colleagues (Young and Flanagan 1998; Young et al. 2003) proposed that EMSs from Impaired Limits and Disconnection and Rejection schema domains are associated with pathological narcissism. This proposal gains support from a study by Oatway and Vignoles (2006) who found that parental coldness and excessive parental admiration together were the strongest predictors of overt narcissism. These are forms of caregiving that are responsible for the development of EMSs from the above mentioned two schema domains. Investigating a normative sample, Torres (2002) found somewhat contradicting relations between EMSs and overt narcissism. Overt narcissism was negatively related to some EMSs from Disconnection and Rejection and Impaired Autonomy and Performance schema domains. Overt narcissists showed elevated levels of Entitlement EMS from Impaired Limits schema domain, whereas EMSs from Other-Directedness and Overvigilance and Inhibition were inconsequently correlated with overt narcissism. Moreover, Zeigler-Hill, Green, Arnau, Sisemore, and Myers (2011, p. 101.) found that "the subscales of the NPI differed considerably in their associations with the early maladaptive schemas".

Only a few studies investigated the relationship between antisocial characteristics and EMSs. In normative samples of adolescents and university students, psychopathy – especially its antisocial and impulsive components – was predicted by more pronounced presence of EMSs from Disconnection and Rejection, Impaired Autonomy and Performance, and Impaired Limits schema domains (Chakhssi, Bernstein and Ruiter 2014; Muris 2006; Torres 2002). With regard to Machiavellianism, authors are aware of one single study examining the relationship between Machiavellian attitudes and EMSs. Láng (2015a) found in a sample of adolescents that Emotional deprivation, Mistrust/Abuse, Entitlement/Grandiosity, and Approval-seeking/Recognition-seeking EMSs were positively related to Machiavellianism, whereas

Enmeshment/Undeveloped self and Self-sacrifice EMSs were negatively associated with Machiavellianism.

2. Aims of the Study, Hypothesis

The aims of our study were twofold. On the one hand, we wanted to test whether we would be able to find a core of the DT in terms of EMS domains (Aim 1). Based on the previously suggested cores of the DT (see Introduction), we hypothesized that Impaired Limits schema domain would be the EMS domain that represents a common EMS domain of all DT traits. Beyond that, we also wanted to explore the distinctive EMS domain patterns that could differentiate the components of the DT from each other (Aim 2).

3. Method

3.1. Sample and Procedure

After receiving informed consent from their parents, 498 adolescents (354 girls; 16.03 ± .93 years of age on average) participated in the study (entitled "Associations between personality traits and interpersonal relations"). All participants were students of secondary schools in Hungary. Questionnaires were completed in groups of 25-35 participants, depending on the size of the class.

We had two reasons for asking adolescents to participate in the study. On the one hand, through secondary schools we had access to a relatively big sample to test our hypothesis.

On the other hand, according to the theory of Young and colleagues (2003), EMSs are fully evolved in adolescence.

3.2. Measures

3.2.1. Short Dark Triad (SD3; Jones and Paulhus 2014)

SD3 is a 27-item self-report measure of three socially aversive personality traits.

Table 2. Descriptives of and Pearson's correlations between theDark Triad traits and schema domains (n = 497)

				r						
				Dark Triad		Schema domains				
		M	SD	Narc	Psych	DR	IAP	IL	OD	OI
Dark Triad	Machiavellianism	28.63	5.15	.325	.579	*.235*	.157	*.415*	*.262*	*.302*
	Narcissism	25.21	6.09		.422	- .175	*- .232*	*.271*	.006	- .121
	Psychopathy	22.41	6.32			.117	.099	*.417*	.106	.098
Schema domains	Disconnection and Rejection	11.59	4.10				.744	.461	.681	.767
	Impaired Autonomy and Performance	10.09	3.64					.475	.659	.720
	Impaired Limits	14.34	4.03						.533	.475
	Other-Directedness	13.67	3.51							.693
	Overvigilance and Inhibition	13.73	3.78							

Note: Narc = Narcissim; Psych = Psychopathy; DR = Disconnection and Rejection; IAP = Impaired Autonomy and Performance; IL = Impaired Limits; OD = Other-Directedness; OI = Overvigilance and Inhibition. Correlations with r > |.09| are significant at the level of .05. Correlations between Dark Triad traits and schema domains with an at least small effect size (r > |.20|) are in italics.

The three scales – each with 9 items – measure Machiavellianism (e.g., 'Most people can be manipulated'; Cronbach's α = .67), narcissism (e.g., 'I know that I am special because everyone keeps telling me so'; Cronbach's α = .79), and psychopathy (e.g., 'Payback needs to be quick and nasty'; Cronbach's α = .75).

Participants indicated their agreement with the items on a 5-point Likert-scale.

Correlations between the components (Table 2) were of expected direction and strength (Furnham, Richards, and Paulhus, 2013).

3.2.2. Young Schema Questionnaire Short Form – 3rd Edition (YSQ-S3; Young 2005)

YSQ-S3 is a 90-item self-report measure with 18 scales representing 18 first order EMSs and 5 second order schema domains (Young et al., 2003). Participants indicated their agreement with the items on a 6-point Likert-scale.

A recent study (Van Vlierberghe, Braet, Bosmans, Rosseel, and Bogels, 2010) showed that the use of the five domains is theoretically the most appealing.

Thus, we decided to use schema domain scores for statistical analysis. List and descriptions of schema domains are presented in Table 1. Internal consistency indices were good to excellent for all five schema domains (.75 < Cronbach's αs < .92).

3.3. Statistical Analyses

We used IBM SPSS Statistics 19.0 for Windows for statistical analyses. Besides descriptive statistics, Cronbach's αs were computed as indices of internal reliability.

Level of significance was set at .05 for all analyses. To test the relationship between each EMS domain and each component of the DT, we used Pearson's correlation.

To avoid false positive results (Type I error), only correlations with at least small effect size ($r > |.20|$) were reported and interpreted. Finally, we used canonical correlation analysis to test the relationship between schema domains and the DT as two sets of interrelated variables.

Correlations between variables and canonical variates were considered to be meaningful only in cases where correlation coefficients (rs) were above $|.35|$.

4. RESULTS

Pearson's correlations between schema domains and components of the DT (Table 2) revealed that Machiavellianism was significantly and positively correlated with all but one schema domains. Adolescents with more pronounced Machiavellian attitude had more frequent expectations about neglect, abuse and rejection (Disconnection and Rejection schema domain); they had more problems with respecting others and pursuing long-term personal goals (Impaired Limits schema domain); they were more likely to suppress their own inclinations in order to gain approval (Other-Directedness schema domain); and they put more emphasis on suppressing their feelings to meet rigid internalized expectations (Overvigilance and Inhibition schema domain). Narcissism was positively associated with Impaired Limits schema domain; thus, more narcissistic adolescents had more problems with respecting others, cooperation, and the pursuit of long-term personal goals. Narcissism was negatively associated with Impaired Autonomy and Performance schema domain, which means that more narcissistic adolescents were relatively free of worries about separation, independence, and successful performance. Psychopathy was significantly and positively associated with Impaired Limits schema domain. Thus, adolescents with more pronounced psychopathic personality traits reported to have more problems with maintaining respectful and mutual relationships and with pursuing long-term personal goals.

Further analysis of the two sets of variables (i.e., EMS domains and DT traits) with canonical correlation revealed three significant functions (all $Fs > 14.051$; $ps < .05$). Results of this analysis are presented in Table 3. For the strongest canonical relationship (Function 1), all three DT components loaded strongly and negatively on a canonical variate that was correlated with a canonical variate of EMS domains with only Impaired Limits loading strongly and negatively on it. Thus, we considered Impaired Limits to represent a central and common characteristic of all three DT traits. For Function 2, Machiavellianism and psychopathy loaded positively and narcissism negatively on a canonical variate that was significantly associated with a canonical variate with all schema domains loading strongly on it. We interpreted this canonical correlation as the relationship between the Dark Dyad (i.e., Machiavellianism and psychopathy; Egan, Chan, and Shorter, 2014) and a general vulnerability to psychopathology or general EMS vulnerability. For Function 3, psychopathy loaded strongly and positively on a canonical variate that was correlated with a canonical variate with strong and negative loadings of Other-Directedness and Overvigilance and Inhibition

EMS domains. This canonical correlation – the weakest of all but still significant – was interpreted as impulsive recklessness as a characteristic connected specifically to psychopathy.

5. Discussion

Several limitations of the study have to be mentioned before discussing its results. First, we only relied on self-report measures in obtaining our data. Moreover, SD3 (Jones and Paulhus 2014) was also unable to differentiate between primary and secondary psychopathy or between overt and covert forms of narcissism. Since results from former studies (Chakhssi et al. 2014; Torres 2002; Zeigler-Hill et al. 2011) have shown that EMSs are differentially associated with the different facets of narcissism and psychopathy, further studies should eliminate this impairment with the use of multifaceted measures for each component of the DT.

Table 3. Canonical solution for Dark Triad predicting schema domains (n = 497)

Variable	Function 1 (dark core - IL)		Function 2 (dark dyad – general schema vulnerability)		Function 3 (psychopathy – impulsive recklessness)	
	Coef	r	Coef	r	Coef	r
Mach	- .309	*- .674*	.788	*.682*	- .897	- .283
Narc	- .692	*- .895*	- .811	*- .440*	- .308	- .079
Psych	- .242	*- .713*	.272	*.386*	1.234	*.585*
rc (R2)	.53 (.29)		.40 (.16)		.28 (.08)	
DR	.186	.037	.449	*.893*	.360	- .044
IAP	.713	.165	.310	*.843*	.964	.186
IL	- 1.070	*- .780*	.146	*.548*	.516	.210
OD	- .169	- .207	- .382	*.572*	- .793	*- .377*
OI	- .092	- .062	.529	*.901*	- 1.068	*- .402*

Note: Mach = Machiavellianism; Narc = Narcissim; Psych = Psychopathy; DR = Disconnection and Rejection; IAP = Impaired Autonomy and Performance; IL = Impaired Limits; OD = Other-Directedness; OI = Overvigilance and Inhibition. Coef = standardized coanonical coefficient; rc = canonical correlation. Correlations greater than |.35| are in italics.

Second, some components of the DT – especially Machiavellianism – might be sensitive to cultural embeddedness. Thus, our results are limited in validity, and cross-cultural comparisons should reveal whether our results could be replicated outside Hungary. However, our study is the first that systematically investigated the relationship between the DT and EMS domains.

Results from both Pearson's correlations and canonical correlations supported the hypothesis and showed that Impaired Limits EMS domain was significantly and positively associated with each DT trait and also with the latent variate composed of all three components of the DT. The central role of Impaired Limits as the core of the DT is in line with several explanations. Previously disagreeableness (Paulhus and Williams, 2002), lack of honesty and humility (Book et al. 2015; Lee and Ashton 2014), manipulativeness and callousness (Jones and Figueredo 2013), and the pursuit of a fast life strategy (Jonason and Webster 2010) were all claimed as the core of the DT. Similarly to the above concepts, Impaired Limits EMS domain also refers to a view of a self that is unable to cooperate, to respect others, and to pursue long-term goals. Thus, Impaired Limits could represent a cognitive structure underlying the several core personality traits and behavioral strategies of the DT that were listed above.

Psychopathy and Machiavellianism positively but narcissism negatively contributed to a latent variate that was associated with a latent variate composed of all maladaptive schema domains. On the one hand, this result is in line with previous findings (Torres 2002) that showed negative associations between overt narcissism and EMSs from all EMS domains except for Impaired Limits. The negative association of narcissism with overall schema vulnerability might also result from the omnipotent and invulnerable self-image of narcissist individuals (Rhodewalt and Peterson 2011). However, this self-enhancing bias seems not to be characteristic of individuals high in psychopathy and Machiavellianism who showed generally elevated levels of EMS domains. This line of reasoning fits well with the concept of Dark Dyad (Egan et al. 2014) as well. According to the concept of Dark Dyad, narcissism should be omitted form the DT – leaving it a Dark Dyad – because it often shows outcome patterns that are distinct from those of Machiavellianism and psychopathy. McHoskey's (McHoskey, Worzel and Szyarto 1998) idea of Machiavellianism as everyday psychopathy might also be considered as a pioneering forerunner of the concept of Dark Dyad.

However, the third function of the canonical correlation linked a latent variate composed solely of psychopathy specifically to a latent variate characterized by the relative absence of Other-Directedness and Overvigilance and Inhibition EMS domains. Thus, although with a smaller effect size, but psychopathy still had its own distinct EMS domain correlates compared to Machiavellianism and narcissism. The relative absence of natural inclinations' suppression (Overvigilance and Inhibition EMS domain) and indifference for others' needs and approval (Other-Directedness) is in line with the impulsive and reckless nature of psychopathic individuals (Neumann and Hare 2008).

CONCLUSION

To sum up, the current study found that Impaired Limits EMS domain constituted the central core belief of the Dark Triad. Moreover, we were able to reveal that an overall vulnerability to the negative effects of EMS domains was characteristic of psychopathy and Machiavellianism but not of narcissism. Finally, a characteristic pattern of EMS domains specific to psychopathy – namely relative absence of Other-Directedness and Overvigilance and Inhibition EMS domains – were also found. Given these distinctive patterns, we speculate that the common core of disagreeableness, callousness, and impulsivity – as represented by the salience of the Impaired Limits schema domain – might have different etiology and might serve different functions in the case of each component of the Dark Triad. Machiavellian deceit and exploitation might be frantic yet unsuccessful efforts to establish a sense of safety in face of hurtful affects resulting from the elevated levels of EMS domains (Láng 2015b). Narcissists' might be simply self-absorbed and inattentive to others (Emmons 1987), which leads to disregard. At last, psychopaths – with their abusive life histories and neurological predisposition (Shirtcliff et al. 2009) – seem to have problems with moderating behavior. This speculative line of reasoning might gain some support from previous theorizing about the DT. According to Jones and Paulhus (2011b), narcissists are motivated by ego-identity goals. This is in accordance with our finding that narcissism was solely correlated with Impaired Limits – a self-absorbed, disagreeable interpersonal stance. Contrasted with narcissists, psychopaths and Machiavellians strive for material rewards (Jones and Paulhus 2011b). Moreover, temporal focus distinguishes Machiavellians from psychopaths. While Machiavellian individuals are more like parasites with long-term goals – they infiltrate, deceive, and exploit on the long run –, psychopaths act as predators and function in a fast search-and-prey mode (Jones 2014). This latter statement is in accordance with the result linking psychopathy but not

Machiavellianism to impulsive recklessness, i.e. the relative absence of Other-Directedness and Overvigilance and Inhibition EMS domains.

Despite its limitations, our study is the first to systematically investigate the relationship between EMS domains and the DT. We believe that our results contribute substantially to the understanding of socially disliked, but vulnerable individuals. Future research should elaborate on how our findings could be translated into the prevention and treatment of Dark Triad related psychological problems.

References

Baron-Cohen, S. (2011). The science of evil: On empathy and the origins of cruelty. New York: Basic Books.

Barry, C. T., and Kauten, R. L. (2014). Nonpathological and pathological narcissism: which self-reported characteristics are most problematic in adolescents?. *Journal of Personality Assessment,* 96, 212-219.

Barry, C. T., and Wallace, M. T. (2010). Current considerations in the assessment of youth narcissism: Indicators of pathological and normative development. *Journal of Psychopathology and Behavioral Assessment*, 32, 479-489.

Bartholomew, K., and Horowitz, L. M. (1991). Attachment styles among young adults: a test of a four-category model. *Journal of Personality and Social Psychology,* 61, 226-244.

Beck, A. T. (1967). Depression: Causes and treatment. Philadelphia: University of Pennsylvania Press.

Blair, R. J. R. (1995). A cognitive developmental approach to morality: Investigating the Psychopath. *Cognition*, 57, 1-29.

Blair, R. J. R. (2013). The neurobiology of psychopathic traits in youths. *Nature Reviews Neuroscience*, 14, 786-799.

Blair, R. J. R., Peschardt, K. S., Budhani, S., Mitchell, D. G. V., and Pine, D. S. (2006). The development of psychopathy. *Journal of Child Psychology and Psychiatry*, 47, 262-276.

Book, A., Visser, B. A., and Volk, A. A. (2015). Unpacking "evil": Claiming the core of the Dark Triad. *Personality and Individual Differences*, 73, 29-38.

Brenning, K., Bosmans, G., Braet, C., and Theuwis, L. (2012). Gender differences in cognitive schema vulnerability and depressive symptoms in adolescents. *Behaviour Change*, 29, 164-182.

Chakhssi, F., Bernstein, D., and Ruiter, C. (2014). Early maladaptive schemas in relation to facets of psychopathy and institutional violence in offenders with personality disorders. *Legal and Criminological Psychology*, 19, 356-372.

DeLisi, M., Peters, D. J., Dansby, T., Vaughn, M. G., Shook, J. J., and Hochstetler, A. (2014). Dynamics of psychopathy and moral disengagement in the etiology of crime. *Youth Violence and Juvenile Justice,* 12, 295-314.

Egan, V., Chan, S., and Shorter, G. W. (2014). The Dark Triad, happiness and subjective well-being. *Personality and Individual Differences*, 67, 17-22.

Elliott, C. H., and Lassen, M. K. (1997). A schema polarity model for case conceptualization, intervention, and research. *Clinical Psychology: Science and Practice*, 4, 12-28.

Emmons, R. A. (1987). Narcissism: theory and measurement. *Journal of Personality and Social Psychology*, 52, 11.

Ferriday, C., Vartanian, O., and Mandel, D. R. (2011). Public but not private ego threat triggers aggression in narcissists. *European Journal of Social Psychology,* 41, 564-568.

Finger, E. C., Marsh, A. A., Blair, K. S., Reid, M. E., Sims, C., Ng, P., Pine, S., and Blair, R. J. R. (2011). Disrupted reinforcement signaling in the orbitofrontal cortex and caudate in youths with conduct disorder or oppositional defiant disorder and a high level of psychopathic traits. *American Journal of Psychiatry*, 168, 152-162.

Frazier, T. W., Youngstrom, E. A., Glutting, J. J., and Watkins, M. W. (2007). ADHD and achievement meta-analysis of the child, adolescent, and adult literatures and a concomitant study with college students. *Journal of Learning Disabilities,* 40, 49-65.

Furnham, A., Richards, S. C., and Paulhus, D. L. (2013). The Dark Triad of personality: A 10 year review. *Social and Personality Psychology Compass,* 7, 199-216.

Harter, S., Low, S., and Whitesell, N. R. (2003). What have we learned from Columbine: The impact of the self-system on suicidal and violent ideation among adolescents. *Journal of Youth Violence*, 2, 3–26.

Hopkins, J. R. (2014). Adolescence: The transitional years. New York: Academic Press.

Ináncsi, T., Láng, A., and Bereczkei, T. (2015). Machiavellianism and Adult Attachment in General Interpersonal Relationships and Close Relationships. *Europe's Journal of Psychology*, 11, 139-154.

Jonason, P. K., and Webster, G. D. (2010). The Dirty Dozen: A concise measure of the dark triad. *Psychological Assessment*, 22, 420–432.

Jonason, P. K., Lyons, M., and Bethell, E. (2014). The making of Darth Vader: Parent–child care and the Dark Triad. *Personality and individual differences,* 67, 30-34.

Jones, D. N., and Figueredo, A. J. (2013). The core of darkness: Uncovering the heart of the Dark Triad. *European Journal of Personality*, 27, 521-531.

Jones, D. N., and Paulhus, D. L. (2011a). Machiavellianism. In M. R. Leary, and R. H. Hoyle (Eds.), Handbook of individual differences in social behavior (pp. 93-108). New York: Guilford Press.

Jones, D. N., and Paulhus, D. L. (2011b). Differentiating the Dark Triad within the interpersonal circumplex. In L. M. Horowitz and S. Strack (Eds.), Handbook of interpersonal psychology: Theory, research, assessment, and therapeutic interventions (pp. 249-268). New York, NY: Wiley.

Jones, D. N., and Paulhus, D. L. (2014). Introducing the Short Dark Triad (SD3) A Brief Measure of Dark Personality Traits. *Assessment,* 21, 28-41.

Kajonius, P. J., Persson, B. N., and Jonason, P. K. (2015). Hedonism, Achievement, and Power: Universal values that characterize the Dark Triad. *Personality and Individual Differences*, 77, 173-178.

Kraut, R. E., and Price, J. D. (1976). Machiavellianism in parents and their children. *Journal of Personality and Social Psychology*, 33, 782-786.

Láng, A. (2015a). Machiavellianism and early maladaptive schemas in adolescents. *Personality and Individual Differences*, 87, 162-165.

Láng, A. (2015b). Borderline Personality Organization predicts Machiavellian interpersonal tactics. *Personality and Individual Differences*, 80, 28-31.

Láng, A., and Birkás, B. (2014). Machiavellianism and perceived family functioning in adolescence. *Personality and Individual Differences*, 63, 69-74.

Láng, A., and Lénárd, K. (2015). The relation between memories of childhood psychological maltreatment and Machiavellianism. *Personality and Individual Differences,* 77, 81-85.

Lee, K., and Ashton, M. C. (2014). The dark triad, the big five, and the hexaco model. *Personality and Individual Differences*, 67, 2-5.

Lilienfeld, S. O., Latzman, R. D., Watts, A. L., Smith, S. F., and Dutton, K. (2014). Correlates of psychopathic personality traits in everyday life: results from a large community survey. *Frontiers in Psychology*, published online. Retrieved from http://www.ncbi.nlm.nih.gov/pmc/articles/PMC4106400/pdf/fpsyg-05-00740.pdf on 14th May, 2015.

Lynam, D. R. (1996). The early identification of chronic offenders: who is the fledgling psychopath?. *Psychological Bulletin*, 120, 209–234.

McHoskey, J. W., Worzel, W., and Szyarto, C. (1998). Machiavellianism and psychopathy. *Journal of Personality and Social Psychology*, 74, 192-210.

McIlwain, D. (2003). Bypassing empathy: A Machiavellian theory of mind and sneaky power. In B. Repacholi and V. Slaughter (Eds.), Individual differences in theory of mind. Macquarie monographs in cognitive science (pp. 39–66). Hove, UK: Psychology Press.

Miller, J. D., Dir, A., Gentile, B., Wilson, L., Pryor, L. R., and Campbell, W. K. (2010). Searching for a vulnerable dark triad: Comparing factor 2 psychopathy, vulnerable narcissism, and borderline personality disorder. *Journal of Personality*, 78, 1529-1564.

Morf, C. C., and Rhodewalt, F. (2001). Unraveling the paradoxes of narcissism: A dynamic self-regulatory processing model. *Psychological Inquiry,* 12, 177-196.

Muris, P. (2006). Maladaptive schemas in non clinical adolescents: Relations to perceived parental rearing behaviours, big five personality factors and psychopathological symptoms. *Clinical Psychology and Psychotherapy,* 13, 405-413.

Murray, J., and Farrington, D. P. (2010). Risk factors for conduct disorder and delinquency: key findings from longitudinal studies. *Canadian Journal of Psychiatry*, 55, 633-642.

Neumann, C. S., and Hare, R. D. (2008). Psychopathic traits in a large community sample: links to violence, alcohol use, and intelligence. *Journal of Consulting and Clinical Psychology*, 76, 893-899.

Ojha, H. (2007). Parent-child interaction and Machiavellian orientation. *Journal of the Indian Academy of Applied Psychology*, 33, 285-289.

Otway, L. J., and Vignoles, V. L. (2006). Narcissism and childhood recollections: A quantitative test of psychoanalytic predictions. *Personality and Social Psychology Bulletin*, 32, 104-116.

Paulhus, D. L., and Harms, P. D. (2004). Measuring cognitive ability with the overclaiming technique. *Intelligence,* 32, 297–314.

Paulhus, D. L., and Williams, K. M. (2002). The dark triad of personality: Narcissism, Machiavellianism, and psychopathy. *Journal of Research in Personality,* 36, 556-563.

Pujara, M., Motzkin, J. C., Newman, J. P., Kiehl, K. A., and Koenigs, M. (2014). Neural correlates of reward and loss sensitivity in psychopathy. *Social Cognitive and Affective Neuroscience*, 9, 794-801.

Raskin, R. N. (1980). Narcissism and creativity: Are they related? *Psychological Reports*, 46, 55–60.

Rauthmann, J. F., and Kolar, G. P. (2013). The perceived attractiveness and traits of the Dark Triad: Narcissists are perceived as hot, Machiavellians and psychopaths not. *Personality and individual differences*, 54, 582-586.

Rhodewalt, F. and Peterson, B. (2011). Narcissism. In M. R. Leary, and R. H. Hoyle (Eds.), Handbook of individual differences in social behavior (pp. 547-560). New York: Guilford Press.

Robins, R. W., and Beer, J. S. (2001). Positive illusions about the self: Short-term benefits and long-term costs. *Journal of Personality and Social Psychology,* 80, 340–352.

Shirtcliff, E. A., Vitacco, M. J., Graf, A. R., Gostisha, A. J., Merz, J. L., and Zahn Waxler, C. (2009). Neurobiology of empathy and callousness: implications for the development of antisocial behavior. *Behavioral Sciences and the Law,* 27, 137-171.

Shorey, R. C., Stuart, G. L., and Anderson, S. (2013). Do gender differences in depression remain after controlling for early maladaptive schemas? An examination in a sample of opioid dependent treatment seeking adults. *Clinical Psychology and Psychotherapy*, 20, 401-410.

Shultz, J. S. (1993). Situational and dispositional predictions of performance: A test of the hypothesized Machiavellianism X structure interaction among sales persons. *Journal of Applied Social Psychology*, 23, 478-498.

Sparks, J. R. (1994). Machiavellianism and personal success in marketing: The moderating role of latitude for improvisation. *Journal of the Academy of Marketing Science,* 22, 393-400.

Szijjarto, L., and Bereczkei, T. (2014). The Machiavellians'"Cool Syndrome": They Experience Intensive Feelings but Have Difficulties in Expressing Their Emotions. Current Psychology, published online. Retrieved from http://download-v2.springer.com/static/pdf/658/art%253A10.1007%252 Fs12144-014-9262-1.pdf?token2=exp=1431341873~acl=%2Fstatic%2F pdf%2F658%2Fart%25253A10.1007%25252Fs12144-014-9262-1.pdf*~hmac=7bfd0c1c0606b8639bc608578aee575a1e09a59de08ebef9da a143eb9cf6c4a7 on 11th May, 2015.

Taubner, S., White, L. O., Zimmermann, J., Fonagy, P., and Nolte, T. (2013). Attachment-related mentalization moderates the relationship between psychopathic traits and proactive aggression in adolescence. *Journal of Abnormal Child Psychology,* 41, 929-938.

The Hofstede Centre (n.d.). Data for Hungary on the 6-D model. Retrieved from http://geert-hofstede.com/hungary.html on 11th May, 2015.

Torres, C. (2002). Early maladaptive schemas and cognitive distortions in psychopathy and narcissism (Doctoral dissertation). Retrieved from http://www.sakkyndig.com/psykologi/artvit/torres2002.pdf on 11th May, 2015.

Twenge, J. M., and Campbell, W. K. (2009). The narcissism epidemic: Living in the age of entitlement. New York: Free Press.

Van Vlierberghe, L., Braet, C., Bosmans, G., Rosseel, Y., and Bögels, S. (2010). Maladaptive schemas and psychopathology in adolescence: On the utility of Young's schema theory in youth. *Cognitive Therapy and Research,* 34, 316-332.

Wilson, D. S., Near, D., and Miller, R. R. (1996). Machiavellianism: A synthesis of the evolutionary and psychological literatures. *Psychological Bulletin,* 119, 285–299.

Young, J. E. (1999). Cognitive therapy for personality disorders: A schema-focused approach (rev. ed.). Sarasota: Professional Resources Press.

Young, J. E., and Flanagan, C. (1998). Schema-focused therapy for narcissistic patients. In E. F. Ronningstam (Ed.), Disorders of narcissism: Diagnostic, clinical, and empirical implications (pp. 239-262). Washington, DC: American Psychiatric Association.

Young, J. E., Klosko, J. S., and Weishaar, M. E. (2003). Schema therapy: A practitioner's guide. New York: Guilford Press.

Zeigler-Hill, V., Green, B. A., Arnau, R. C., Sisemore, T. B., and Myers, E. M. (2011). Trouble ahead, trouble behind: Narcissism and early maladaptive schemas. *Journal of Behavior Therapy and Experimental Psychiatry*, 42, 96-103.

In: Psychopathology
Editor: Jeremy Williams
ISBN: 978-1-63485-745-1

Chapter 4

Avoidance: Implications for Psychopathology and Advances in Research

Santiago Barajas[1,*], Luis Garra[2] and Marisa García-Pérez[3]
[1]University Hospital of Guadalajara, Spain
[2]University of Castilla-La Mancha, Spain
[3]Madrid, Spain

Abstract

The concept of avoidance is central to the conceptualization and diagnostic criteria of the Axis I anxiety disorders described by the *Diagnostic and Statistical Manual of Mental Disorders* (4th ed., text rev., DSM-IV-TR; American Psychiatric Association, 2000). Its study has been expanded from motor behaviors in the presence of phobic stimuli to other areas. In the short term, avoidance reduces distress, but in the long term contributes to the maintenance of anxiety. With regard to depression, Ferster (1973) postulated a central role for avoidance in his depression theory. For this author, depressed people escape from aversive internal and external stimuli and frequently avoid related situations. Depression would be characterized by passivity as opposed to action. In

* Corresponding Author address: Dr. Santiago Barajas. Hospital Universitario de Guadalajara. C/ Donante de Sangre s/n. 19002 Guadalajara. Spain. Email: sbarajas@sescam.jccm.es.

this sense, Behavioral Activation as a treatment for depression (Jacobson, Martell, & Dimidjian, 2001; Martell et al., 2001) represents a renewed interest in the concept of avoidance. The relevance of avoidance study is also expanding into other areas of psychopathology, such as psychotic disorders (Vilardaga, Hayes, Atkins, Bresee, & Kambiz, 2013). In this case, some authors propose that avoiding feelings of low self-worth can contribute to paranoid thinking (Udachina, Varese, Myin-Germeys, & Bentall, 2014).

Three main types of avoidance can be distinguished: behavioral avoidance, which includes putting off decisions, turning down opportunities, isolating oneself, and giving up on tasks before they are completed; cognitive avoidance, which refers to a wide variety of coping strategies such as rumination, intentionally trying to suppress thoughts, and attempting to dissociate from negative experiences; and, experiential avoidance, which includes according to Hayes, Wilson, Gifford, Follette, & Strosahl (1996) both avoidance and escape in all of their forms, as long as they are used as methods of altering the form or frequency of experiences and the contexts that occasion them.

The present chapter also reviews the main instruments for assessing avoidance as well as treatment suggestions.

Keywords: avoidance, psychopathology, cognitive-behavioral avoidance, experiential avoidance, avoidance assessment

INTRODUCTION

It is not a matter of avoiding the pain for the pain is inevitable;
it is a matter of choosing the consequences of pain.
(Maurice Maeterlinck, 1862-1949)

Avoidance is a core process in many forms of psychopathology (Barlow, Allen, & Choate, 2004; Barlow et al., 2011). It has been proposed that many emotional disorders are related to efforts to avoid unexpected, excessive or aversive emotional experiences (Barlow, 2002; Martell, Addis, & Jacobson, 2001). Such experiences occur frequently, not only in the clinical population but in the general population as well, for example, 68% of a sample of 300 students had experienced at least one unexpected emotional experience in the last three months (Barlow et al., 2004). In a sense, avoidance strategies can be thought to hinder the extinction of emotional responses. Krypotos, Effting, Kindt, and Beckers (2015) in a magnificent review of theoretical models, laboratory procedures and advances on avoidance learning, affirm that avoidance is quickly becoming a topic of prime empirical interest not only in experimental psychology but also in clinical psychology and psychiatry as well as in behavioral neuroscience. Avoidance is a key characteristic of adaptive and maladaptive fear. Maladaptive avoidance is in fact a central characteristic of a wide spectrum of mental disorders (American Psychiatric Association, 2013). The *Diagnostic and Statistical Manual of Mental Disorders* (DSM-5; American Psychiatric Association, 2013) has included avoidance in several diagnostic criteria that previously referred to fear only.

According to Servatius (2016), avoidance encompasses thoughts and efforts toward prevention of future aversive experiences and events. By comparison, avoidance is a fairly sophisticated construct. Avoidance is the situational evaluation of likelihoods, efficacy of responses, and costs. Therefore, in many circumstances those avoiding are *expected* to be experiencing fear. However, the empirical literature provides ample evidence that the processes are distinct. The bounding conditions of avoidance are not only the duration of threat (acute/sustained), but the perceived intensity of threat, its perceived proximity, and the utility of responses or efforts. These features illustrate that avoidance acquired with arbitrary responses differ in a number of parameters from those modifying reflexive responses or 'natural' responses, which are in turn distinct from fear responses. Diathesis models of mental illness capture avoidance biases as dynamic interactions of vulnerabilities (genes, epigenetics, personality, and developmental phases) with risk factors (psychological stressors, physical injuries) ultimately expressed as psychopathology (Servatius, 2016).

In the present chapter we also consider avoidance as a key concept in psychopathology and we assume that avoidance be it behavioral, cognitive, or emotional, would be present in the majority of mental disorders. This type of avoidance would produce problems in daily life because of its elevated frequency or intensity. For example, someone with a major depressive disorder would avoid contact with other people, because he would not want to see others exhibiting a better mood than his. In panic disorder with agoraphobia, people would avoid situations to prevent them from experiencing unpleasant sensations or to prevent someone else from observing their physiological responses. A person suffering from borderline personality disorder could present self-harm behavior to avoid coping with highly challenging situations, or to escape from painful thoughts, or to imagine unrealistic future events instead of dealing with real present problems. Similarly, alcohol abuse could be considered as an avoidance behavior because it allows someone to avoid personal problems rather than taking an active role and assuming his responsibility to change them. It could even suggest that in schizophrenia, paranoid thinking could functionally be an extreme way to avoid facing traumatic experiences, or facing stressful situations for which he has no coping skills._According to Krypotos et al., (2015), avoidance and escape seem to be distinct subtypes of defensive behaviors, and they might play a different role in mental disorders. Although Mowrer (1951) proposed that escape/avoidance is motivated by high fear levels, multiple results contradict this hypothesis, because these actions also are performed in the absence of fear. Both experimental data and clinical findings suggest that fear may sometimes, but not always, be involved in the maintenance of avoidance. For these authors, the observation that fear may not be necessary for avoidance has clear clinical implications. Avoidance can be acquired not only through direct experience but can be acquired by vicarious learning or instructional learning, even recent evidence shows other indirect pathways as symbolic generalization (Krypotos et al., 2015).

Regarding generalization of avoidance, Cameron, Schlund and Dymond (2015) have indicated that in animals, both fear and avoidance of potentially threatening stimuli may generalize to perceptually related stimuli and situations. The behavioral consequences of generalization mean that aversive learning experiences with specific threats may lead to the inference that classes of related stimuli are threatening, potentially dangerous, and need to be avoided, despite differences in physical form. Although they have pointed out that little is known about avoidance generalization in humans, they have demonstrated for the first time, the equivalence of instructed-learning and observational-learning pathways of avoidance acquisition on the generalization of avoidance behavior. Their findings show that generalized avoidance is a resilient behavioral consequence of fear learning and may emerge in the absence of a direct avoidance learning history, suggesting that generalized avoidance remains persistent following extinction testing (Cameron et al., 2015).

With respect to gender differences in avoidance, Blalock and Joiner (2000) summarize that in the category of behavioral avoidance, women are more likely than men to use emotional venting, self-care, and relaxation, whereas men are more likely to use alcohol and drugs as a form of behavioral avoidance. These authors also consider that there is evidence for greater use of cognitive avoidance by women, although in some studies men used denial and fantasy to a greater extent than women did. They found in a study with undergraduate students that cognitive avoidance was associated with increases in depressive and anxious symptoms under stressful conditions in women, but not in men.

Avoidance and Psychopathology

Avoidance and Anxiety

The concept of avoidance has been central to the conceptualization and diagnostic criteria of the Axis I anxiety disorders described by the *Diagnostic and Statistical Manual of Mental Disorders* (4th ed., text rev.: DSM-IV-TR; American Psychiatric Association, 2000). Its study has been expanded from motor behaviors in the presence of phobic stimuli to other areas. For example, people with anxiety disorders may avoid certain places and situations because they are contextual reminders of an anxiety episode. In the short term, avoidance reduces distress, but in the long term contributes to the maintenance of anxiety.

According to Aupperle and Paulus (2010), avoidance can be considered a drive motivated in response to stimuli and situations that threaten the integrity of the individual, i.e., fear or pain inducing stimuli. Avoidance is also an active choice process, i.e., a decision that is made to sacrifice potential rewards in order to avoid potential negative outcomes. Therefore, inherent in the notion of an anxiety disorder is conflict between approach-related drives (e.g., to seek positive social interactions, to leave the house) and avoidance-related drives (e.g., to prevent being humiliated or having a panic attack) (Aupperle & Paulus, 2010). These authors propose that approach-avoidance valuation may be dysfunctional for individuals with anxiety disorders and they suggest three possible explanatory hypotheses: a) over-representation of avoidance valuation; b) under- or over-representation of approach valuation; and c) insufficiency in integrating and arbitrating approach- and avoidance-related valuations. In this sense, the first one would be presumably related to dysfunction within amygdala and/or insular regions. The second one would be likely related to ventral striatal dysfunction. And, the third one would be likely related to orbitofrontal cortex and/or prefrontal cortex dysfunction (Aupperle & Paulus, 2010).

Dymond and Roche (2009) have pointed out that although avoidance has played an important role in the etiology and maintenance of anxiety, there has been surprisingly little basic behavior-analytic research on human avoidance, with most research based on cognitive and associative learning processes.

Although the two-factor model (Mowrer, 1951) has been the main theory to explain acquisition and maintenance of avoidance through both classical and operant conditioning, this theory cannot explain those cases in which there is no association between unconditioned and neutral stimulus and those in which there is a maintenance of anxiety under real extinction conditions. In such cases, processes as derived relational responding and the transformation of functions might be crucial to developing a sophisticated analysis of anxiety. According to Dymond and Roche (2009), the analysis of derived relational processes has demonstrated the important fact that neutral stimuli can gain discriminative functions indirectly; that is, in the absence of the usual process for establishing discriminative control and in the absence of reinforcement.

Avoidance and Depression

With regard to depression, Ferster (1973) postulated a central role for avoidance in his depression theory. For this author, depressed people escape from aversive internal and external stimuli and frequently avoid related situations. These efforts preempt positively reinforced behavior and their frequent use leads to a narrowing of the behavioral repertoire. Therefore, depression would be characterized by passivity as opposed to action. Behavioral Activation as a treatment for depression (Jacobson, Martell, & Dimidjian, 2001; Martell et al., 2001; Mazzucchelli, Kane, & Rees, 2009) represents a renewed interest in the concept of avoidance. Ottenbreit and Dobson (2004) suggest that the functional analysis of depression, as first proposed by Ferster (1973), focuses on avoidance as a coping strategy. Thus, depressed individuals tend to isolate themselves, avoid stressful situations, and take little action when faced with a stressful event. Coping avoidance thoughts and behaviors include avoiding thinking about goals or solutions, putting off decisions, turning down opportunities, isolating oneself, and giving up on tasks before they are completed. The functional perspective of depression proposes that inactivity, avoidance and isolation interfere with the possibilities of exposing oneself to success or reinforcement, because they prevent the individual from searching for and testing solutions to problems.

In a prospective study with 1211 individuals assessed three times over a ten year period, Holahan, Moos, Holahan, Brennan and Schutte (2005) found that avoidance coping at baseline was associated with both more chronic and more acute life stressors four years later. Using structural equation models, these authors proved that those intervening life stressors linked baseline avoidance coping and depressive symptoms ten years later, controlling for the influence of initial depressive symptoms. Holahan et al., (2005) point out that their results were applicable as much for women as for men. So, they proposed avoidance coping as a key mechanism. Also, according to Blalock and Joiner (2000) longitudinal studies suggest that coping strategies characterized by avoiding stressful situations and using passive cognitive responses to life´s negative events lead to a more depressed mood. Conversely, the use of strategies characterized by proactive efforts to manage stressful events can result in lower levels of depression.

Avoidance and Other Disorders

The effects of avoidance behavior have been documented not only on depression but on psychopathology in general (Kashdan, Barrios, Forsyth & Steger, 2006). The study of avoidance is also expanding into other areas of psychopathology, such as psychotic disorders (Vilardaga, Hayes, Atkins, Bresee, & Kambiz, 2013), body dysmorphic disorder (Wilson, Wilhelm, & Hartmann, 2014), post-traumatic stress disorder (Bordieri, Tull, McDermott, & Gratz, 2014), hoarding disorder (Ayers, Castriotta, Dozier, Espejo, & Porter, 2014), stuttering (Georgieva, 2014), chronic pain (Crombez, Eccleston, Van Damme, Vlaeyen, & Karoly, 2012), trichotillomania (Norberg, Wetterneck, Wood, & Conelea, 2007) or psychogenic nonepileptic seizures (Dimaro et al., 2014). The relevance of avoidance study in psychotic disorders is particularly noteworthy; in this case, it has been proposed that avoiding feelings of low self-worth can contribute to paranoid thinking (Udachina, Varese, Myin-Germeys, & Bentall, 2014). For Udachina et al., (2014), their results are consistent with the attributional model of paranoia which proposes that paranoid delusions are a product of avoidance of negative views about the self (Bentall, Corcoran, Howard, Blackwood, & Kinderman, 2001) and support the hypothesis that intolerance and avoidance of aversive mental states contribute to the development of paranoid ideas. Regarding hallucinations, people use to consider them as a threat to their physical or psychological well-being; this kind of interpretation would produce a series of avoidance responses that would increase the probability of the self-discrepant thoughts returning, so that the person enters a sort of ‘‘vicious circle” (García-Montes, Pérez-Álvarez, Soto-Balbuena, Perona-Garcelán, & Cangas, 2006). Also, García-Montes, Pérez-Álvarez and Cangas-Díaz (2006) have pointed out that auditory hallucinations could be understood as a type of experiential avoidance of attributing one´s own thoughts (the listened voice) to an external source, thus avoiding responsibility for them.

AVOIDANCE SUBTYPES

Blalock and Joiner (2000) found evidence for the existence of two basic dimensions of avoidance coping, cognitive avoidance coping and behavioral avoidance coping, using confirmatory factor analysis with the Avoidant Coping Scales of the Moos´s Coping Responses Inventory (Moos, 1988). This inventory includes items categorized as cognitive avoidance and others categorized as behavioral avoidance. The different dimensions of avoidance have also been studied by Ottenbreit and Dobson (2004) using their Cognitive-Behavioral Avoidance Scale (CBAS), which not only examines the dimensions of cognitive and behavioral avoidance, but also of social/nonsocial and active/passive avoidance.

We consider that three main types of avoidance can be distinguished: behavioral avoidance, which includes such behaviors as putting off decisions, turning down opportunities, isolating oneself, and giving up on tasks before they are completed; cognitive avoidance, which refers to a wide variety of coping strategies such as rumination, intentionally trying to suppress thoughts, and attempting to dissociate from negative experiences; and, experiential avoidance, which includes according to Hayes, Wilson, Gifford, Follette, & Strosahl (1996) both avoidance and escape in all of their forms, as long as they are used as methods of altering the form or frequency of experiences and the contexts that occasion them.

Behavioral Avoidance

Despite the central importance of behavioral avoidance for understanding the development and maintenance of anxiety disorders, there is little research on the underlying mechanisms of behavioral avoidance in humans, and past research specifically has been focused on responses toward single fear relevant stimuli (Pittig, Schultz, Craske, & Alpers, 2014). Although this past research offered extensive insights into avoidance responses within a controlled laboratory setting, the sole focus on avoidance of a single stimulus may not be completely translatable to complex avoidance behavior and its pathological quality in anxiety disorders. According to Pittig et al., (2014), the selection of adaptive behavior in complex situations is the key for human survival and well-being. Moreover, adaptive behavior protects the individual from harm but also enables him to obtain rewards (e.g., food, social contact, or secondary rewards such as money). For these authors, in healthy individuals avoidance is functional if it prevents an actual threat, whereas in people with anxiety disorders avoidance is more recurrent and persistent and not related to a realistic threat to the patient.

Situations avoided by anxious individuals usually contain incentives or rewards, which are missed due to avoidance. Furthermore, these individuals are often explicitly aware of these benefits, even for their most feared situations (Kashdan, Elhai, & Breen, 2008), and, thus, are torn between the choice to approach or to avoid (Pittig et al., 2014). A solution to this approach-avoidance conflict requires some kind of decision-making process to determine behavior. In this regard, avoidance behavior can be conceptualized as a shift toward avoidant decisions, which represent a costly outcome of the approach-avoidance conflict (Pittig et al., 2014). In a series of two experiments, these authors found that avoidant decisions were pronounced in highly trait-anxious participants who exhibited higher fear responses, and that fear conditioning could lead to avoidant decision-making, especially in vulnerable individuals. For these researchers, an emotional decision-making style of this kind may be a link between aversive experience and the development of habitual pathological avoidance, and they point out that introducing rewards for this approach may counteract avoidant decisions (Pittig et al., 2014).

Cognitive Avoidance

Avoidance of intrusive memories is a predictive factor of depressive and anxiety symptoms, although depressed individuals frequently use thought suppression they recognize it to be an inefficient coping mechanism (Williams & Moulds, 2007). Moreover, this kind of avoidance seems a lost cause because it has been calculated that during waking hours (sixteen hours) a mean of four thousand thoughts appears in a day (Klinger, 1996). Also, mind wandering in real world is considerably higher than in laboratory experiments; in this way, mind wandering occurs in 46.9% of people and in at least 30% during every activity except making love (Killingsworth & Gilbert, 2010). These authors found those data developing an application for mobile phone and they analyzed real-time reports of thoughts, feelings, and actions of 2,250 adults as they went about their daily activities.

Rumination is a frequent type of cognitive avoidance. Rumination is defined as a repetitive pattern of thoughts and behaviors that repetitively focus the individual's attention on his or her negative feelings and the nature and implications of those feelings (Nolen-Hoeksema, 1991). High ruminators may avoid the private experience of negative affect through rumination and in so doing, may actually worsen their negative mood. This response style results in longer lasting and more severe episodes of low mood. Over the past two decades, rumination has evolved as a critical construct in understanding the development and persistence of depressed mood. Hundreds of articles have addressed rumination related topics, and consistent evidence for the role of ruminative thought processes in depression has emerged (Smith & Alloy, 2009). Smith and Alloy (2009) in a review article about the rumination concept, conclude that is a multifaceted, multidimensional construct that has been studied in a variety of contexts and in relation to a variety of psychological and health outcomes. For these authors, although it is clear that rumination is important in the development of depression and anxiety, it can be difficult to determine how it is best characterized, best measured, and best used to predict certain outcomes.

Within the context of emotion regulation, rumination has been characterized as an avoidant coping strategy. In this sense, avoidance of private experiences is detrimental because it prevents individuals from responding to aversive stimuli and often has the paradoxical effect of increasing avoided material (Hayes et al., 1996; Wenzlaff & Wegner, 2000). According to Smith and Alloy (2009), several theories suggest that rumination is a misguided emotion regulation strategy, specifically, that individuals engage in rumination because they believe it will help them solve problems, analyze and/or eliminate discrepancies between current and desired status, aid in goal attainment, or process information related to stressful or traumatic events. They also suggest that rumination may be best understood in the context of a larger theory; specifically, rumination is an emotion regulation strategy that is driven by positive metacognitive beliefs about its efficacy in remediating perceived discrepancies, but ruminative thinking serves to effectively avoid processing of negative emotion (Smith & Alloy, 2009).

Borkovec, Alcaine and Behar (2004) have pointed out that worry is another kind of cognitive avoidance. Worry is a cognitive attempt to solve the problem of a possible future danger; it functions to avoid the occurrence of temporally distant bad events. The worry process appears to be negatively reinforced both by immediate suppression of sympathetic reactions to anxiety provoking material and by the more long-term nonoccurrence of predicted feared events. Worry may also be superficial in its content, reflecting an avoidance of more distressing thoughts and emotion deriving from past traumas, negative childhood attachment experiences, or current interpersonal difficulties (Borkovec, Alcaine & Behar, 2004).

Experiential Avoidance

Experiential avoidance is the phenomenon that occurs when a person is unwilling to remain in contact with particular private experiences (e.g., bodily sensations, emotions, thoughts, memories, images, behavioral predispositions) and takes steps to alter the form or frequency of these experiences or the contexts that occasion them, even when these forms of avoidance cause behavioral harm (Hayes et al., 1996). The term avoidance in this context explicitly includes both avoidance and escape in all of their forms. Although the short term effect of experiential avoidance is positive (reduction of the avoided event), the long term effects are negatives because of the increase in the frequency of such events. Such events become pathological when avoidance persists even when it is useless or life distorting (Hayes et al., 1996). According to Torneke, Luciano and Valdivia (2008), the main problem is when the private events with aversive functions become the target of avoidance, because our ability as humans to control them is very limited. Namely, the rules about controlling the emergence of private events and how to stop them do not work in the way the rules prescribe. Furthermore, the harder one try the more one will contact what they want to get rid of. Finally, as the individual engages in deliberate avoidance efforts, other behaviors which were fundamentally controlled by positive reinforcement are blocked, rendering in an unfulfilled life in the long run (Torneke, Luciano y Valdivia, 2008). From this perspective, many of the mental disorders depicted in formal diagnostic taxonomies (DSM and ICD) could be conceptualized as unhealthy methods of experiential avoidance.

Moreover, experiential avoidance would be a basic component of human condition because is built on language. So, usually works as a learned behavior by negative reinforcement. From this point of view, experiential avoidance would be included in the continuous *adaptive behavior/non-adaptive behavior*, and an excessive thought fusion would result in using non-adaptive strategies (Wilson & Luciano, 2002). Along these lines, Kashdan et al., (2006) noted that everyone experiences moments of pain and suffering, which are a part of the total spectrum of human emotions. These include potentially intense moments of distress, such as panic attacks, and a range of evaluative thoughts, such as doubts about oneself and about one's ability to handle a given situation. The form and content of these events are part of being human and living in the present moment, and are not in themselves problematic or dysfunctional. Moreover, working toward valuable goals requires confronting a wide range of emotional experiences, many of them painful. Finally, it must be considered that experiential avoidance is a process not a theory, Frame Relational Theory of human language and cognition is the underlying theory (Hayes, Barnes-Holmes, & Roche, 2001).

Blackledge and Hayes (2001) have proposed several potential pathways to explain how experiential avoidance contributes to psychopathology. One pathway is that deliberate avoidance strategies are usually verbal and involve the avoided item (e.g., "I won't think about using heroin today" includes the symbolic representation of using heroin). Because of this fact, the avoided item may actually become more accessible and likely to influence further cognition and behavior (Wenzlaff & Wegner, 2000). A second pathway is that private experiences are often classically conditioned, and thus may not be amenable to verbal control strategies. Chawla and Ostafin (2007) also have studied the role of experiential avoidance in the etiology, maintenance, and treatment of maladaptive behavior and psychopathology. After an empirical review of 28 studies, they suggested that an unwillingness to be in contact with aversive private experience and taking action to alter that experience does indeed influence psychopathology. Although they pointed out some inconsistencies between studies, the broad picture of the evidence suggests that experiential avoidance (a) influences the likelihood of substance use relapse, (b) mediates the relation between traumatic events and general psychological distress, (c) predicts severity of symptoms in some specific disorders such as generalized anxiety disorder and trichotillomania, and (d) mediates the relationship between maladaptive coping and self-regulatory strategies, and psychological distress (Chawla & Ostafin, 2007).

Experiential avoidance has been studied in a variety of problems and many studies have found a direct relation between experiential avoidance and the symptoms associated with most psychological disorders (Hayes et al., 1996). In a sense, it has been found that experiential avoidance is related with some relevant factors that can contribute to develop of psychopathology. For example, Kashdan et al., (2006) found that experiential avoidance mediated the effects of emotional responses styles, maladaptive coping, and uncontrollability on anxiety-related distress (e.g., anxiety sensitivity, trait anxiety, suffocation fears, and body sensation fears); mediated the effects of two emotion regulation strategies (i.e., suppression and reappraisal) on daily negative and positive experiences; and was associated with diminished: daily positive affective experiences, healthy life appraisals and frequency of positive events. Finally, experiential avoidance also has shown an inverse relation with health and quality of life measures (Butler & Ciarrochi, 2007; Hayes, Luoma, Bond, Masuda, & Lillis, 2006; Ruiz, 2010).

Experiential avoidance has been recognized, implicitly or explicitly, within most systems of therapy (e.g., psychodynamic, gestalt, behavioral, and cognitive therapies) (Blackledge & Hayes, 2001). And it explicitly takes a central role in most 'third wave' therapies: Dialectical Behavior Therapy (Linehan, 1993), Mindfulness-Based Cognitive Therapy for Depression (Segal, Williams, & Teasdale, 2006) and Acceptance and Commitment Therapy (Hayes, McCurry, Afari, & Wilson, 1991). In the latter, the term experiential avoidance disorder has been coined, which can be understood as an ineffective generalized behavioral class of verbally regulated avoidance that can be described according to the classical paradigm of self-control, with the addiction of more recent formulations on verbal behavior and derived relational responding (Luciano, Rodríguez, & Gutiérrez, 2004). For these authors, experiential avoidance disorder can be thought as a special instance of a lack of self-control where the person has come, through personal history, to value "the need of feeling well" as an absolute priority in order to embark on committed valued actions.

The opposite pole of experiential avoidance would be named psychological acceptance. Psychological acceptance involves the adoption of an intentionally open, receptive, flexible, and nonjudgmental posture with respect to moment-to-moment experience and implies a voluntary and values-based choice to enable or sustain contact with private experiences or the events that will likely occasion them (Hayes, Strosahl, & Wilson, 2011). Psychological acceptance also allows one to spend more time actively living, making choices to assist completion of goals or sorting out problems, rather than spending time and mental resources on controlling psychological events (Butler & Ciarrochi, 2007).

AVOIDANCE ASSESSMENT

To date, the CBAS (Cognitive Behavioral Avoidance Scale; Ottenbreit y Dobson, 2004) is the only self-report measure of cognitive-behavioral avoidance. The CBAS is a multidimensional measure that consists of 31 items. The response format entail a five-point Likert scale reflecting similarity ratings (1 = not at all true for me, 2 = somewhat true for me, 3 = moderately true for me, 4 = very much true for me, and 5 = extremely true for me). Total scores range from 31 to 155, where the higher the score the higher the avoidance level. People must indicate how each statement applies to them in general, in order to obtain a trait measure of avoidance. Thus, the items do not refer to a recent period of time, as is for example the case of Beck´s depression and anxiety inventories.

The factor analysis of the CBAS carried out by Ottenbreit and Dobson (2004) showed four factors that accounted for a total of 44.95% of the variance in item responses. The Behavioral Social factor accounted for 27.54% and consisted of eight items (e.g., "I tend to make up excuses to get out of social activities"). The Cognitive Nonsocial factor accounted for 7.87% and consisted of ten items (e.g., "While I know that I have to make some important decisions about school/work, I just do not get down to it"). The Cognitive Social factor accounted for 5.30% and consisted of seven items (e.g., "I try not to think about problems in my personal relationships"). And the Behavioral Nonsocial factor accounted for 4.24% and consisted of six items (e.g., "I quit activities that challenge me too much"). Ottenbreit and Dobson (2004) made their study with 391 undergraduate students at the University of Calgary. They found correlations between the four subscales that ranged from .39 to .57 and they suggested that the subscales measured distinct, but related, constructs. They also found high correlations between subscale scores and the total scale score (range: .78 - .80), indicating that a composite avoidance score is appropriate. The psychometric properties of the scale were quite satisfactory; the alpha coefficient for the total scale was .91 and for the four subscales ranged from .75 to .86. These authors also conducted correlations with criterion measures to determine if avoidance, as measured by the CBAS, was related to depression and anxiety. For that purpose, they used the BDI-II (Beck, Steer, & Brown, 1996) and STAI (Spielberger, Gursuch, & Lushene, 1970) and they found moderate correlations (.48 and .58 respectively). There is no information about cut off points or mean score.

Others authors have also found significant correlations for CBAS. For example, Moulds, Kandris, Starr y Wong (2007) with a sample of 104

Australian undergraduate students, found correlations ranging from .73 to .80 between each subscale score and the total score. They also found significant correlations between the four subscales, ranging from .31 to .56, which were consistent with those found by the original authors. These authors also found significant correlations between the CBAS and the Beck's inventories of anxiety and depression, specifically, .49 with BAI and .62 with BDI-II. Along the same lines, Carvalho and Hopko (2011) found a correlation of .45 with BAI and a correlation of .75 in the case of BDI-II. Moreover, Kanter, Rusch, Busch and Sedivy (2009) found correlations in the expected line using the BADS (Behavioral Activation for Depression Scale; Kanter, Mulick, Busch, Berlin, & Martell, 2007) in a community sample with depressive symptoms. More recently, Ottenbreit, Dobson and Quigley (2014) have also found a significant positive relation between avoidance and rumination, specifically a correlation of .40 between CBAS and RRS (Ruminative Responses Scale; Nolen-Hoeksema & Morrow, 1991). All these data contribute to strengthen the psychometric properties of CBAS.

The CBAS has been adapted to German (Röthlin et al., 2009) and Spanish (Barajas, Garra, & Ros, 2016). The psychometric properties are adequate in both cases, in the German version the alpha coefficient was .92 for the total scale and ranged for subscales from .70 to .87. In the Spanish version, the alpha coefficient for the total scale was .95 and ranged from .77 to .93 for subscales. Whereas studies with CBAS English version were only made with samples of undergraduate students (Carvalho & Hopko, 2011; Moulds et al., 2007; Ottenbreit & Dobson, 2004), as much the German version as the Spanish version have been applied to outpatients, normal controls and undergraduate students. Therefore, we can conclude that the CBAS is a reliable instrument for use in different types of population.

Moreover, the main measure of experiential avoidance is the Acceptance and Action Questionnaire (AAQ-II; Bond et al., 2011). This questionnaire assesses the constructs of experiential avoidance, psychological inflexibility and acceptance. Bond et al., (2001) have published the results obtained with 2,816 subjects distributed into six samples in three studies, and have provided data of two AAQ-II versions, one made of seven items and the other one made of ten items. Items are evaluated using a Likert-type scale that run from 1 (never true) to7 (always true), with higher scores indicating greater levels of psychological inflexibility (experiential avoidance). For Bond et al., (2011), greater levels of inflexibility, indicated by higher AAQ-II scores, should be related to poorer life functioning, worse general mental health, higher levels of depression, anxiety, and stress. They even suggest that higher levels of psychological inflexibility may serve as a risk factor for mental ill.

For the 10-item version, Bond et al., (2011) informed a bifactorial structure, where one factor accounted for the 41.47% of the variance and the other one for the 4.94%. The mean score obtained by 206 undergraduate students was 30.69 (*SD* = 9.91). The alpha coefficient was .87, while in 7-item version was .88. Using the 7-item version in another study with 583 bank employees, they found a test-retest reliability of .81 and .79 at 3- and 12-months, respectively. Although Bond et al., (2011) considered the 7-item version as the final version of the AAQ-II, they pointed out that the 10-item version is not significantly weaker and both correlate at *r* = .96. Thus, it should not be assumed that non-English translations and empirical studies that had previously appeared using the 10-item version were invalid.

The AAQ-II was not designed as a tool for diagnosing mental disorders. Therefore, although does not have cut-off points as other measures that were intended for such use (e.g., BDI-II, BAI), Bond et al., (2011) suggest the range of 24-28 or above as a preliminary indication of which scores on the AAQ-II may indicate a clinically relevant level of distress. The AAQ-II has demonstrated appropriate discriminant validity. Regarding convergent validity, these authors found significant and elevated correlations both with BDI-II as BAI. Finally, the AAQ-II was not associated with age, gender, or race.

Avoidance has been studied not only through self-report measures but also through experimental tasks. For example, there are several studies that compare the performance of individuals with high experiential avoidance (AAQ score a standard deviation or more over the mean) and low experiential avoidance (AAQ score equal o below the mean) on different tasks. In this way, Sloan (2004) examined the relationship between emotional reactivity to pleasant, unpleasant, and neutral emotion-eliciting stimuli and experiential avoidance. This author separated sixty-two participants into high experiential avoiders and low experiential avoiders, and found that the former reported greater emotional experience to both unpleasant and pleasant stimuli than the latter. Karekla, Forsyth and Kelly (2004) in another study with healthy undergraduates divided in two groups (with the same criteria described previously) that underwent a series of inhalations of carbon dioxide-enriched air, found that individuals high in experiential avoidance endorsed more panic symptoms, more severe cognitive symptoms, more fear, and panic, than individuals with lower experiential avoidance. With equivalent criteria, Zettle, Petersen, Hocker and Provines (2007) compared the performance of undergraduate students on a challenging perceptual-motor task while simultaneously were induced of unpleasant sensations, and they found that high avoidant participants reported being more likely to engage in catastrophizing and to be distressed by sensations induced during the task, than their low avoidant counterparts. Moreover, Cochrane, Barnes-Holmes, Barnes-Holmes, Stewart and Luciano (2007) made another study in which a student group completed a simple matching task that required them to choose whether or not to look at an aversive visual image. These authors found that high avoidance participants took longer to emit a correct response that produced an aversive rather than a neutral picture. Additionally, the high avoidance individuals reported greater levels of anxiety following the experiment even though they rated the aversive images as less unpleasant and less emotionally arousing than their low avoidant counterparts. Some evidence has even been found indicating that people with higher experiential avoidance levels showed a lower level of concentration on a high cognitive demand task (López et al., 2010).

Although all these studies were conducted on non-clinical samples, some results also point to the relevance of avoidance in the clinical population when using an experimental task. For example, Barajas (2015) designed an avoidance task that consisted of presenting 60 visual stimuli from the IAPS (International Affective Picture System. Lang, Bradley and Cuthbert, 2005), 20 of them with positive valence, 20 neutral and 20 with negative valence, and studied the performance of a clinical sample and a control group. The results revealed significantly higher avoidance levels in the clinical sample than in the control group when performing the task. Namely, the clinical group avoided significantly more negative pictures than the control group. Also, a correlation was found in both groups between avoidance and the symptomatology of anxiety (BAI) and depression (BDI-II). The avoidance level was not related to gender or age (Barajas, 2015).

AVOIDANCE TREATMENT

Based on theory and data emerging from the fields of learning, emotional development and regulation, and cognitive science, Barlow et al., (2004) pointed out that, following a standard psychoeducational phase common to all psychotherapeutic approaches, one of the three fundamental therapeutic components relevant to the treatment of emotional disorders is preventing emotional avoidance. This treatment takes place in the context of provoking emotional expression (emotional exposure) through situational, internal, and somatic (interoceptive cues), as well as through standard mood-induction exercises, and differs from patient to patient only in the situational cues and exercises utilized (Barlow et al., 2004).

Thus, the first step for avoidance treatment would be a psychoeducational component whose main objective would be become aware of the avoidant behavior and its consequences in the short and long term. This psychoeducational component would include giving feedback based on functional analysis. At this stage, it is also important enhancing motivation for change, because people with psychopathology usually have a long story of avoidance behaviors and they find difficult to change them. For this purpose, validation of personal experiences and reinforcement of adequate coping behaviors are necessary. Finally, we have to set specific, operative and simple initial objectives, to obtain results in the shortest possible time. That is, intervention should begin by easier modifiable avoidance behaviors.

Regarding phobic stimuli, exposure is the treatment choice and this should be in vivo instead of in imagination. Regarding type of response, if this is an active response (escape), programmed reduction of frequency, intensity or duration also can be useful, especially when the person does not tolerate exposure. If it is a passive response (inhibition, procrastination), then behavior activation is the adequate intervention. This should be participatory, gradual, focused on valuable objectives and of short duration at the beginning. In this case, behavior activation also entails an exposure component and the main objective is to tolerate unpleasant emotional states.

Considering the form of the avoidance response (cognitive, behavioral or emotional) we suggest the following intervention procedures. For predominant cognitive avoidance responses (e.g., rumination, fantasize, distraction, thought suppression) it would be advisable using emotional exposure emphasizing the cognitive component. Moreover, if as it has been postulated rumination is a kind of cognitive avoidance, practicing mindfulness could be an useful procedure to help to be aware of ruminative processes (as of any other cognitive process) and to diminish such negative tendency. Furthermore, it has been hypothesized that mindfulness implies a contact with external and internal events just as they are and increases willingness to tolerate uncomfortable emotions and sensations (Levitt, Brown, Orsillo, & Barlow, 2004). In this sense, low levels of mindfulness could imply avoidance of unpleasant internal or external events, while practicing mindfulness would imply a component of exposure, even though this term was not used in its theoretical origins. According to Linehan (1993), one of the main therapeutic effects of mindfulness training is related to exposure to negative emotions. For this author, prolonged observation of thoughts and emotions, without avoiding or escaping from them, is an example of exposure. By paying mindful attention to negative emotional states, patients can learn that there is no reason to fear or avoid them, given that these states will eventually disappear. Recently, an inverse relationship between mindfulness and cognitive-behavioral and experiential avoidance has been found (Barajas & Garra, 2014). Mindfulness can thus be considered a useful procedure for encouraging exposure to problematic stimuli in each case, while mindlessness states may correspond to avoidance coping.

In those cases where the main problem is behavioral avoidance response (e.g., escape, isolation, safety behaviors, drug or substance use), in addition to exposure, applying programmed reduction, behavioral activation, differential reinforcement of other behaviors and/or social skills training may also be necessary.

Finally, when treating emotional avoidance response (e.g., weeping, rage, demanding attention, dissociative symptoms or dependent behaviors) emotional exposure must be used, in this case emphasizing the emotional component versus the cognitive one. Mindfulness, social skills training, extinction and differential reinforcement of other behaviors will also be supplementary techniques.

REFERENCES

American Psychiatric Association (2000). *Diagnostic and statistical manual of mental disorders* (4th ed., text rev.). Washington, DC: Author.

American Psychiatric Association (2013). *Diagnostic and Statistical Manual of Mental Disorders: DSM5*. Arlington,VA: Author.

Aupperle, R. L., & Paulus, M. P. (2010). Neural systems underlying approach and avoidance in anxiety disorders. *Dialogues in Clinical Neuroscience, 12*, 517-531.

Ayers, C. R., Castriotta, N., Dozier, M. E., Espejo, E. P., & Porter, B. (2014).Behavioral and experiential avoidance in patients with hoarding disorder. *Journal of Behavior Therapy and Experimental Psychiatry, 45*, 408-414.

Barajas, S., & Garra, L. (2014). Mindfulness and psychopathology: Adaptation of the Mindful Attention Awareness Scale (MAAS) in a Spanish sample. *Clínica y Salud, 25*, 49-56.

Barajas, S. (2015). Evitación y psicopatología: Un estudio a través de una tarea experimental y su relación con medidas de autoinforme [Avoidance and psychopathology: A study through an experimental task and its relation with self-report measures]. *Revista de Psicopatología y Psicología Clínica, 20*, 63-73.

Barajas, S., Garra, L., & Ros, L. (2016). Avoidance in anxiety and depression: Adaptation of the Cognitive-Behavioral Avoidance Scale in a Spanish sample. Manuscript submitted for publication.

Barlow, D. H. (2002). *Anxiety and its disorders: the nature and treatment of anxiety and panic* (2nd ed.). New York: Guilford Press.

Barlow, D. H., Allen L.B., & Choate, M.L. (2004). Toward a unified treatment for emotional disorders. *Behavior Therapy, 35,* 205-230.

Barlow, D. H., Farchione, T.J., Fairholme, C.P., Ellard, K.K., Boisseau, C.L., Allen, L.B., & Ehrenreich-May, J.T. (2011). *Unified protocol for transdiagnostic treatment of emotional disorders: Therapist guide* (1st ed.). New York: Oxford University Press.

Beck, A. T., Steer, R. A., & Brown, G. K. (1996). *Beck Depression Inventory—II manual*. San Antonio, TX: The Psychological Corporation.

Bentall, R.P., Corcoran, R., Howard, R., Blackwood, N., & Kinderman, P. (2001). Persecutory delusions: A review and theoretical integration. *Clinical Psychology Review, 21,* 1143-1192.

Blackledge, J. T., & Hayes, S. C. (2001). Emotion regulation in acceptance and commitment therapy. *Clinical Psychology Science and Practice, 10,* 161–165.

Blalock, J. A., & Joiner, Jr., T. E. (2000). Interaction of cognitive avoidance coping and stress in predicting depression/anxiety. *Cognitive Therapy and Research, 24*, 47-65.

Bond, F. W., Hayes, S. C., Baer, R.A., Carpenter, K., Guenole, N., Orcutt, H.K., (…), & Zettle, R.D. (2011). Preliminary psychometric properties of Acceptance and Action Questionnaire-II. A revised measure of psychological inflexibility and experiential avoidance. *Behavior Therapy, 42*, 676-688.

Bordieri, M. J., Tull, M. T., McDermott, M. J., & Gratz, K. L. (2014). The moderating role of experiential avoidance in the relationship between posttraumatic stress disorder symptom severity and cannabis dependence. *Journal of Contextual Behavioral Science, 3,* 273-278.

Borkovec, T. D., Alcaine, O., & Behar, E. (2004). Avoidance theory of worry and generalized anxiety disorder. In R.G. Heimberg, C.L. Turk, & D.S.

Mennin (Eds.) *Generalized anxiety disorder: Advances in research and practice* (pp.77-108). New York: Guilford Press.

Butler, J. & Ciarrochi, J. (2007). Psychological acceptance and quality of life in the elderly. *Quality of Life Research, 16,* 607-615.

Cameron G., Schlund M.W., & Dymond, S. (2015) Generalization of socially transmitted and instructed avoidance. *Frontiers in Behavioral Neuroscience, 9,* 159.

Carvalho, J. P., & Hopko, D.R. (2011). Behavioral therapy of depression: Reinforcement as a mediating variable between avoidance and depression. *Journal of Behavior Therapy and Experimental Psychiatry, 42*, 154-162.

Chawla, N. & Ostafin, B. (2007) Experiential Avoidance as a Functional Dimensional Approach to Psychopathology: An Empirical Review. *Journal of Clinical Psychology, 63,* 871–8.

Cochrane, A., Barnes-Holmes, D., Barnes-Holmes, Y., Stewart, I. & Luciano, C. (2007). Experiential avoidance and aversive visual images: Response delays and event related potentials on a simple matching task. *Behaviour Research and Therapy, 45*, 1379-1388.

Crombez, G., Eccleston, C., Van Damme, S., Vlaeyen, J. W., & Karoly, P. (2012). Fear-avoidance model of chronic pain: the next generation. *The Clinical journal of pain, 28,* 475-483.

Dimaro, L. V., Dawson, D.L., Roberts, N.A., Brown, I., Moghaddam, N.G., & Reuber, M. (2014). Anxiety and avoidance in psychogenic nonepileptic seizures: The role of implicit and explicit anxiety. *Epilepsy and Behavior, 33,* 77-86.

Dymond, S., & Roche, B. (2009). A contemporary behavior analysis of anxiety and avoidance. *The Behavior Analyst, 32,* 7–27.

Ferster, C.B. (1973). A functional analysis of depression. *American Psychologist, 28*, 857-870.

García-Montes, J.M., Pérez-Álvarez, M., Soto-Balbuena, C., Perona-Garcelán, S., & Cangas, A.J. (2006). Metacognitions in patients with hallucinations and obsessive-compulsive disorder: The superstition factor. *Behaviour Research and Therapy, 44*, 1091–1104.

García-Montes, J. M., Pérez-Álvarez, M., & Cangas-Díaz, A. (2006). Aproximación al abordaje clínico de los síntomas psicóticos desde la Aceptación. *Apuntes de Psicología, 24*, 293-307.

Georgieva, D. (2014). Intensive non-avoidance group therapy with stutterer adults: preliminary results. *Codas, 26,* 122-130.

Hayes, S. C., Barnes-Holmes, D. & Roche, B. (Eds.) (2001). *Relational frame theory: A post-Skinnerian account of human language and cognition*. New York: Kluwer Academic/Plenum Publishers.

Hayes, S. C., Luoma, J. B., Bond, F., Masuda, A. & Lillis, J. (2006). Acceptance and Commitment Therapy: Model, processes and outcomes. *Behaviour Research and Therapy, 44*, 1-25.

Hayes, S. C., McCurry, S. M., Afari, N. & Wilson, K. (1991). *Acceptance and commitment therapy (ACT). A manual for the treatment of emotional avoidance*. Reno, NV: Context Press.

Hayes, S.C., Strosahl, K.D., & Wilson, K.G. (2011). *Acceptance and commitment therapy: The process and practice of mindful change* (2nd ed.). New York: The Guilford Press.

Hayes, S.C., Wilson, K.G., Gifford, E.V., Follette, V.M. & Strosahl, K.D. (1996). Experiential avoidance and behavioral disorders: A functional dimension approach to diagnosis and treatment. *Journal of Consulting and Clinical Psychology, 64,* 1152-1168.

Holahan, C. J., Moos, R. H, Holahan, C. K., Brennan, P. L. & Schutte, K.K. (2005). Stress generation, avoidance coping and depressive symptoms: a10-year model. *Journal of Consulting and Clinical Psychology, 73*, 658-666.

Jacobson, N. S., Martell, C. R., & Dimidjian, S. (2001). Behavioral activation treatment for depression: returning to contextual roots. *Clinical Psychology: Science and Practice, 8*, 225-270.

Karekla, M., Forsyth, J.P. & Kelly, M.M. (2004). Emotional avoidance and panicogenic responding to a biological challenge procedure. *Behavior Therapy, 35*, 725-746.

Kanter, J. W., Mulick, P. S., Busch, A. M., Berlin, K.S. & Martell, C.R. (2007). The Behavioral Activation for Depression Scale (BADS): psychometric properties and factor structure. *Journal of Psychopathology and Behavioral Assessment, 29*, 191-202.

Kanter, J.W., Rusch, L.C., Busch, A.M. & Sedivy, S.K. (2009). Validation of the Behavioral Activation for Depresion Scale (BADS) in a community sample with elevated depressive symptoms. *Journal of Psychopathology and Behavioral Assessment, 31*, 36-42.

Kashdan, T.B., Barrios, V., Forsyth, J.P., & Steger, M.F. (2006). Experiential avoidance as a generalized psychological vulnerability: comparisons with coping and emotion regulation strategies. *Behaviour Research and Therapy, 44*, 1301-1320.

Kashdan, T.B., Elhai, J.D., & Breen, W.E. (2008). Social anxiety and disinhibition: An analysis of curiosity and social rank appraisals, approach-avoidance conflicts, and disruptive risk-taking behavior. *Journal of Anxiety Disorders, 22,* 925–939.

Killingsworth, M. A. & Gilbert, D. T. (2010). A wandering mind is an unhappy mind, *Science, 330*, 932.

Klinger, E. (1996). The contents of thoughts: interference as the downside of adaptive normal mechanisms in thought flow. In I.G. Sarason, G.R. Pierce, & B. R. Sarason (Eds.). *Cognitive interference: theories, methods and findings* (pp. 3-24). NJ: Lawrence Erlbaum Associates.

Krypotos A. M., Effting M., Kindt, M., & Beckers, T. (2015) Avoidance learning: a review of theoretical models and recent developments. *Frontiers in Behavioral Neuroscience, 9,* 189.

Lang P. J., Bradley M. M. & Cuthbert B.N. (2005). *International affective picture system (IAPS): Affective ratings of pictures and instruction manual. Technical Report A-6.* University of Florida, Gainesville, FL. (retrieved from: http://csea.phhp.ufl.edu/Media.html).

Levitt, J. T, Brown, T. A., Orsillo, S.M., & Barlow, D.H. (2004). The effects of acceptance versus suppression of emotion on subjective and psychophysiological response to carbon dioxide challenge in patients with panic disorder. *Behavior Therapy, 35*, 747-766.

Linehan, M. M. (1993). *Cognitive-behavioral treatment of borderline personality disorder.* New York: Guilford Press.

López, J. C., Ruiz, F. J., Feder, J., Barbero, A., Suárez, J.J., Rodríguez, J.A. & Luciano, C. (2010). The role of experiential avoidance in the performance on a high cognitive demand task. *International Journal of Psychology and Psychological Therapy, 10*, 475-488.

Luciano, C., Rodríguez, M., & Gutiérrez, O. (2004). A proposal for synthesizing verbal contexts in Experiential Avoidance Disorder and Acceptance and Commitment Therapy. *International Journal of Psychology and Psychological Therapy, 4,* 377-394.

Martell, C. R., Addis, M. E. & Jacobson, N.S. (2001). *Depression in context. Strategies for guided action*. New York: W.W. Norton.

Mazzucchelli, T., Kane, R., & Rees, C. (2009). Behavioral activation treatments for depression in adults: a meta-analysis and review. *Clinical Psychology: Science and Practice, 16,* 383-411.

Moos, R. H. (1988). *Coping Responses Inventory Manual.* Odessa, FL: Psychological Assessment Resources, Inc.

Mowrer, O. H. (1951). Two-factor learning theory: summary and comment. *Psychological Review*. 58, 350–354.

Nolen-Hoeksema, S. & Morrow, J. (1991). Effects of rumination and distraction on naturally occurring depressed mood. *Cognition and Emotion, 7,* 561-570.

Nolen-Hoeksema, S. & Morrow, J. (1991). A prospective study of depression and posttraumatic stress symptoms after a natural disaster: the 1989 Loma Prieta earthquake. *Journal of Personality and Social Psychology, 61*, 115–121.

Norberg, M. M., Wetterneck, C. T., Woods, D. W., & Conelea, C. A. (2007). Experiential avoidance as a mediator of relationships between cognitions and hair-pulling severity. *Behavior Modification, 31*, 367-381.

Ottenbreit, N. D. & Dobson, K.S. (2004). Avoidance and depression: the construction of the Cognitive-Behavioral Avoidance Scale. *Behaviour Research and Therapy, 42*, 292-313.

Ottenbreit, N. D., Dobson, K.S., & Quigley, L. (2014). An examination of avoidance in major depression in comparison to social anxiety disorder. *Behaviour Research and Therapy, 56,* 82-90.

Pittig, A., Schultz, A. R., Craske, M.G., & Alpers, G.W. (2014). Acquisition of Behavioral Avoidance: Task-Irrelevant Conditioned Stimuli Trigger Costly Decisions. *Journal of Abnormal Psychology, 123,* 314–329.

Röthlin, P., Holtforth, M.G., Bergomi, C., Berking, M., Ottenbreit, N.D., & Caspar, F. (2009). Vermeidung und deprssion: Die psychometrische evaluation der deutschen version der Cognitive-Behavioral Avoidance Scale (CBAS) [Avoidance and depression: The psychometric evaluation of the German version of the "Cognitive-Behavioral Avoidance Scale" (CBAS)]. *Diagnostica, 56,* 46-55.

Ruiz, F. J. (2010). A review of Acceptance and Commitment Therapy empirical evidence: correlational, experimental psychopathology, component and outcome studies. *International Journal of Psychology and Psychological Therapy, 10*, 125-162.

Segal, Z. V., Williams, J. M. G., & Teasdale, J. D. (2002). *Mindfulness-Based Cognitive Therapy for Depression: A New Approach to Preventing Relapse.* New York: Guilford Press.

Servatius, R.J. (2016). Avoidance: From Basic Science to Psychopathology. *Frontiers in Behavioral Neuroscience, 10,* 15.

Sloan, D. M. (2004). Emotion regulation in action: Emotional reactivity in experiential avoidance. *Behaviour Research and Therapy, 42,* 1257-1270.

Smith, J. M. & Alloy, L.B. (2009). A roadmap to rumination: a review of the definition, assessment, and conceptualization of this multifaceted construct. *Clinical Psychology Review, 29,* 116-128.

Spielberger, C. D., Gursuch, R. L., & Lushene, R. E. (1970). *Manual for the State–Trait Anxiety Inventory (Self Evaluation Questionnaire).* Palo Alto, CA: Consulting Psychologists Press.

Torneke, N., Luciano, C. & Valdivia, S. (2008). Rule governed behavior and psychological problems. *International Journal of Psychology and Psychological Therapy, 8,* 141-146.

Udachina, A., Varese, F., Myin-Germeys, I., & Bentall, R.P. (2014). The role of experiential avoidance in paranoid delusions: An experience sampling study. *British Journal of Clinical Psychology, 53,* 422-432.

Vilardaga, R., Hayes, S.C., Atkins, D.C., Bresee, C. & Kambiz, A. (2013). Comparing experiential acceptance and cognitive reappraisal as predictors of functional outcome in individuals with serious mental illness. *Behaviour Research and Therapy, 51,* 425-433.

Wenzlaff, R. M., & Wegner, D. M. (2000). Thought suppression. *Annual Review of Psychology, 51,* 59–91.

Williams, A. D. & Moulds, M. L. (2007). Cognitive avoidance of intrusive memories: Recall vantage perspective and associations with depression. *Behaviour Research and Therapy, 45,* 1141-1153.

Wilson, K. G. & Luciano, C. (2002). *Terapia de aceptación y compromiso: un tratamiento conductual orientado a los valores.* Madrid: Pirámide.

Wilson, A. C., Wilhelm, S., & Hartmann, A. S., (2014). Experiential avoidance in body dysmorphic disorder. *Body Image, 11,* 380-383.

Zettle, R. D., Petersen, C. L., Hocker, T. R. & Provines, J. L. (2007). Responding to a challenging perceptual-motor task as a function of level of experiential avoidance. *The Psychological Record, 57,* 49-62.

Biographical Sketch

SANTIAGO BARAJAS
Clinical Psychologist
University Hospital of Guadalajara
C/Donante de Sangre s/n
19002, GUADALAJARA, SPAIN
sbarajas@sescam.jccm.es

I. EDUCATION AND TRAINING.

- PhD – Doctoral Thesis. Title: "Cognitive-behavioral avoidance, psychological acceptance, and mindfulness in the psychopathology of anxiety and depression". Department of Psychology, University of Castilla-La Mancha, Spain. Awarded highest grade.
- Doctoral Program: Clinical Psychology. Department of Personality, Assessment and Psychological Treatment. University Complutense of Madrid. Awarded highest grade.
- Master of Science in Behavior Modification. University Complutense of Madrid, Spain.
- Bachelor of Science in Clinical Psychology (five year program). University Complutense of Madrid, Spain.
- Licensed Clinical Psychologist to work in the Spanish National Health Service. Passing a rigorous public examination process and completing four years of residency are required for obtaining this license.
- Registered EuroPsy Psychologist and Registered EuroPsy Specialist in Psychotherapy, both awarded by the European Federation of Psychologists Associations.

II. PROFFESIONAL APPOINTMENTS.

Currently:
Clinical Psychologist
Department of Clinical Psychology. University Hospital of Guadalajara. Health Service of Castilla-La Mancha (SESCAM). Spain.
Rigorous public examination process required to secure position.

Previously:
Consultant of Mental Health
Health Service Office, Government of Castilla-La Mancha, Toledo, Spain.

III. PUBLICATIONS.

- Barajas, S., Garra, L. & Ros, L. (submitted for publication). Avoidance in anxiety and depression: Adaptation of the Cognitive-Behavioral Avoidance Scale in a Spanish sample.
- Barajas, S. & Garra, L. (submitted for publication). Emotional reactivity, avoidance and mindfulness: A comparison between patients with anxiety and depression and non-patients.
- Barajas, S. (2015). Evitación y psicopatología: Un estudio a través de una tarea experimental y su relación con medidas de autoinforme [Avoidance and psychopathology: A study through an experimental task and its relation with self-report measures]. Revista de Psicopatología y Psicología Clínica, 20, 63-73. http://dx.doi.org/ 10.5944/rppc.vol.1.num.1.2015.14409.
- Barajas, S. & Garra, L. (2014). Mindfulness and psychopathology: Adaptation of the Mindful Attention Awareness Scale (MAAS) in a Spanish sample. *Clínica y Salud, 25*, 49-56. http://dx.doi.org/ 10.1016/S1130-5274(14)70026-X.
- Barajas, S.; Torrubias, R. y Díaz, C. (2004). Trastornos mentales de inicio en la infancia, niñez o adolescencia. En L. Chamorro (Coord.): *Guía de manejo de los trastornos mentales en atención primaria.* (pp. 215-232). Barcelona: Ars Medica. ISBN-84-9706-068-7.
- Barajas, S. (2002). Subtipos de trastorno obsesivo-compulsivo. Asociación con síntomas de ansiedad, depresión y preocupaciones [Subtypes of obsessive-compulsive disorder, differential characteristics of pure obsessive people and relationship with symptoms of anxiety, depression and worry]. *Clínica y Salud*, 13, 207-231.
- Barajas, S. (2001). Evaluación de la calidad asistencial en un servicio de salud mental, a través de la percepción y evaluación de pacientes con trastorno obsesivo-compulsivo [Evaluation of the quality of a mental health service through the perception and evolution of patients suffering from obsessive-compulsive disorder]. *Clínica y Salud,* 12, 305-326.

IV. ACADEMIC EXPERIENCE.

Currently:

Clinical Professor. University of Alcalá, Spain.

Professor of Master's Degree Program at University of Almería and University of Alcalá. Spain.

Previously:

Assistant Professor. Department of Psychology. University of Castilla-La Mancha, Spain.

In: Psychopathology
Editor: Jeremy Williams
ISBN: 978-1-63485-745-1

Chapter 5

THE INTERGENERATIONAL IMPACT OF TRAUMA: INDIVIDUAL, FAMILY AND COMMUNITY IMPLICATIONS

A. Gnazzo, M. Khademi, V. Guerriero, J. Manoogian, A. Kalayjian, G. C. Zavattini and G. de Campora
Department of Dynamic and Clinical Psychology,
Faculty of Medicine and Psychology, Sapienza,
University of Rome, Rome, Italy

ABSTRACT

The intergenerational transmission (IT) of trauma can be defined as the influence of a disruptive experience perpetuated from a generation to another. Disruptive experiences can promote the onset psychopathological symptoms, compromising both the individual and the interpersonal functioning. Thus, literature (Kaitz et al., 2009; Pat-Horenczyk et al., 2014) has highlighted that the presence of this psychopathological pattern affect the way the parent respond to the emotional and physical needs of the child, which in turn may lead toward emerging difficulties of the child itself. Despite these evidences, only a few studies (Schwerdtfeger et al., 2013; Starr et al., 2014) have investigated the presence of different trajectories for the transmission of traumatic symptoms suggesting that the intergenerational transmission of traumatic symptoms can follow two different routes: direct and indirect transmission. Direct transmission is represented by specific effects of the parents' symptomatic behaviors, while the indirect transmission is described as the overall parental difficulty shown because of his/her own traumatic history.

Aim of the current review is to report those studies where the intergenerational transmission (IT) of the trauma has been taken into account according to three main perspectives: 1) the IT impact on the individual functioning; 2) the family dynamics involved in the IT of trauma; and 3) the community/social implications related to the IT.

1. Definition of Trauma

This chapter addresses the intergenerational transmission of trauma (ITT). First, a definition of trauma will be provided according to the most recent diagnostic guidelines (APA, 2013). Second, a deepen attention will be paid to the construct of ITT.

Trauma may be defined as a stressful situation or terrible event that has an emotional or physical impact on the victim (Aschenbrenner, 2013). This impact can compromise the person's ability to cope and function optimally (Alayarian, 2008), however, not all experiences of trauma lead to a trauma-related disorder or symptoms. The effect of the traumatic experience may be mediated by an individual's ability to cope well with the traumatic experience (Cherry & Galea, 2015; Westphal & Bonanno, 2007). This "resilience" to trauma decreases the likelihood of experiencing psychological distress and increases the likelihood of adaptation to the context, and is attributed to intrapersonal characteristics such as coping style (Bonanno, 2004) but may also depend on intrapersonal factors such as social support and social comparison (Hooberman, Rosenfeld, Rasmussen, & Keller, 2010).

The fifth edition of the Diagnostic and Statistical Manual of Mental Disorders (DSM-5; APA, 2013) incorporates the definition of trauma into Posttraumatic Stress Disorder (PTSD), in the new chapter on Trauma-and Stressor-Related Disorders. The diagnostic criteria included are:

> "exposure to actual or threatened death, serious injury or sexual violation. The exposure must result from one or more of the following scenarios, in which the individual: • directly experiences the traumatic event;• witnesses the traumatic event in person;• learns that the traumatic event occurred to a close family member or close friend (with the actual or threatened death being either violent or accidental); • experiences first-hand repeated or extreme exposure to aversive details of the traumatic event (not through media, pictures, television or movies unless work-

> related).The disturbance, regardless of its trigger, causes clinically significant distress or impairment in the individual's social interactions, capacity to work or other important areas of functioning. It is not the physiological result of another medical condition, medication, drugs or alcohol." (APA, 2013, p. 271)

Events which usually lead to PTSD include war, a terrorist attack, captivity, being taken hostage, torture and violent personal assault (Javidi, & Yadollahie, 2011), as well as natural disasters like wildfire, tornado, hurricane, flood, and earthquakes (Papanikolaou, Adamis, Mellon, & Prodromitis, 2011). After these events, the victims may experience symptoms including severe anxiety, dissociative symptoms, dissociative amnesia, poor concentration, sleep disturbance, and derealization (APA, 2013). In addition, several studies have found that between 21% and 94% of PTSD victims have symptoms of depression (Ginzburg, 2007; Hashemian et al., 2006; Sundquist, Johansson, DeMarinis, Johansson, & Sundquist 2005), 39% to 97% have symptoms of anxiety (Hashemian et al., 2006; Sundquist et al., 2005) and 11% to 67% have symptoms of both anxiety and depression in addition to the PTSD symptoms (Brady & Clary, 2004; Hashemian et al., 2006).

Alongside the experiences that threaten the survival and integrity of the individual, there are other adversities that may put individuals at greater risk for the development of a trauma, such as losses, abandonments, witnessed violence and institutionalization. These events are also traumatic for some people and cause of psychopathological symptoms that do not fall under the diagnosis of PTSD but are manifested in the form of mood or dissociative disorders, substance abuse, and so on (Lu, Mueser, Rosenberg, & Jankowski, 2008; Whelan- Goodinson, Ponsford, Johnston, & Grant, 2009). These symptoms negatively affect the quality of life of individuals who have gone through the traumatic event; they can last many years and affect the working and emotional lives of the victims. At the same time, many studies (Daoud et al., 2012; Elias et al., 2012; Kellermann, 2015) have observed that the offspring of victims of traumatic events show adverse symptoms ascribed to the experiences that their parents lived through. In literature this occurrence is known as "transmission of trauma" or ITT.

2. Transmission of Trauma Across Generation

The term ITT is generally used to describe the effects of trauma on victims' children. To date, the widest source of information about ITT comes from research on collective trauma such as the Holocaust, World War II, the Armenian genocide and the oppression of Indigenous peoples (Bezo & Maggi, 2015). Children of collective trauma survivors have reported anger, guilt, depressive mood (Wiseman et al., 2006), shame (Karenian et al., 2011), lower socio-emotional functioning (Scharf, 2007) and increased suicidal attempts (Elias et al., 2012) as compared to children of parents who were not survivors.

Studies have addressed the issue of ITT from an integrated framework of biological, psychodynamic, sociocultural and family systems (Kellermann, 2015). From a biological perspective, trauma transmission occurs as a result of a genetic or biochemical predisposition. These findings are derived from studies (Bohacek & Mansuy, 2013; Kellermann, 2013; Provençal & Binder, 2015; Rampp, Binder & Provençal, 2014; Yehuda & Bierer, 2009), which found permanent genetic changes as a result of trauma. An epigenetic mark is a change to a gene or to the DNA environment that will subsequently alter how the DNA is read into the RNA. An epigenetic transformation occurs as a result of changes in the external environment that may affect the internal environment. These studies provide evidence that the brain can be rewired after trauma and can permanently alter genes that are passed to future generations. According to the psychodynamic models, ITT occurs when the children of survivors absorb the emotions that are not fully processed at a conscious level by parents (Kellermann, 2001). To explain the suffering within the families of traumatized parents, a phenomenon known as the "conspiracy of silence" has been proposed, leading the Survivor parents to be emotionally withdrawn (Braga, Mello, & Fiks, 2012; Fromm, 2011; Giladi & Bell, 2013). Thus, the transmission of trauma is considered a result of the unconsciously displaced emotions (Katz, 2003; Kellermann, 2001; Shmotkin, Shrira, Goldberg, & Palgi, 2011). In comparison with psychoanalytic models, sociocultural theories focus on conscious and direct effects of survivor parents on their children. From this perspective, it is accepted that the survivor parents may represent inadequate role models for their children. These children learn by observing and imitating their parents and therefore may assume the behaviors and emotional states of their parents (Kellermann, 2001). Regarding the family system perspective, emphasis is placed on the communicational and interactional style of the interactions between survivor parents and their children. In many cases a very closed family system has been observed, in which parents are concerned for their children and children are concerned for their parents (Klein-Parker, 1988). In this mutual identification the children of survivors live in the past experienced by their parents (Kellermann, 2001). With this framework in mind, we believe that it is important to describe, more specifically, the impact of trauma on individual functioning and on family dynamic, as well as the community/social implications of ITT.

3. The Impact of ITT on Individual Functioning

Literature has shown that the impact of traumatic event is not limited to the person exposed to that particular event only, rather it effects the people directly linked to the survivors, especially offspring (Dekel & Goldblatt, 2008; Giladi & Bell, 2013; Lev-Wiesel, 2007). Most of this information is from studies on World War II, the Holocaust, mass genocides and the oppression of Indigenous peoples. As reported by Kellermann (2015) the more a person experiences traumatic events, the more he or she suffers from PTSD (Hong & Efferth, 2015; Neuner et al., 2004; Schoedl, Costa, Fossaluza, Mari & Mello, 2014) and the more this condition relates to trauma, which is passed on to the offspring (Kellermann, 2015). This suggests a strong relationship between parental PTSD and symptomatology in offspring (Barel et al., 2010; Bombay et al., 2011; Daoud et al., 2012; Elias et al., 2012; Kellermann, 2015; Lemstra et al., 2012; Pearce et al., 2008). Kellermann (2001) conducted a comprehensive meta-analysis of 35 studies, which examined the mental state of offspring of Holocaust survivors. Accordingly, this population reported issues related to the separation-individuation process, impairments in self-esteem, difficulties with affect regulation, and a preoccupation with death, compared to the control group (Kellermann, 2001). Daud and colleagues (2005) studied the offspring of Lebanese and Iraqi refugee parents who had been subjected to torture and found that children of tortured parents had more anxiety, depression, post-traumatic stress symptoms, attention deficit and behavioral disorders when compared to the control group of non-traumatized refugee families.

In general, offspring of survivors report a higher prevalence of depression (Muong, 2009; Razavi, Razavi-Ratki, Nojomi, & Namiranian, 2012; Shceeringa & Zeanah, 2008) and anxiety (Leen-Feldner, Feldner, Bunaciu, & Blumenthal, 2011) compared to an average adult group. An association between parent survivors' symptoms and both children psychopathology (Beardslee, Gladstone & O'Connor, 2011; Dekel &

Goldblatt, 2008; Lambert, Engh, Hasbun, & Holzer, 2012) and behavioral problems, such as higher rate of aggression (Ahmadzadeh & Malekian, 2004) has also been found. Studies among children of Holocaust survivors have shown that only paternal symptomatology may predict offspring psychiatric disorders, including PTSD, for both men (Yehuda, Bell, Bierer, & Schmeidler, 2008) and women (Cohen, Hien, & Batchelder, 2008). Studies conducted on other populations of survivors has shown similar results as the studies on Holocaust survivors and their offspring. For example, Vaage and colleagues (2011), in a study of children of Vietnamese refugees found that children's *Total Difficulties Scores*, measured by *Strengths and Difficulties Questionnaire* (SDQ; Goodman, 2001), were positively associated with a paternal diagnosis of PTSD. These children appeared to be less obedient and reported more fears and loneliness than the control group. Interestingly, compared to peers in the control group, children of Vietnamese refugees reported similar levels of happiness and restlessness. This highlights the possibility that the traumatic history of parents does not necessarily shape the degree of happiness and restlessness of their children.

The severity of parental symptoms and difficulties in handling their personal traumatic history tend to affect their caregiving skills, harming the attachment representations and intra-family communication (Almqvist & Broberg, 2003; Giromini et al., 2016; Measham & Rousseau, 2010; Lambert et al., 2014). Mental representations of traumatized individuals may be assessed through the use of Adult Attachment Interview[1] (AAI; Main Goldwyn, & Hesse, 2003) which reveals disorientation or disorganization during the discussion of potentially traumatic episodes, including abandonment, loss or sexual and physical abuse. During the administration of the interview, a sudden deterioration of the narrative quality expressed in lapses in metacognitive monitoring of speech and/or reasoning, suggests a disorganized state of mind (Lyons-Ruth & Jacobvitz, 2008). These individuals are classified as *unresolved/disorganized* in association to one of the three organized AAI classifications (*secure, dismissing* and *preoccupied*). Attachment disorganization has been linked to dissociative pathology (Barone & Lionetti, 2013; Liotti & Farina, 2011; Steele & van der Hart, 2014) and the parental disorganized state of mind may negatively influence an adult's ability to take

[1] The AAI is a semi-structured interview used to assess the state of mind regarding childhood experiences with caregivers. Attachment representation are classified as *secure* (F), *dismissing* (Ds) or *preoccupied* (E) depending on the interviewee's coherence of narrative referring to the discrepancy between sematic and episodic memories about early attachment experiences (Hesse, 2008).

care of the child and encourage the transmission of disorganization between generations (Lyons-Ruth & Jacobvitz, 2008; Solomon, & George, 2011). These aspects will be further discussed in the following section.

According to literature, the traumatic memories of the survivor parents can be transmitted to their children through epigenetic marks subjecting these children to significant chromosomal changes (Kellermann, 2015). Epigenetics is the study of heritable changes in gene expression that are not due to changes in the underlying DNA sequence and occur as a result of environmental stress or major emotional trauma which impact the chromosomes (Meaney & Szyf, 2005). Inheritance through epigenetic mechanisms has been studied (Bohacek & Mansuy, 2013; Kellermann, 2013; Provençal & Binder, 2015; Rampp, Provençal, & Binder, 2014; Thomson, 2015; Yehuda & Bierer, 2009) and several animal laboratory studies have shown that the animals can inherit a parental memory of trauma, and respond as if they had lived the traumatic event (Debiec & Sullivan, 2014; Dias & Ressler, 2014). The same mechanism, at the genetic level, may also impact humans (Gallagher, 2013). The epigenetic perspective is seeking to integrate both hereditary and environmental factors, assuming that biological and psychosocial factors are in close interaction with each other (Crews et al., 2014; Hofer, 2014).

As previously stated, individual functioning is one of the perspectives we can consider in order to better understand the underlying functions of ITT. Family level is intrinsically involved in the individual functioning and the following section will address this perspective in relation to impairment of parental functioning.

4. Family Dynamics Related to ITT

Intergenerational transmission of traumatic symptoms can follow two different routes: direct and indirect transmission (Schwartz, Dohrenwend, & Levav, 1994; Schwerdtfeger et al., 2013). Direct transmission – as previously discussed - is represented by specific effects of the parents' symptomatic behaviors, while indirect transmission is described as the overall parental difficulty shown because of his/her own traumatic history. This section will focus on the indirect transmission of trauma on offsprings, paternal features and the implications for routine activities of the family (Ruscio et al., 2002; Cohen et al., 2003).

Research in this area has generally shown traumatized parents to be less emotionally or functionally available to their children (de Campora, Giromini,

Larciprete, Li Volsi & Zavattini, 2014; Dyb, Jensen, & Nygaard, 2011; Schwerdtfeger et al., 2013; Schwerdtfeger & Geoff, 2007). Several studies have also shown that mothers with PTSD symptoms appear to be less sensitive and responsive (Di Folco, de Campora & Zavattini, *in press*; Schechter et al., 2010; Van Ee, Kleber & Mooren, 2012;), more avoidant (Schechter et al., 2008) and more hostile and controlling when interacting with their children (Davies, Slade, Wright, & Stewart, 2008). Other studies have shown a close association between parental symptoms of PTSD and both internalizing and externalizing behavior problems of their children (Enlow et al., 2011; Lombardo & Motta, 2008). Banyard, Williams and Siegel (2003) highlighted that parental symptoms of PTSD were associated with lower levels of parenting satisfaction, increased child neglect and use of physical punishment. Indeed, parents with PTSD symptoms may experience difficulties regulating their own arousal and, consequently, experience difficulties modulating the infant's arousal (de Campora & Meldolesi, 2014; Tull, Barrett, McMillan, & Roemer, 2007). Samper, Taft, King and King (2004) studied parent–child relationships among 250 male Vietnam veterans with children included in the National Vietnam Veterans Readjustment Study (NVVRS; Kulka et al., 1990). Results indicated that parental avoidance and emotional numbing symptoms, related to PTSD, were significantly related to a perceived lower quality of the parent–child relationship and parenting satisfaction. Similar results were obtained in a study (Berz, Taft, Watkins, & Monson, 2008) on 60 female Vietnam veterans who had biological children, included in NVVRS (Kulka et al., 1990). Results showed a significant negative relationship between both hyperarousal and avoidance/numbing symptoms, related to PTSD and lower parenting satisfaction and lower quality of the parent-child relationship.

One of the most concrete assumptions regarding parental unavailability is linked to the hypothesis that avoidance and numbing symptoms of PTSD have a negative impact on parenting (Ruscio, Weathers, King, & King, 2002) influencing adults' internal representations of attachment (Salo, Qouta, & Punamaki, 2005). Survivors often experience a flood of processes not yet fully processed, that may lead to a blurring of identity and may also elicit problematic relationships with their children. Barocas and Barocas (1973) asserted that the survivor has a vulnerability relating to the object world. Recently, Somer and Nizri (2013) found that children of survivors felt deeply affected by their parents' traumatic experiences but also needed to distance themselves from over-identifying with their traumatized parents, displaying a difficulty in managing intimacy.

The attachment-based model of trauma transmission has shown that in a disorganized attachment relationship the infant is likely to have an unclear and incoherent strategy for using the caregiver as a secure base in response to a parent acting as a source of fear for the child (Main & Solomon, 1986; 1990). This relationship is characterized by parental unresolved/disorganized states of mind (Hesse & Main, 2000) that may reflect parental caregiving in the presence of traumatic experiences (Carlson Yates, & Sroufe, 2009; Liotti, 2004) and may lead to a fragmented sense of self in the child (Lyons-Ruth, Dutra, Schuder, & Bianchi, 2006; Pace, Cavanna, Guiducci & Bizzi, 2015). A 1995 meta-analysis by van IJzendoorn of nine studies investigating the relationship between AAI and Strange Situation Procedure[2] (SSP; Ainsworth, Blehar, Waters, & Wall, 1978) classifications, showed that 53% of children with disorganized attachment pattern had unresolved/disorganized mothers. Attachment research has demonstrated that "unresolved adults" (unresolved for trauma or loss assessed with the AAI) behave in a frightened or frightening way (Lyons-Ruth & Jacobvitz, 2008), which can be frightening to the child (Madigan, Moran, & Pederson, 2006). This in turn increases the risk of these parents having children with a disorganized attachment pattern (Madigan, Moran, & Pederson, 2006).

Main and Solomon (1986), during their studies on SSP, observed that children's disorganized attachment pattern can be defined by a series of behaviors exhibited in stressful situation and in the presence of parents. Typically, children with disorganized attachment exhibited contradictory behaviors, misdirected or stereotypical behaviors, freezing behaviors, and apprehension towards, or fear of the parents after separation (Main & Morgan, 1996). Disruptive/aggressive and dissociative disorders usually emerge (Hesse & Main, 2000), as well as elevated cortisol levels in stressful situations, externalizing problems, controlling behavior and symptoms of posttraumatic stress disorder (PTSD) in childhood and adolescence (Ellis, MacDonald, Lincoln & Cabral, 2008) and dissociative behavior in adulthood (van Ijzendoorn, Schuengel, & Bakermans–Kranenburg, 1999). Field, Om, Kim, and Vorn (2011) conducted a study with 200 children of Cambodian survivors and found a significant relationship between higher levels of parental trauma symptoms and higher degree of role-reversal in parent-child relationship (i.e.,

[2] SSP is an experimental procedure conducted to observe the child attachment behaviors during separation and reunion episodes from the parent. It allows to classified the child attachment pattern into three main attachment style (*secure, insecure-avoidant and insecure-ambivalent/resistant*) (Ainsworth et al., 1978) and one *disorganized* attachment style (Main & Soloman, 1990).

the parent required care and attention from a child incompatible with the age of the child) and overprotective parenting that, in turn, was linked to greater anxiety and depression in the child.

There have been some indications that the transmission of trauma may in fact be more complex. A meta-analysis (Madigan, Bakermans-Kranenburg, Van Ijzendoorn, Moran, Pederson, & Benoit, 2006) on the disorganized attachment transmission found only moderate effect sizes for the associations between, unresolved/disorganized attachment and infant disorganized pattern and only a small part of variance of the association between unresolved states of mind and disorganized attachment was explained by parental behavior. These results highlight the necessity of investigating other factors which may influence the development of a disorganized attachment pattern. Along these lines, Schechter (2003) investigated the intergenerational transmission of attachment between severely traumatized women and their children and found that the severity of interpersonal trauma did not predict negative maternal narratives of children, otherwise maternal reflective functioning[3] was a predictive factor of maternal descriptions of the children. Similarly, Berthelot and colleagues (Berthelot, Ensink, Bernazzani, Normandin, Luyten, & Fonagy, 2015) highlighted that infant attachment disorganization is only partially explained by mothers' unresolved trauma and trauma-specific reflective function in a sample of children and mothers with a history of childhood maltreatment.

In addition to the attachment bond, a key element featuring the family functioning is the family communication style or the intra-family trauma communication style (Dalgaard & Montgomery, 2015). These terms refer to different ways parents communicate their PTSD symptoms (Dalgaard et al., 2016; Feniger-Schaal et al., 2016) and the basic assumption is that insufficiently worked-through trauma experiences, may transfers from the parents' mind to the child's mind, unless verbalized (Dalgaard et al., 2016). Wiseman and colleagues (2002), have investigated the intra-family communication in offspring of Holocaust survivors, using a combination of the Core Conflict Relationship Theme[4] (CCRT) and a narrative qualitative

[3] Reflective Functioning (RF; Fonagy, Target, Steele, & Steele, 1998) is an operationalization of mentalization in the context of attachment theory. It refers to the ability to understand oneself and others mental states underlying behaviors.

[4] Framework developed by Luborsky (1977) to study narratives. Through this method it's possible to understand central relationship patterns and issues related to relational narratives. The CCRT has composed by three scale: "*wish*", what he subject wanted from other people; "*response of other*", the way in which react other people to the response of subject; "*self*", how the subject react to their response.

analysis. Their findings demonstrated a strong relationship between the family communication style and the psychological symptoms shown by the offspring, and including internal conflict and guilt around needing to be independent, while simultaneously fearing separation. Authors described a peculiar family communication style, which they called "knowing-not knowing" (Jucovy, 1985), which was characterized by the offspring's non-verbal knowledge of their parents' traumatic experiences. A "dialectical tension" was believed to exist between knowing and not knowing about the horrors their parents experienced. "The known is at times unconscious because the individual does not know at least consciously that he or she knows" (Wiseman & Barber, 2008, p. 239). Several core themes emerged in the narratives, including profound feelings of anger, anxiety and helplessness, as well as joy and pride. The CCRT model revealed the main relational themes of an inherent wish for closeness with parents and at the same time a wish for autonomy and independence. One adult child of a survivor shared "I should protect my parents (mutual overprotection) by giving up my basic wishes and avoiding confrontations at all cost" (Wiseman & Barber, 2008, p. 232).

The timing and the way traumatic experiences are disclosure to the child have also been found to be relevant, even more than the disclosure or nondisclosure of past trauma itself. Measham and Rousseau (2010) as well as Rousseau, Measham, and Nadeau, (2013) found that among refugee families from non-Western cultures a moderate parental approach to disclosure of past trauma was associated with psychological adjustment in children. In "modulated disclosure" intra-family communication style is focused on the timing and the particular manner of disclosure, and these are linked to parental sensitivity to the child's cognitive and emotional needs. These findings demonstrate how intergenerational trauma can be transmitted both consciously and unconsciously and within the first significant relationship.

5. The Community/Social Implications of ITT

"There have been a variety of terms used to describe the multigenerational nature of distress in communities, including *collective trauma, intergenerational trauma, multigenerational trauma, and historical trauma.* [...] Historical trauma is collective in that many members of a community view the events as acute losses and experience corresponding trauma reactions. It is understood as compounding insomuch as events occurring at different time periods (often across generations) come to be seen as parts of a single traumatic trajectory" (Evans-Campbell, 2008, pp. 320-321).

As described by Withback and colleagues (2004) the study of the *Historical trauma* originated in the 1960s with psychoanalysts who wanted to study the effect of World War II on the Holocaust survivors and their families. The term "historical trauma" indicates that a traumatic event occurred over the course of many years and transmitted across generations, among groups of people who share specific affiliation or group identities such as ethnicity, nationality or religious affiliation (Evans-Campbell, 2008) as well as a shared history of oppression, victimization, or massive group trauma exposure (Campbell & Evans-Campbell, 2011; Karenian et al., 2011; Wexler et al., 2009). Several survivor groups such as African Americans, Armenians refugees, native American and Alaska Natives (AIAN), Cambodian, Japanese Americans, Mexicans and Mexican Americans, Palestinian youth, Russians, Vietnamese and, of course Holocaust Survivors (Evans-Campell, 2008) helped to understand the mechanisms and the effects of these disruptive events on these populations at large. Usually the reaction to traumatic events is strongly related to two dimensions, individual/familial, and the community which represents a broader representation of the person and the family.

The different way in which the community may respond to traumatic events may include the breakdown of traditional culture and values, the loss of traditional rites of passage and internalized racism (Gone, 2014; Prussing, 2014). Literature has shown that communities, which have histories of trauma, are more vulnerable to psychopathological symptoms in later generations (Kellermann, 2015). From the intergenerational point of view, Kellermann (2001) showed that the first, second and even third generation offspring of Holocaust survivors display heightened post-traumatic stress symptoms (Barel et al., 2010). Similar results were found in study by Karenian and colleagues (2011) on children of Armenian survivors, who found elevated post-traumatic stress symptoms among these children. In a study (Daoud et al., 2012) on offspring of displaced Palestinians, Authors found lower self-rated health, poorer socio-economic status, and higher stress in comparison to offspring of families who were not displaced. Several studies on the offspring of persecuted indigenous peoples have found that historical trauma is associated with increased exposure to sexual violence (Pearce et al., 2008), increased risk of drug abuse (Lemstra et al., 2012), higher risk of depressive symptoms (Bombay et al., 2011), and an increase in suicidal thoughts and attempts (Elias et al., 2012).

The communication of historical trauma seems to be relevant for ITT at the community level, as well as at the family level (Evans-Campell, 2008), once again, suggesting the phenomenon of "conspiracy of silence" (Danieli, 1998). When the survivors tried to talk about their terrible experience they were not heard or believed leading them to not talk about their traumatic experiences and to suffer with the rest of the society - the "non survivors" - moreover, increasing their feelings of isolation, loneliness, and mistrust. This situation was far from favorable to the elaboration of the traumatic experiences, in fact it was so destructive that their offspring would never be able to understand the horrific nature of survivor experiences, while at the same time they lived with the effect of the trauma through the intergenerational transmission of those unspoken traumatic experiences (Danieli, 2007). The offspring continue to live emotionally those events for many years and generations (Brave Heart, 1998; 2000) and suffer their effects on their health, mental health, and identity (Evans-Campell, 2008). This family functioning was described by Bar-On (1995) in his biographical study where "untold" stories where transmitted to the second generation who "became sensitive to their parents' needs to keep silent responding with a 'double wall' the parents did not tell and the children did not ask" (Bar-On, 1995, page 326).

Attachment theory studied ITT also at the community level. In attachment theory, experiences owing to lack of resolution of mourning in case of loss or traumatic experiences may be indicative of a disorganized attachment (Hesse, 1999; van IJzendoorn, 1995). Several survivors may well suffer from prolonged unresolved trauma and develop a disorganized attachment (Hesse, 1999). A 1998 randomized group study on second generation Jewish persons showed that survivor parents were described as less affectionate and more committed/protective towards their children than did the parents of the control group and the children described their childhood as characterized by parental preoccupation of the losses in wartime and with more problems with separation and individuation (Bar-On et al., 1998). Rowland-Klein and Dunlop (1998) suggested that war trauma experienced by Holocaust survivors may be transferred to the third generation as well. ITT was studied across three generations of Holocaust survivors (grandmother), the mothers and the infants in 98 families (Sagi-Schwartz et al., 2003). Data showed that grandmothers differed significantly from non survivors for the irresolution at the Adult Attachment Interview (AAI) but the mothers did not differ on attachment patterns, traumatic stress, anxiety, and maternal behavior toward their infants. Also, contrary to expectations, data did not show any intergenerational transition of trauma however, between mothers and infants, which may presumably reflect a protective role-played by the mothers. In light of these results, we underline the importance of a deeper investigation of these aspects by comparing results obtained with instruments used within attachment theory with tools from other theoretical frameworks.

CONCLUSION

This chapter has provided an overview of the understandings of trauma, and how the trauma can impact and pass across generations known as ITT. As we have seen, the traumatic or stressful events may have intergenerational effects at individual, family and community levels of functioning (Kellermann, 2015), in addition to having an impact on the people who are directly exposed to the traumatic event. The more extensive knowledge about ITT comes from literature on mass trauma, such as World War II, Holocaust, mass genocide and the oppression of Indigenous peoples (Bezo & Maggi, 2015; Berz et al., 2008; Evans-Campbell, 2008; Samper et al., 2004; Vaage et al., 2011) and has shown a close relationship between the PTSD symptoms of the parents and risk of psychopathology in the offspring.

Given the literature, what appear to emerge is that the more the parents were exposed to trauma, the more the children show posttraumatic symptoms or psychopathology (Belsky, 2008; Guerriero, Gnazzo, Zavattini & de Campora, 2015). The underlying mechanisms of this relationship are not entirely clear, and literature suggests several different frameworks including a biological, psychodynamic, sociocultural and family systems point of view (Kellermann, 2015) in order to build an integrated perspective. Family dynamics and the community may influence ITT at the individual level, but in turn their functioning may depend on the individual level of functioning.

In seeking to study the intergenerational impact of trauma within an integrated framework, several authors (Bohacek & Mansuy, 2013; Kellermann, 2013; Provençal & Binder, 2015; Rampp, Provençal, & Binder, 2014; Thomson, 2015; Yehuda & Bierer, 2009) suggest that the impact of trauma may be inherited from the traumatized parents through epigenetic mechanisms. What happens is a permanent genetic change as a result of trauma that will alter the DNA and these DNA alterations in the parents are then transmitted to the child (Kellermann, 2015). The epigenetic paradigm attempts to overcome the notion that ITT was caused exclusively by environmental factors, such as the family functioning or community functions The epigenetic perspective is trying to integrate both hereditary and environmental factors, assuming that biological and psychosocial factors are in close interaction with each other (Crews et al., 2014; de Campora, Larciprete, Delogu, Meldolesi & Giromini, 2016; Hofer, 2014). In regards to this, literature is seeking to introduce a new diagnostic entity into the PTSD, the *transgenerational stress disorder*, a separate subtype of PTSD specific for the offspring of survivors (Kellerman, 2015).

It is important to emphasize that not all experiences of trauma lead to trauma-related disorder or symptoms and there are indications that ITT does not takes place in all families of survivors (Sagi-Schwartz, van IJzendoorn, Bakermans-Kranenburg, 2008; Van IJzendoorn, Bakermans-Kranenburg, & Sagi-Schwartz, 2008)). Research literature suggests that in these cases, resilience factors may mediate the effects of the traumatic experience (Cherry & Galea, 2015; Laghi, Baiocco, Ghezzi, Petrocchi & Pace, 2012; Westphal & Bonanno, 2007)).

A review of the literature reveals that no particular attention has been given to the possible areas of intervention in order to prevent the impact of traumatic experiences across generations. The key might be to increment the resilience factors (Gnazzo, Guerriero, Di Folco, Zavattini & de Campora, 2015), at both the individual level and family/community level. Future studies are needed to increase our knowledge, and to deepen the investigation into the impact of ITT according to an integrated perspective.

REFERENCES

Ahmadzadeh, G. H., & Malekian, A. (2004). Aggression, anxiety, and social development in adolescent children of war veterans with PTSD versus those of non-veterans. *Journal of Research in Medical Sciences*, 9(5), 231-234.

Ainsworth, M. D. S., Blehar, M., Waters, E., & Wall, S. (1978). *Patterns of attachment: Observations in the Strange Situation and at home*. Hillsdale, N]: Erlbaum.

Alayarian, A. (2008). *Consequences of denial: The Armenian genocide.* London: Karnac Books.

Almqvist, K., & Broberg, A. G. (2003). Young children traumatized by organized violence together with their mothers–The critical effects of damaged internal representations. *Attachment & Human development, 5*(4), 367-380. doi:10.1080/14616730310001633447.

American Psychiatric Association (2013). *Diagnostic and statistical manual of mental disorders: DSM-5.* Washington, D.C.: American Psychiatric Association.

Aschenbrenner, K. (2013). Ripples Against the Other Shore: The Impact of Trauma Exposure on the Immigration Process Through Adjudicators. *Michigan Journal of Race & Law, 19*(53).

Banyard, V. L., Williams, L. M., & Siegel, J. A. (2003). The impact of complex trauma and depression on parenting: An exploration of mediating risk and protective factors. *Child maltreatment, 8*(4), 334-349. doi:10.1177/1077559503257106.

Bar-On, D. (1995). *Fear and hope: Three generations of five Israeli families of Holocaust survivors.* Cambridge, Mass.: Harvard University Press.

Bar-On, D., Eland, J., Kleber, R. J., Krell, R., Moore, Y., Sagi, A., & van IJzendoorn, M. H. (1998). Multigenerational perspectives on coping with the Holocaust experience: An attachment perspective for understanding the developmental sequelae of trauma across generations. *International Journal of Behavioral Development, 22*(2), 315-338. doi:10.1080/0165 02598384397.

Barel, E., Van IJzendoorn, M. H., Sagi-Schwartz, A., Bakermans-Kranenburg, M. J. (2010). Surviving the Holocaust: a meta-analysis of the long-term sequelae of a genocide. *Psychological Bulletin, 136*(5), 677-98. doi: 10.1037/a0020339.

Barocas, H. A., & Barocas, C. B. (1973). Manifestations of concentration camp effects on the second generation. *American Journal of Psychiatry, 130*(7), 820-821. doi:10.1176/ajp.130.7.820.

Barone, L., & Lionetti, F. (2013). Trauma, attachment disorganization cues and risk factors in the life span. *Psicologia clinica dello sviluppo, 17*(1), 3-26.

Beardslee, W. R., Gladstone, T. R., & O'Connor, E. E. (2011). Transmission and prevention of mood disorders among children of affectively ill parents: A review. *Journal of the American Academy of Child & Adolescent Psychiatry, 50*(11), 1098-1109. doi:10.1016/j.jaac.2011. 07.020.

Belsky, J. (2008). War, trauma and children's development: Observations from a modern evolutionary perspective. *International Journal of Behavioral Development, 32*(4), 260-271. doi: 10.1177/0165025 408090969.

Berthelot, N., Ensink, K., Bernazzani, O., Normandin, L., Luyten, P., & Fonagy, P. (2015). Intergenerational transmission of attachment in abused and neglected mothers: The role of trauma-specific reflective functioning. *Infant mental health journal*, *36*(2), 200-212. doi:10.1002/imhj.21499.

Berz, J. B., Taft, C. T., Watkins, L. E., & Monson, C. M. (2008). Associations between PTSD symptoms and parenting satisfaction in a female veteran sample. *Journal of Psychological Trauma*, *7*(1), 37-45. doi:10.1080/19322880802125969.

Bezo, B., & Maggi, S. (2015). Living in "survival mode:" Intergenerational transmission of trauma from the Holodomor genocide of 1932–1933 in Ukraine. *Social Science & Medicine*, *134*, 87-94. doi:10.1016/j.socscimed.2015.04.009.

Bohacek, J., & Mansuy, I. M. (2013). Epigenetic inheritance of disease and disease risk. *Neuropsychopharmacology*, *38*(1), 220-236. doi:10.1038/npp.2012.110.

Bombay, A., Matheson, K., & Anisman, H. (2011). The impact of stressors on second generation Indian residential school survivors. *Transcultural Psychiatry*, *48*(4), 367-391. doi:10.1177/1363461511410240.

Bonanno, G. A. (2004). Loss, trauma, and human resilience: Have we underestimated the human capacity to thrive after extremely aversive events? *American Psychologist*, *59*, 20–28. doi:10.1037/0003-066x.59.1.20.

Brady, K. T., Clary, C. M., 2004. Affective and anxiety comorbidity in post-traumatic stress disorder treatment trials of sertraline. *Com. Psychiatry* 44, 360–369. doi:10.1016/s0010-440x(03)00111-1.

Braga, L. L., Mello, M. F., & Fiks, J. P. (2012). Transgenerational transmission of trauma and resilience: a qualitative study with Brazilian offspring of Holocaust survivors. *BMC Psychiatry*, *12*(1), 1, 134. doi:10.1186/1471-244x-12-134.

Brave Heart, M. Y. B., & DeBruyn, L. M. (1998). The American Indian Holocaust: Healing historical unresolved grief. *American Indian and Alaska Native Mental Health Research, 8*, 56-78. doi:10.5820/aian.0802.1998.60.

Brave Heart, M. Y. H. (2000). Wakiksuyapi: Carrying the historical trauma of the Lakota. *Tulane Studies in Social Welfare*, 21(22), 245-266. doi:10.1037/e318922004-025.

Campbell, C. D., & Evans-Campbell, T. (2011). Historical trauma and Native American child development and mental health: An overview. American Indian and Alaska Native children and mental health: *Development, context prevention, and treatment*, 1-26.

Carlson, E. A., Yates, M. T., & Sroufe, L. A. (2009). *Development of dissociation and development of the self. Dissociation and the dissociative disorders*. New York: Routledge.

Cherry, K. E., & Galea, S. (2015). Resilience after trauma. In D. Ajdukovic, S. Kimhi & M. Lahad (Eds.), *Resiliency: Enhancing Coping with Crisis and Terrorism* (pp. 35-40). The Netherlands: IOS Press.

Cohen, H., Zohar, J., & Matar, M. (2003). The relevance of differential response to trauma in an animal model of posttraumatic stress disorder. *Biological psychiatry, 53*(6), 463-473. doi:10.1016/s0006-3223(02)01 909-1.

Cohen, L. R., Hien, D. A., & Batchelder, S. (2008). The impact of cumulative maternal trauma and diagnosis on parenting behavior. *Child Maltreatment, 13*(1), 27-38. doi:10.1037/e591542013-001.

Crews, K. R., Gaedigk, A., Dunnenberger, H. M., Leeder, J. S., Klein, T. E., Caudle, K. E., & Prows, C. A. (2014). Clinical Pharmacogenetics Implementation Consortium guidelines for cytochrome P450 2D6 genotype and codeine therapy: 2014 update. *Clinical Pharmacology & Therapeutics, 95*(4), 376-382. doi:10.1038/clpt.2013.254.

Dalgaard, N. T., & Montgomery, E. (2015). Disclosure and silencing: A systematic review of the literature on patterns of trauma communication in refugee families. *Transcultural Psychiatry, 52*(5), 579-593. doi:10.1177/1363461514568442.

Dalgaard, N. T., Todd, B. K., Daniel, S. I., & Montgomery, E. (2016). The transmission of trauma in refugee families: Associations between intra-family trauma communication style, children's attachment security and psychosocial adjustment. *Attachment & Human Development, 18*(1), 69-89. doi:10.1080/14616734.2015.1113305.

Danieli, Y. (Ed.)(1998). *International handbook of multigenerational legacies of trauma*. New York: Kluwer Academic/ Plenum Publishing Corporation.

Danieli, Y. (2007). Assessing trauma across cultures from a multigenerational perspective. In J. P. Wilson & C. S.-K. Tang (Eds.), *Cross-cultural assessment of psychological trauma and PTSD* (pp. 65-89). New York, NY: Springer.

Daoud, N., Shankardass, K., O'Campo, P., Anderson, K., Agbaria, A. K., 2012. Internal displacement and health among the Palestinian minority in Israel. *Social Science & Medicine, 74*(8), 1163-1171. doi:10.1016/ j.socscimed. 2011.12.041.

Daud, A., Skoglund, E., & Rydelius, P. A. (2005). Children in families of torture victims: Transgenerational transmission of parents' traumatic experiences to their children. *International Journal of Social Welfare, 14*(1), 23-32. doi:10.1111/j.1468-2397.2005.00336.x.

Davies, J., Slade, P., Wright, I., & Stewart, P. (2008). Posttraumatic stress symptoms following childbirth and mothers' perceptions of their infants. *Infant Mental Health Journal*, *29*(6), 537-554. doi: 10.1002/imhj.20197.

Debiec, J., & Sullivan, R. M. (2014). Intergenerational transmission of emotional trauma through amygdala-dependent mother-to-infant transfer of specific fear. *Proceedings of the National Academy of Sciences, 111*(33), 12222-12227. doi:10.1073/pnas.1316740111.

Dekel, R., & Goldblatt, H. (2008). Is there intergenerational transmission of trauma? The case of combat veterans' children. *American Journal of Orthopsychiatry, 78*(3), 281-289. doi.org/10.1037/a0013955.

de Campora, G., Giromini, L., Larciprete, G., Li Volsi, V., & Zavattini, G. C. (2014). The impact of maternal overweight and emotion regulation on early eating behaviors. Eating behaviors, 15(3), 403-409. doi: 10.1016/ j.eatceh.2014.04.013.

de Campora, G., & Meldolesi, C. (2014). Indexes of psychopathology risk in gestational overweight. *Giornale italiano di psicologia*, 41(3), 601-610.

Dias, B. G., & Ressler, K. J. (2014). Parental olfactory experience influences behavior and neural structure in subsequent generations. *Nature Neuroscience, 17*(1), 89-96. doi:10.1038/nn.3594.

Di Folco, S., de Campora, G., Zavattini, G. C. (in press). Sintonie e dissintonie nei legami precoci: traiettorie di valutazione e considerazioni cliniche nei contesti ad alto rischio per lo sviluppo infantile. *Maltrattamento e Abuso all'infanzia.*

Dyb, G., Jensen, T. K., & Nygaard, E. (2011). Children's and parents' posttraumatic stress reactions after the 2004 tsunami. *Clinical Child Psychology and Psychiatry*, *16*(4), 621-634. doi: 10.1177/1359104510 391048.

Elias, B., Mignone, J., Hall, M., Hong, S. P., Hart, L., & Sareen, J. (2012). Trauma and suicide behaviour histories among a Canadian indigenous population: An empirical exploration of the potential role of Canada's residential school system. *Social Science & Medicine, 74*(10), 1560-1569. doi:10.1016/j.socscimed.2012.01.026.

Ellis, B. H., MacDonald, H. Z., Lincoln, A. K., & Cabral, H. J. (2008). Mental health of Somali adolescent refugees: the role of trauma, stress, and perceived discrimination. *Journal of consulting and clinical psychology, 76*(2), 184. doi:10.1037/0022-006x.76.2.184.

Enlow, M. B., Kitts, R. L., Blood, E., Bizarro, A., Hofmeister, M., & Wright, R. J. (2011). Maternal posttraumatic stress symptoms and infant emotional reactivity and emotion regulation. *Infant Behavior and Development, 34*(4), 487-503. doi:10.1016/j.infbeh.2011.07.007.

Evans-Campbell, T. (2008). Historical trauma in American Indian/Native Alaska communities a multilevel framework for exploring impacts on individuals, families, and communities. *Journal of Interpersonal Violence, 23*(3), 316-338. doi:10.1177/0886260507312290.

Feniger-Schaal, R., Noy, L., Hart, Y., Koren-Karie, N., Mayo, A. E., & Alon, U. (2016). Would you like to play together? Adults' attachment and the mirror game. *Attachment & Human Development*, *18*(1), 33-45. doi:10. 1080/14616734.2015.1109677.

Field, N. P., Om, C., Kim, T., & Vorn, S. (2011). Parental styles in second generation effects of genocide stemming from the Khmer Rouge regime in Cambodia. *Attachment & Human Development*, *13*(6), 611-628. doi:10. 1080/14616734.2011.609015.

Fonagy, P., Target, M., Steele, H., & Steele, M. (1998). *Reflective-functioning manual, version 5.0, for application to adult attachment interviews.* London: University College London.

Fromm, M. G. (Ed.). (2011). *Lost in Transmission*. London: Karnac Books.

Gallagher, J. (2013). *'Memories' Pass Between Generations. BBC News*. Retrived 25/04/2016 from http://www.bbc.com/news/health-25156510.

Giladi, L., & Bell, T. S. (2013). Protective factors for intergenerational transmission of trauma among second and third generation Holocaust survivors. *Psychological Trauma: Theory, Research, Practice, and Policy, 5*(4), 384–391. doi:10.1037/a0028455.

Ginzburg, K., (2007). Comorbidity of PTSD and depression following myocardial infarction. *Journal of Affective Disord*ers, *94*, 135–143. doi:10.1016/j.jad.2006.03.016.

Giromini, L., de Campora, G., Brusadelli, E., D'Onofrio, E., Zennaro, A., Zavattini, G. C., & Lang, M. (2015). Validity and Reliability of the Interpersonal Competence Questionnaire: Empirical Evidence from an Italian Study. *Journal of Psychopathology and Behavioral Assessment*, 1-11. doi:10.1007/s10862-015-9499-5.

Gnazzo, A., Guerriero, V., Di Folco, S., Zavattini, G. C., & de Campora, G. (2015). Skin to skin interactions. Does the infant massage improve the couple functioning?. *Frontiers in psychology*, 6:1468. doi: 10.3389/fpsyg. 2015.01468.

Gone, J. P. (2014). Reconsidering American Indian historical trauma: Lessons from an early Gros Ventre war narrative. *Transcultural Psychiatry, 51*(3), 387-406. doi:10.1177/1363461513489722.

Guerriero, V., Gnazzo, A., Zavattini, G. C., & de Campora, G. (2015). Quando la relazione non funziona: il maltrattamento su bambini con Disturbo dello Spettro Autistico. Una revisione della letteratura. *Maltrattamento e abuso all'infanzia*, 3, 55-83. doi: 10.3280/mal2015-003004.

Hashemian, F., Khoshnood, K., Desai, M. M., Falahati, F., Kasl, S., & Southwick, S. (2006). Anxiety, depression, and posttraumatic stress in Iranian survivors of chemical warfare. *JAMA Journal of the American Medical Association*, *296*(5), 560-566. doi:10.1001/jama.296.5.560.

Hesse, E. (1999). The adult attachment interview: Historical and current perspectives. In J. Cassidy and P. Shavers (Eds.), *Handbook of Attachment: Theory, research, and clinical applications* (395-433). New York: The Guilford Press.

Hesse, E., & Main, M. (2000). Disorganized infant, child, and adult attachment: Collapse in behavioral and attentional strategies. *Journal of the American Psychoanalytic Association*, *48*(4), 1097-1127. doi:10.1177/00030651000480041101.

Hofer, M. A. (2014). The emerging synthesis of development and evolution: A new biology for psychoanalysis. *Neuropsychoanalysis*, *16*(1), 3-22. doi:10.1080/15294145.2014.901022.

Hong, C., & Efferth, T. (2015). Systematic Review on Post-Traumatic Stress Disorder Among Survivors of the Wenchuan Earthquake. *Trauma, Violence, & Abuse.* doi:10.1177/1524838015585313.

Hooberman, J., Rosenfeld, B., Rasmussen, A., & Keller, A. (2010). Resilience in trauma exposed refugees: The moderating effect of coping style on resilience variables. *American Journal of Orthopsychiatry*, *80*(4), 557–563. doi:10.1111/j.1939-0025.2010.01060.x.

Javidi, H. & Yadollahie, M. (2012). Post-traumatic stress disorder. *The International Journal of Occupational and Environmental Medicine*, *3*, 2-9.

Jucovy, M. E. (1985). Telling the Holocaust story: A link between the generations. *Psychoanalytic Inquiry, 5,* 31–50. doi:10.1080/07351698509533574.

Karenian, H., Livaditis, M., Karenian, S., Zafiriadis, K., Bochtsou, V., & Xenitidis, K. (2011). Collective trauma transmission and traumatic reactions among descendants of Armenian refugees. *International Journal of Social Psychiatry*, *57*(4), 327-337. doi:10.1177/0020764009354840.

Katz, M. (2003). Prisoners of Azkaban: Understanding intergenerational transmission of trauma due to war and state terror (with help from Harry Potter). *Journal for the Psychoanalysis of Culture and Society*, *8*(2), 200-207. doi:10.1353/psy.2003.0037.

Kellermann, N. P. (2001). Transmission of Holocaust trauma-An integrative view. *Psychiatry*, *64(*3), 256-267. doi:10.1521/psyc.64.3.256.18464.

Kellermann, N. P. (2013). Epigenetic transmission of Holocaust Trauma: Can nightmares be inherited?. *The Israel Journal of Psychiatry and Related Sciences*, *50*(1), 33-9.

Kellermann, N. P. (2015). Epigenetic transgenerational transmission of Holocaust trauma: A Review. Unpublished paper. Retrived 28/04/2016 from https://www.researchgate.net/profile/Natan_Kellermann/publication/284350803_Epigenetic_transgenerational_transmission_of_Holocaust_trauma_A_Review/links/5651e9dd08ae1ef929754433.pdf.

Klein-Parker, F. (1988). Dominant attitudes of adult children of Holocaust survivors toward their parents. In *Human adaptation to extreme stress* (pp. 193-218). US: Springer. doi:10.1007/978-1-4899-0786-8_9.

Kulka, R. A., Schlenger, W . E., Fairbank, J. A., Hough, R. L., Jordan, B. K.., Marmar, C. R., & Weiss, D. S., Grady, D. A. (1990). *Trauma and the Vietnam War generation: Report of findings from the National Vietnam Veterans Readjustment Study.* New York: Brunner/Mazel, Publisher.

Laghi, F., Baiocco, R., Ghezzi, E., Petrocchi, N., Pace, C. S. (2012). La fiducia nell'attaccamento ai genitori e ai pari e i disturbi del comportamento alimentare in adolescenza. *Psicologia Clinica dello Sviluppo, 16*(3), 557-578. doi:10.1449/38839.

Lambert, J. E., Engh, R., Hasbun, A., & Holzer, J. (2012). Impact of posttraumatic stress disorder on the relationship quality and psychological distress of intimate partners: A meta-analytic review. *Journal of Family Psychology*, 26(5), 729. doi:10.1037/a0029341.

Lambert, J. E., Holzer, J., & Hasbun, A. (2014). Association between parents' PTSD severity and children's psychological distress: a meta-analysis. *Journal of Traumatic Stress*, 27(1), 9-17. doi: 10.1002/jts.2189.

Leen-Feldner, E. W., Feldner, M. T., Bunaciu, L., & Blumenthal, H. (2011). Associations between parental posttraumatic stress disorder and both offspring internalizing problems and parental aggression within the National Comorbidity Survey-Replication. *Journal of Anxiety Disorders, 25*(2), 169-175. doi:10.1016/j.janxdis.2010.08.017.

Lemstra, M., Rogers, M., Thompson, A., Moraros, J., & Buckingham, R. (2012). Risk indicators associated with injection drug use in the Aboriginal population. *Aids Care*, *24*(11), 1416-1424.

Lev–Wiesel, R. (2007). Intergenerational transmission of trauma across three generations: A preliminary study. *Qualitative Social Work, 6*(1), 75-94. doi:10.1080/09540121.2011.650678.

Liotti, G. (2004). Trauma, dissociation, and disorganized attachment: Three strands of a single braid. *Psychotherapy: Theory, research, practice, training*, *41*(4), 472. doi:10.1037/0033-3204.41.4.472.

Liotti, G., & Farina, B. (2011). *Sviluppi traumatici: eziopatogenesi, clinica e terapia della dimensione dissociativa*. R. Cortina.

Lombardo, K. L., & Motta, R. W. (2008). Secondary trauma in children of parents with mental illness. *Traumatology*, 14(3), 57–67. doi:10.1177/1534765608320331.

Lu, W., Mueser, K. T., Rosenberg, S. D., & Jankowski, M. K. (2008). Correlates of adverse childhood experiences among adults with severe mood disorders. *Psychiatric Services, 59*(9), 1018-1026. doi:10.1176/ps.2008.59.9.1018.

Lyons-Ruth, K., & Jacobvitz, D. (2008). Attachment disorganization: Genetic factors, parenting contexts, and developmental transformation from infancy to adulthood.

Lyons-Ruth, K., Dutra, L., Schuder, M. R., & Bianchi, I. (2006). From infant attachment disorganization to adult dissociation: relational adaptations or traumatic experiences?. *The Psychiatric clinics of North America*, *29*(1), 63. doi:10.1016/j.psc.2005.10.011.

Madigan, S., Bakermans-Kranenburg, M. J., Van Ijzendoorn, M. H., Moran, G., Pederson, D. R., & Benoit, D. (2006). Unresolved states of mind, anomalous parental behavior, and disorganized attachment: A review and meta-analysis of a transmission gap. *Attachment & Human Development*, *8*(2), 89-111. doi:10.1080/14616730600774458.

Madigan, S., Moran, G., & Pederson, D. R. (2006). Unresolved states of mind, disorganized attachment relationships, and disrupted interactions of adolescent mothers and their infants. *Developmental Psychology, 42*(2), 293-304. doi:10.1037/0012-1649.42.2.293.

Main, M. & Morgan, H. (1996). Disorganization and disorientation in infant Strange Situation behavior: Phenotypic resemblance to dissociative states? In L. Michelson & W. Ray. (Eds.), *Handbook of Dissociation: Theoretical, Empirical and Clinical Perspectives*, (107-138). New York: Plenum. doi:10.1016/s0145-2134(97)00168-3.

Main, M., & Solomon, J. (1986). Discovery of an insecure-disorganized/disoriented attachment pattern. In T. B. Brazelton, M. W. Yogman, (Ed), *Affective development in infancy*, (pp. 95-124). Westport, CT, US: Ablex Publishing.

Main, M., & Solomon, J. (1990). Procedures for identifying infants as disorganized/disoriented during the Ainsworth Strange Situation. *Attachment in the preschool years: Theory, research, and intervention, 1*, 121-160.

Meaney, M. J., & Szyf, M. (2005). Maternal care as a model for experience-dependent chromatin plasticity?. *Trends in Neurosciences, 28*(9), 456-463. doi:10.1016/j.tins.2005.07.006.

Measham, T., & Rousseau, C. (2010). Family disclosure of war trauma to children. *Traumatology, 16*(4), 85-96. doi:10.1177/1534765610365915.

Muong, S. (2009). *The effects of parental unresolved trauma on second generation Cambodian adolescents.* Palo Alto University.

Neuner, F., Schauer, M., Karunakara, U., Klaschik, C., Robert, C., & Elbert, T. (2004). Psychological trauma and evidence for enhanced vulnerability for posttraumatic stress disorder through previous trauma among West Nile refugees. *BMC Psychiatry, 4*(1), 4-34.

Pace C.S., Cavanna, D., Guiducci, V., & Bizzi, F. (2015). When parenting fails: alexithymia and attachment states of mind in mothers of female patients with eating disorders. Frontiers in Psychology, section Psychology for Clinical Settings, 6, Article 1145, 1-11. doi:10.3389/fpsyg.2015.01145.

Papanikolaou, V., Adamis, D., Mellon, R. C., Prodromitis, G., & Kyriopoulos, J. (2011). Double disaster: mental health of survivors of wildfires and earthquake in a part of Greece. *Psychology, 2*(02), 132-137 doi:10.4236/psych.2011.22021.

Pearce, M. E., Christian, W. M., Patterson, K., Norris, K., Moniruzzaman, A., Craib, K. J. & Spittal, P. M. (2008). The Cedar Project: Historical trauma, sexual abuse and HIV risk among young Aboriginal people who use injection and non-injection drugs in two Canadian cities. *Social science & medicine, 66*(11), 2185-2194. doi:10.1016/j.socscimed. 2008.03.034.

Provencal, N., & Binder, E. B. (2015). The effects of early life stress on the epigenome: from the womb to adulthood and even before. *Experimental Neurology, 268*, 10-20. doi:10.1016/j.expneurol.2014.09.001.

Prussing, E. (2014). Historical trauma: Politics of a conceptual framework. *Transcultural Psychiatry, 51*(3), 436-458. doi:10.1177/1363461514531316.

Rampp, C., Binder, E. B., & Provençal, N. (2014). Epigenetics in posttraumatic stress disorder. *Progress in Molecular Biology and Translational Science, 128,* 29-50.

Razavi, S. H., Razavi-Ratki, S. K., Nojomi, M. M., & Namiranian, N. (2012). Depression and general anxiety in the prisoner of war's children: a cross sectional study. *Medical Journal of the Islamic Republic of Iran, 26*(4), 179-184.

Rousseau, C., Measham, T., & Nadeau, L. (2013). Addressing trauma in collaborative mental health care for refugee children. *Clinical child psychology and psychiatry, 18*(1), 121-136. doi:10.1177/135910451 2444117.

Rowland-Klein, D., & Dunlop, R. (1998). The transmission of trauma across generations: Identification with parental trauma in children of Holocaust survivors. *Australian and New Zealand Journal of Psychiatry, 32*(3), 358-369. doi:10.3109/00048679809065528.

Ruscio, A. M., Weathers, F. W., King, L. A., & King, D. W. (2002). Male war-zone veterans' perceived relationships with their children: The importance of emotional numbing. *Journal of Traumatic Stress, 15*(5), 351-357. doi: 10.1023/A:1020125006371.

Sagi-Schwartz, A., van IJzendoorn, M. H., & Bakermans-Kranenburg, M. J. (2008). Does intergenerational transmission of trauma skip a generation? No meta-analytic evidence for tertiary traumatization with third generation of Holocaust survivors. *Attachment & human development, 10*(2), 105-121. doi:10.1080/14616730802113661.

Sagi-Schwartz, A., Van IJzendoorn, M. H., Grossmann, K. E., Joels, T., Grossmann, K., Scharf, M., & Alkalay, S. (2003). Attachment and traumatic stress in female Holocaust child survivors and their daughters. *American Journal of Psychiatry, 160*(6), 1086-1092. doi:10.1176/appi.ajp. 160.6.1086.

Salo, J. A., Qouta, S., & Punamäki, R. L. (2005). Adult attachment, posttraumatic growth and negative emotions among former political prisoners. *Anxiety, Stress, and Coping, 18*(4), 361-378. doi:10.1080/10615 800500289524.

Samper, R. E., Taft, C. T., King, D. W., & King, L. A. (2004). Posttraumatic stress disorder symptoms and parenting satisfaction among a national sample of male Vietnam veterans. *Journal of Traumatic Stress, 17*(4), 311-315. doi:10.1023/b:jots.0000038479.30903.ed.

Scharf, M. (2007). Long-term effects of trauma: Psychosocial functioning of the second and third generation of Holocaust survivors. *Development and Psychopathology, 19*(02), 603-622. doi:10.1017/s0954579407070290.

Schechter, D. S. (2003). Intergenerational communication of maternal violent trauma: Understanding the interplay of reflective functioning and posttraumatic psychopathology. *Relational Perspectives Book Series, 23*, 115-142.

Schechter, D. S., Coates, S. W., Kaminer, T., Coots, T., Zeanah Jr, C. H., Davies, M., & McCaw, J. E. (2008). Distorted maternal mental representations and atypical behavior in a clinical sample of violence-exposed mothers and their toddlers. *Journal of Trauma & Dissociation, 9*(2), 123-147. doi:10.1080/15299730802045666.

Schechter, D. S., Willheim, E., Hinojosa, C., Scholfield-Kleinman, K., Turner, J. B., McCaw, J, & Myers, M. M. (2010). Subjective and objective measures of parent-child relationship dysfunction, child separation distress, and joint attention. *Psychiatry, 73*(2), 130-144. doi:10.1521/psyc.2010.73.2.130.

Scheeringa, M. S., & Zeanah, C. H. (2008). Reconsideration of harm's way: Onsets and comorbidity patterns of disorders in preschool children and their caregivers following Hurricane Katrina. *Journal of Clinical Child & Adolescent Psychology, 37*(3), 508-518. doi:10.1080/15374410802148178.

Schoedl, A. F., Costa, M. P., Fossaluza, V., Mari, J. J., & Mello, M. F. (2014). Specific traumatic events during childhood as risk factors for posttraumatic stress disorder development in adults. *Journal of Health Psychology, 19*(7), 847-857. doi:10.1177/1359105313481074.

Schwartz, S., Dohrenwend, B. P., & Levav, I. (1994). Nongenetic familial transmission of psychiatric disorders? Evidence from children of Holocaust survivors. *Journal of Health and Social Behavior*, 385-402. doi:10.2307/2137216.

Schwerdtfeger, K. L & Geoff, B. N. (2007). Intergenerational transmission of trauma: Exploring mother-infant prenatal attachment. *Journal of Traumatic Stress 20*, 39–51. doi:10.1002/jts.20179.

Schwerdtfeger, K. L., Larzelere, R. E., Werner, D., Peters, C., & Oliver, M. (2013). Intergenerational Transmission of Trauma: The Mediating Role of Parenting Styles on Toddlers' DSM-Related Symptoms. *Journal of Aggression, Maltreatment & Trauma, 22*(2), 211-229. doi:10.1080/10926771.2013.743941.

Shmotkin, D., Shrira, A., Goldberg, S. C., & Palgi, Y. (2011). Resilience and vulnerability among aging Holocaust survivors and their families: An intergenerational overview. *Journal of Intergenerational Relationships, 9*(1), 7-21. doi:10.1080/15350770.2011.544202.

Solomon, J., & George, C. (Eds.). (2011). *Disorganized attachment and caregiving*. New York, NY: Guilford Press.

Somer, E., & Nizri, M. (2013). Intimate Relationships among Second Generation Holocaust Survivors in Israel–A Qualitative Analysis of Coping with the Parents' Heritage. *Klinische Sozialarbeit, 9*(4), 9-10.

Steele, K., & Van der Hart, O. (2013). Understanding attachment, trauma and dissociation in complex developmental trauma disorders In A. Danquah & K. Berry (Eds.) *Attachment theory in adult mental health: A guide to clinical practice* (pp. 78-94). Abingdon, UK: Routledge.

Sundquist, K., Johansson, L. M., DeMarinis, V., Johansson, S. E., & Sundquist, J. (2005). Posttraumatic stress disorder and psychiatric co-morbidity: symptoms in a random sample of female Bosnian refugees. *European Psychiatry, 20*(2), 158-164. doi:10.1016/j.eurpsy.2004.12.001.

Tull, M. T., Barrett, H. M., McMillan, E. S., & Roemer, L. (2007). A preliminary investigation of the relationship between emotion regulation difficulties and posttraumatic stress symptoms. *Behavior Therapy, 38(*3), 303-313. doi:10.1016/j.beth.2006.10.001.

Vaage, A. B., Thomsen, P. H., Rousseau, C., Wentzel-Larsen, T., Ta, T. V., & Hauff, E. (2011). Paternal predictors of the mental health of children of Vietnamese refugees. *Child and Adolescent Psychiatry and Mental Health, 5*(2). doi:10.1186/1753-2000-5-2.

van Ee, E., Kleber, R. J., & Mooren, T. (2012). War trauma lingers on: Associations between maternal posttraumatic stress disorder, parent–child interaction, and child development. *Infant Mental Health Journal, 33*(5), 459-468. doi:10.1002/imhj.21324.

Van IJzendoorn, M. (1995). Adult attachment representations, parental responsiveness, and infant attachment: a meta-analysis on the predictive validity of the Adult Attachment Interview. *Psychological bulletin, 117*(3), 387-403. doi:10.1037/0033-2909.117.3.387.

Westphal, M., & Bonanno, G. A. (2007). Posttraumatic growth and resilience to trauma: Different sides of the same coin or different coins? *Applied Psychology, 56*(3), 417-427. doi:10.1111/j.1464-0597.2007.00298.x.

Wexler, L. M., DiFluvio, G., & Burke, T. K. (2009). Resilience and marginalized youth: Making a case for personal and collective meaning-making as part of resilience research in public health. *Social Science & Medicine*, *69*(4), 565-570.

Whelan-Goodinson, R., Ponsford, J., Johnston, L., & Grant, F. (2009). Psychiatric disorders following traumatic brain injury: their nature and frequency. *The Journal of Head Trauma Rehabilitation, 24*(5), 324-332.

Wiseman, H., & Barber, J. P. (2008). *Echoes of the trauma*. New York: Cambridge University Press.

Wiseman, H., Barber, J. P., Raz, A., Yam, I., Foltz, C., & Livne-Snir, S. (2002). Parental communication of Holocaust experiences and interpersonal patterns in offspring of Holocaust survivors. *International Journal of Behavioral Development*, *26*(4), 371-381.

Wiseman, H., Metzl, E., & Barber, J. P. (2006). Anger, guilt, and intergenerational communication of trauma in the interpersonal narratives of second generation Holocaust survivors. *American Journal of Orthopsychiatry, 76*(2), 176-84.

Yehuda, R., & Bierer, L. M. (2009). The relevance of epigenetics to PTSD: Implications for the DSM-5. *Journal of Traumatic Stress, 22*(5), 427-434.

Yehuda, R., Bell, A., Bierer, L. M., & Schmeidler, J. (2008). Maternal, not paternal, PTSD is related to increased risk for PTSD in offspring of Holocaust survivors. *Journal of Psychiatric Research, 42*(13), 1104-1111.

In: Psychopathology
Editor: Jeremy Williams

ISBN: 978-1-63485-745-1

Chapter 6

On Pre- and Postnatal Mental Health Intervention Concepts

***Goetz Egloff*[1,*] *and Dragana Djordjevic*[2,†]**
[1]Practice for Psychoanalysis, Mannheim, affil,
University of Heidelberg, Heidelberg, Germany
[2]University Children's Clinic, Niš, Serbia, affil,
University of Heidelberg, Heidelberg, Germany

Abstract

In order to prevent the development of psychopathology symptoms in individuals psychiatry, psychoanalysis, and infant mental health research have conceptualized early intervention approaches. Since especially the postnatal relationship between baby and mother/father has been examined extensively in the last decades, some progress has been accomplished as to how parents-to-be can be prepared for parenthood. Parental competencies have also been well-examined; e.g., intuitive parental competencies which are processed within a time frame of 200 to 600 milliseconds are supposed to be universal, potentially existing in any person, and in the relational objects the baby has. Personal factors such as psychopathology can compromise the expression of intuitive parental competencies, however societal factors seem to be underestimated as to

* Corresponding author: Tel.: +49 62140040687; fax: +49 62140040687. E-mail address: goetz.egloff@alumni.uni-heidelberg.de; g.egloff.medpsych.ma@email.de.
† E-mail address: dragana.djordjevic@alumni.uni-heidelberg.de.

psychic functioning. Apart from intrapsychic and interpersonal factors, societal superstructure might influence the level of psychic functioning and of developing of psychopathology symptoms in general. While structured interventions preparing for parenthood cannot make up for societal shortcomings they can give parents-to-be hands-on advice as well as give them access to their emotional experiences. In Germany, a few intervention programs for parents-to-be exist, focusing on bonding, on relational issues, and on educational practices. For pre-schoolers there are structured interventions for kindergartens, including the involvement of parents.

In the chapter, the above mentioned interventions are presented along with aspects of developmental psychopathology, especially of violence in its different facets. Also, an insight into personal factors' influences on intuitive parental competencies is given. Prenatal and postnatal educational tasks especially for secondary school education can be derived from the intervention concepts outlined, most of which should be viable for extenuating the development of psychopathology symptoms.

Keywords: infant mental health prevention, prenatal and postnatal psychopathology, early intervention concepts

1. Introduction

The scientific knowledge of prenatal and perinatal experiencing in humans that Otto Rank first solicited in his concept of birth trauma at the beginning of the 20th century (Rank 1998) went unrecognized for quite a long time. Since in the last decades this has changed (cp. Janus 2013; cp. Egloff 2013) and nowadays even embryo and fetus are subject of scientific psychosocial research, prenatal, perinatal, and postnatal impairment and trauma are generally acknowledged to have significant impact on human development. Also, mothers' experiences of delivery have been examined and elaborated on (Thiel Bonney & Cierpka 2004; cp. Ballestrem, Strauss, Haefner & Kaechele 2001; cp. Egloff 2012a). Although some behavioral theorists tend to underestimate the impact of transgenerational conveying of specific relational modes, it has become obvious that early socialization factors interfere in forming children's personality. Psychoanalysis and infant mental health research, taken as sub-disciplines of psychopathology, now offer a large amount of knowledge to a) understand human development, to b) conceptualize pathology thereof, and to c) derive interventions from. In a family dynamics perspective, the concept of relational individuation ('bezogene Individuation' [Stierlin, Ruecker Embden, Wetzel & Wirsching 1977; Stierlin 1994]) elaborates on the principle that 'the higher the level of individuation in a family member, family, or group is, the higher the level of personal relating becomes, and is required at the same time.' This concept of co-individuation which originally aimed at the psychic identities of members of a family system generally supports the principle of socialization modes in Lloyd deMause's psychogenetic personality concept (deMause 2000; Janus 2008b). Implicitly, it throws bright light on the modes of manifestation of psychopathology in transgenerational dynamics, and even takes into account physiologically-based premature birth in humans (Janus 2016). From a neuroscientific perspective, Roth (2016) has outlined the latest conceptualization of pre- and early postnatal processes; three 'limbic levels' correlate with a) temperament, b) early experiencing, and c) subsequent socialization, of which at least the latter may be responsive to compensatory intervention, i.e., mental health intervention. Psyche, in this concept, is strictly related to brain physiology – an approach as interesting as it is questionable (cp. Fuchs 2007), at least to some extent. Nevertheless, it was shown that early experience alters brain function and structure in humans (Als et al. 2004).

However, in a postnatal perspective of earliest bio-psycho-social infant development within a family, in the infant-mother-dyad the infant undergoes basic experiencing of being in the world. A dialogical (Birkenbeil 1987) momentum as early as in pre- and postnatal phase can be seen as point of departure of developing, or not, a social character within family, groups, and society. Similarly, Kirshner's depiction of Rene Kaes' approach hints at the group preceding the individual; yet the individual must not to be dissolved in intersubjectivity (Kirshner 2010). An overview on the international discussion and literature of psychopathology in its human developmental nascencies (Wiefel et al. 2007) sums up diagnostic problems and options of treatment of infants and toddlers from a rather descriptive viewpoint, without the inclusion of OPD-oriented dynamic categories of disturbances, though. An OPD-oriented dynamics concept for infants and toddlers published in the same year (Cierpka & Windaus 2007) which encompasses conflict, structure and relation perspectives is especially important for developing a focus-oriented treatment approach. In a recent overview it was shown that OPD-2 is increasingly used in studies (Juan, Pescio & Roussos 2014).

Generally, in psychopathology also a bodily personality concept (Fuchs 2007) should be considered to be a basis, just like Notman (2012) defines the somatic self as the patient's subjective experiencing juxtaposed with objective bodily data, including medical illness. With that, not only practical questions of the autonomy of patients arise automatically (Maier 2014) but the concept of subject autonomy is generally challenged. This is also due to Freud's observation, "Der Reflexvorgang bleibt das Vorbild auch aller psychischen Leistung [The reflex act remains the type of every psychic activity as well]," (Freud 1900) which he stated to put psychic mechanisms in connection with automatic reflex processing in order to emphasize the predominance of unconscious psychic processes – which nowadays are sought to be viewed in terms of bodily correlates, too. Almost a hundred years later, important information about intuitive responses, those being in a middle position between innate reflex behavior and more 'rational' behavior, was brought up thanks to video micro analyses of dyadic interactions of babies and parents. In this context, parental competencies are referred to as intuitive competencies (Papoušek & Papoušek 1987; cp. Djordjevic 2010; cp. Djordjevic & Egloff 2016). They are elicited within a time frame of 200 to 600 milliseconds. Not only mothers, also fathers, children, and other relational objects have been observed to show these; they are universal and to be found in persons of any age, any gender, and in any culture (Fernald et al. 1989). Even though several questions of cultural and natural determinants in parenting still go unresolved (Bornstein 2007), there has to be a deep phylogenetic imprint in humans as to early communication acts, as Papoušek has pointed out. Rene Spitz, in the 1960s, had observed that the physical presence of the mother, i.e., of one relational object, is the basic precondition for healthy infant mental development (Spitz 1967; Spitz 1976). The severe social deprivation of hospitalized and institutionalized children which grow up without a care-giver responding to their needs within a latency of the mentioned 200 to 600 milliseconds, shows compromised development of children in all aspects – physically, mentally, and emotionally (Hellbruegge 1966; Hellbruegge, Becker Freyseng, Menara & Schamberger 1973). Social pediatrics has continually transformed this knowledge into practice, by that paying tribute to psychoanalysis and experimental research, and, often going unnoticed, preventing human beings from developing of psychopathology symptoms.

2. Personal and Societal Factors

The actual societal childcare level depends on the societal reality of existing care-giving options that mirror the actual societal value scheme. The level of expressing intuitive parental competencies is, of course, dependent on mental states of parents. Especially post-partum depression in mothers has been the subject of extensive research investigations (e.g., Papoušek 2000; Ballestrem, Strauss, Haefner & Kaechele 2001; Ambrosini & Stanghellini 2013). In interaction with their newborns, depressive mothers show decreased responsiveness, increased passivity and/or intrusiveness, increased withdrawal, and decreased expression of positive emotions, and they tend to regulate affects of their newborns in an insufficient way (Reck et al. 2004). Papoušek and von Hofacker (1998) have generally pointed out the connections between psychopathology traits in mothers and maladaptive patterns in their intuitive competencies. Familial strain of different kinds can also lead to dysfunctional relational patterns; missing or inadequate internal educational models in parents can have a similar effect (Papoušek & Papoušek 1983). A whole panoply of intrapsychic and interpersonal factors can compromise levels of expressing intuitive parental competencies. However, clinical case reports of psychopathology in adults mostly get a grip on family dynamics from a retrospective point of view (Egloff & Becker 2011), and any retrospective operationalization of intuitive competencies is difficult.

How about the dependence of the level of expressing intuitive parental competencies on the current societal framework itself? This issue, significant as it presumably is (Djordjevic & Egloff 2011), has widely gone unrecognized. Interaction between psychological and socio-economical factors, as in Erich Fromm's perspective of human development (Birkenbeil 1987), is more than merely a negligible factor predisposing psychic experience. Instead it is self-perpetuating, retroactive, inherent to the system, and with the current societal trend goes along with a tendency of fragmentation and with the identity shadings a virtualized society offers (Egloff 2012b). Lately, Fuchs (2014) has outlined contemporary phenomena of phantomization and disembodiment which in the context of virtualized societies pose the question of empathy at stake: is it possible anyway?

In a Habermas perspective, worldly life tends to be colonized by systems; systems interfere with personal self-realization, tending to intrude into the private sphere of people, damaging the reproduction of worldly life, that is of resources of sense-making, of solidarity, and of personality itself (Habermas 1981). His rationale of generating of social pathology phenomena, like personal loss of sense-making, anomie, and psychopathology follows the logic of cultural techniques of rationalization – in case they are not modified to fit people's personal needs.

Some 'new social deprivation' might heavily compromise psychic functioning; there is a tendency in many people to silently accept and justify a neoliberal fashion of an allegedly economic rationale, at least in western

Europe. Obscure neoliberal individualizing of life as an outgrowth of obscure group fantasies (cp. Kurth 2005) might consequentially lead to limitations of basic human ego-functions, compromising the forming of inner psychic space, maybe even suppressing mentalization itself. Bringing psychic flexibility down might consequentially be denuding people of any power, or vision (cp. Layton 2014). Exactly the inner psychic space in humans might be the point of departure of developing of psychopathology, or not. Presumably, it cannot be viewed as being detached from societal framework. So, 'new social deprivation' might consequentially promote a process of societal depravation that would be hard to control, if ever. In case its rambunctious nature were nurtured by poor psychic structure in people, stopping of such a process might take generations.

Any moderate or, poorly organized, psychic structure will quickly decompensate with increasing strain; some aspects of psychopathology might be the outcome of exactly this motion. Again, as the actual societal motion toward even more neoliberal individualization tends to fragmentation and anomie, it goes along with decreasing group coherence and increasing identity issues. Such a mode promotes adaptation and assimilation in personality foremost and is thus in opposition to the forward motion of progressive consciousness (cp. Janus 2008b; cp. Janus 2015a). The consequences of this motion for the following generations might be much more severe than it is actually believed. Sennett (1998), Ehrenberg (2004), or Juengst (2004) in Germany, have elaborated on these aspects on a micro and a macro level in a sociology perspective. Also, neuroscientists like Roth have pointed out socio-political implications of this motion, as well as on the psychological effects of societal value establishing (Roth 2011). Of course, new ways of living in neoliberal societies go along with much freedom and a lot of opportunities never known before, on the other hand, structural frangibilities can easily be observed everywhere.

3. Developmental Pathology Aspects

Human development can strike out in many directions. Pathology in the broad sense of the word, showing in more or less observable action, means development taking a wrong course. The most pivotal role in developmental pathology might be played by aggression and violence, as it shows in externalized action with huge destructive potential. Individuals with aggressive and violent behavior inflict injuries on others, either physically, psychically, or both. They may express threats, or destroy objects. Aggressive and violent behavior, as social scientists like Hurrelmann (1992) or Heitmeyer (1994; cp. Moeller Leimkuehler & Bogerts 2013) have shown, is mainly to be understood as a 'social disease' that is generated by intrapsychic, interpersonal and societal conflicts. It shows in contexts such as family, kindergarten, and school. Yet, the location of conflicts is not necessarily identical with the location of expressed aggression or violence. Conflicts at home may be enacted in school or kindergarten, and experiences of victimization and conflict may be brought back home, leading to aggressive behavior, e.g., in sibling or in parent interaction. At any rate, aggressive behavior is mostly used as a personal solution of interpersonal conflicts, and is expressive of escalating situations that seem to leave no other option of communication (Ratzke et al. 1997). As to a multi-factorial concept of generating of aggressive and violent behavior, it follows that it is mostly important to intervene early in the socialization process of children. Not only is the personal organization of emotions subjected to early childhood (Grossmann 2003) but interactional processes of recognition (e.g., modelled after Lacan following Kojève's interpretation of Hegel [cp. Kirshner 2003, 221]) allow forming of subjectivity. In the infant development concept of LaChance Adams (2007), mutuality leads to shared vision; after all, intersubjective experiencing allows the creation of subjectivity (Flechner 2005), even when intersubjectivity alone may not map the individual in their entirety (cp. Kirshner 2010). Taking into account that regulatory disorders in infants are obviously correlated with insufficient dealings within the family system, especially the family but also institutional surroundings of early childhood, such as kindergarten and pre-school, play a significant role in influencing personal individuation. The research findings on regulatory disorders (Papoušek, Schieche & Wurmser 2004; Cierpka 2012; cp. Bolten 2013) partially go together with regressive levels of family systems (cp. Fuerstenau 2002; cp. Egloff & Becker 2011). Such a perspective includes not only a systemic view but also makes up for the shortcomings of attachment assessment methods which do not examine triads, let alone examine combinations of attachment partners which would be much more informative (Grossmann & Grossmann 2007, 19; cp. Egloff 2015). This is not to denigrate the valuable attachment research findings regularly confirming dyadic patterns of early interaction to be conveyed to subsequent relations and dealings (Grossmann & Grossmann 2007; cp. Taubner & Juen 2010), instead it is to be taken as an intercession for a more panoramic view of relations.

Psychopathology in general can be conceptualized in terms of developmental pathology; yet, it is only one of many etiopathology approaches. In a recent synopsis of the genesis of delusional disorders, approaches from different perspectives are summed up in a phenomenological approach, a psychodynamic one, neuro- and other psychological approaches, a genetic approach, and biological approaches (Marneros 2012, 339-372). Not only can the latter ones be merged in a developmental perspective, as can clinically be seen in several facets (cp. Kilgus & Rea 2014). The phenomenological approach can serve the developmental perspective culturally and clinically (cp. Andresen 2014). As is often the case, etiopathology of psychic disorders can only partially be traced back (cp. Rochford 2014). Conversely trusting the symptom, diverse traits of complex trauma can be observed out of which aggression and violence emerge (Vance 2014). But when it comes to instrumental aggression, another issue goes unresolved unless an even broader perspective is taken; that is why this will be discussed in the following section. Beforehand it has to be said that aggressive impulses in their most neutral form of expansion and initiative are not to be eliminated. They are to be transformed in pro-social modes of application instead, so that potentially destructive aggression will be re-directed before it is realized. Expansion and initiative belong to the individual process of growing up and thus are to be supported, whereas destructive aggression has to undergo a subtle transformation into behavioral modes that are socially acceptable.

4. Aspects of Violence

4.1. On Subjective Violence

Quite often, aggressive children have a dysfunctional family background (Cierpka 1999). In these families, parents are not capable of taking enough care of their children, either physically or psychically. Sometimes there is lack of attachment in the mother-infant-relation existing from birth on, or there are disorders of early attachment that have developed in baby's first year of age (Grossmann et al. 1989). As said before, different sorts of psychopathology in parents affect the infant's emotional development; the parent-infant-relation encompasses a multitude of interactional processes that are prone to dysfunction. Intuitive parental competencies fundamentally influence the infant's emotional development and are vulnerable (cp. Papoušek & Cierpka

2012). Even social status, overall status of societal development, and other factors may compromise these competencies, as can be concluded from very different research perspectives (e.g., Jovanovich 2008; Layton 2014; Graybow, Eighmey & Fader 2015). Especially the experiential evidence of objective societal change in everyday dealings cannot be rejected (cp. Petschauer 2015). Dysfunctional and non-coherent educational practices in some families which can puzzle and disturb children and direct their development toward dysfunctional modes of behavior may even be amplified by the loss of societal structures; at least it may disturb families in developing consistent educational modes (Egloff 2012b).

Findings on subjective violence and aggressive behavior indicate an early lack of empathy in children, a lack of impulse control, and a lack of anger management in connection with early deprivation phenomena (cp. Cierpka, Schick & Egloff 2004; Cierpka & Schick 2006). Deviant behavior in the shape of criminal behavior can be viewed as developmental pathology, especially if lack of empathy (Lacy 2014), or lack of emotional reactivity (Vance 2014) can be diagnosed. The latter is clinically said to be in a small subset of 'psychopaths' only (Vance 2014); yet at this very point the question of instrumental aggression is unresolved and better be viewed in a perspective of objective violence.

Even when in offenders the lack of reflective functioning (Taubner 2008a; 2008b) seems to be the key to their violent acting, and their experiences of abuse and aggressive behavior can be linked to the lack of individual mentalization (Taubner & Curth 2013), developmental pathology without a societal systems context remains incomplete. Early intervening in individuals, in case it is not only to act as a spotter, is thus to be put in a catalog of thrust of policy that incorporates societal framework.

Aggressive children have often been victims of violence themselves (Levold, Wedekind & Georgi 1993; Cierpka & Cierpka 1997) and have learned to react in violent ways. While TV programs of violent contents tend to mediate violence as a means of conflict solution, children consuming many of these programs are used to violent dealings with their peers more often than those who do not consume many of these programs, as Bandura (1973) already showed decades ago. Transposed to today's circumstances, one can easily imagine an increase in everyday violent dealings. Arguing the converse, to some extent, may be correct, too, as there have been veritable changes in societies. Still, the last decades have seen an aggravation of depravation, at least in western Europe.

An important role in socialization is played by educational institutions, which even while offering personal development to children, must also be viewed in terms of repressive force whatsoever. This goes beyond the personal concept of children infallibly experiencing boundaries (Valtin 1995) which is a correct observation but does not convey structural violence in the background of societal relations. Educational institutions – school probably more than kindergarten – are always places of structural violence in which children are not only put under requirements of discipline, accomplishment, and selection but face societal claims under the color of ideological production (cp. Kurth 2003). The consumer subject is constituted through mass culture; consumption also finds its precipitation in institutions of education, and vice versa. Mass culture imparts to the subject to be in desire of something, preferably of something that can be bought. Thus consumer desire can serve the denial of the subject's subordination to productive relations and instead push not only consumerism but exacerbate individual psychopathology, let alone promote egotism and de-solidarization in general.

From a mass culture point of view, any subjective expression that is in contrast to mainstream behavior might be a solution-type compromise that is workable on a personal level and is due to the dialectic of acquiescence and resistance in mass culture. Under such circumstances and along their personal biographic experiencing – counterintuitive as it may partially seem – it cannot be surprising when some children react violently, even when such behavior may only be one among several solutions of the individual: depressive and narcissistic reactions are clinically well-known in this context. So empirical results cited must be taken with some reserve, bearing in mind that they will only portray sections from reality, namely from that what can more or less be observed aligning itself to the research design.

4.2. On Objective Violence

In Žižek's concept of violence (Žižek 2008), objective violence should be differentiated from the subjective kind. Objective violence is, contrary to subjective violence which is committed by individuals and groups, the given structural grid of objective reality in which people exist and act. It is not easy to be observed since it is defined as stemming from the mere functioning of systems. Whereas subjective violence is clearly visible and shows in acts of crime, objective violence is the given frame in which ideology evolves and influences the subject. The contours of society are inherently shaped by societal systems of economics and politics (cp. Habermas 1981). The seemingly smooth functioning of society itself may bear the deadly conditions of its own existence, generating outbursts of individual, subjective violence with often catastrophic consequences. Outbursts of individual, subjective violence thus can be derived from objective violent structures – which is not in the nature of an apology but can serve as a device of a societal status taxonomy. Analogously, what may be conceptualized as personal shortcomings in individuals might also be traced back to objective violent structures of societal depravation. The common notion of e.g., panic disorders (cp. Rochford 2014) is on a micro level. However, on a macro level, subjective aggression in acting violently might serve as the subjective antidote to the very panic that objective reality has yielded.

What has to be allowed for is that the internal conflicts the subject has to resolve might also be determined by the ideological structure that dominates their surroundings. What may look like internal processes that can be accessed psychologically may also be the result of internalized productive relations that better be understood sociologically. In case that society precedes the subject (cp. Kirshner 2010; cp. Egloff 2015), these relations form a specific, yet individually processed relation of the subject to their surroundings, and to existence itself. To some extent, societal ideology, even from a moderate point of view, must be taken as foisted on the subject. Down the line, the subject's relation to existence may either more or less remain on a fantasmatic level tending to repress reality with its class, or milieu differences, or develop toward a more realistic level of relation to existence including the acknowledgment of its being based upon differential class, or milieu belongings. The fantasmatic level, it seems, can only be overcome through socio-emotional learning and self-reflection, if ever. To some extent, a certain amount of aporia might have to be acknowledged within this conceptualization.

Objective violence, at least in today's western European shape, is determined by neoliberalism with a high degree of personal freedom going along with potential fragmentation and anomie. This tendency is obvious even in clinical contexts (Graybow, Eighmey & Fader 2015). In everyday dealings, multiple factors such as group dynamics, mass media, and regressive retroactive needs make for over-identification with mainstream behavior, for rejection of differences and for anticipatory obedience, especially since societal alternatives seem more or less outdated. Quite rigid attitudes and commandments, outspoken or not, go along with the so-called postmodern neoliberal concept of society. The personal overload may generally be based on subject-requirements-in-themselves – which are about the pursuit of realizing and mastering of personal and societal goals –, yet nowadays the individual seems subjected to the logic of escalation more and more. What is nowadays defined as human capital is an amalgamation of individuality and difference at the same time, an interpellation exploited through management programs either (Klinger 2015). In the long run, there might be clinical relevance to this.

Especially so-called post-adolescence turns out to be a more and more difficult phase, not only in western societies (cp. Samardzic & Nikolic 2014). Given the entanglement in the socialization process with its many requirements (Egloff 2015), the question must be raised whether or not a subject can be a subject undamaged at all (Maiso 2010; Maiso 2013). Still, for pragmatic reasons, it should be useful to intervene on a micro level of family relations as well as on a macro level of societal change (cp. Richter, Strotzka & Willi 1976) and take to an emancipatory position. Again, this exactly means facing what Habermas (1981) has conceptualized as social pathology: personal loss of sense-making, anomie, and psychopathology as results of cultural techniques of rationalization. So intervening on a micro level must, on the one hand, get a grip on inner family issues, on the other hand it must serve as an emancipatory act, too – at least as long as societal structures have not changed toward the better.

5. Intervention Concepts

5.1. Pre- and Postnatal Aspects

It has taken long to establish medical evaluation beyond mere physical issues, however mental health is still far from having an integrated pre- and postnatal psychology and psychopathology perspective. Structured programs reaching out to prenatal aspects of mental health have been developed quite recently in Germany. Options of in-time-intervening have been outlined (Cierpka 2007), and new interdisciplinary collaborations have emerged (cp. Ziegenhain & Kuenster 2012; Hertel et al. 2014). Also, psychopathology concepts of phenomenology, like e.g., pathogenetic situation (cp. Fuchs 2007; cp. Marneros 2012; Ambrosini & Stanghellini 2013), have been applied to cultural and natural concepts of human conditions.

On an individual level, educational programs have successfully been established in many educational institutions in Germany (Egloff, Djordjevic &

Cierpka 2015; Seel & Hanke 2015), yet there is still a lack of offers that will start earlier, even when offers have become better within the last ten years (cp. Cierpka, Gross, Egle & Stasch 2006). The majority of early intervention programs available have mostly been adaptations from the US. Comparisons between US and German programs have proven to be difficult due to structural differences in health services (Benz & Sidor 2013).

In an international perspective, recent meta-analyses have shown that programs starting during pregnancy were evaluated as the best when they had a high frequency of home visits (Taubner, Wolter & Rabung 2015). There are findings of advantages of close and personal relating to one another, which comes close to a therapeutic setting in which a good working alliance is in charge, making dealings with transference patterns easier to handle (cp. Samardzic & Nikolic 2014). Moreover, maternal symptom burden was relieved the most in a setting with psychotherapeutic elements established for premature birth coping (Jotzo & Poets 2005). Generally, maternal symptom burden relief has been the most observed effect in programs while there were only small effects of interventions on maternal competencies re-enforcement. Also, only small effects on child development have been observed, and these have been lower and more heterogeneous than effects on mothers-to-be. Then again, having more than twenty sessions has proven helpful for the infant's physical development (cp. Taubner, Wolter & Rabung 2015).

So far there is evidence of evaluation of early communication influences on development and learning processes in children (Rakonjac & Dobrijevic 2013), of interaction, of interconnectedness, and of processes of symbolic communication in general (Mead 1973). Even though the overall phylogenetic human developmental process has been depicted extensively, and the ontogenetic aspects of pre- and perinatal development have largely augmented the concepts of postnatal development (Janus 2008b; Janus 2013; Nyssen & Janus 1997), further augmentations are needed (cp. Djordjevic & Egloff 2011). Infant mental health observations showed slight but distinct negative influences of infant crying and sleeping problems on the child's subsequent social development (Sidor, Fischer, Eickhorst & Cierpka 2013); infants' regulatory problems contribute substantially to external and internal psychic problems in early childhood (Sidor, Fischer & Cierpka 2013). Furthermore, early eating disorders are seen in connection with preterm delivery (Erb, Thiel Bonney & Cierpka 2014).

Neurodevelopmental outcome of preterm newborns, especially extremely preterm newborns, is still highly problematic and connected with so-called 'new morbidity' (Lorenz 2000; Wolke, Ratschinski, Ohrt & Riegel 1994;

Wolke & Meyer 1999; Marlow, Wolke, Bracewell & Samara 2005; cp. Djordjevic 2010), therefore some new approaches in neonatal intensive care units have been developed and implemented (cp. Djordjevic 2010; Djordjevic 2015). Also, in-time-intervening programs for pediatricians and primary care practitioners have been developed (Papoušek, Rothenburg, von Hofacker & Cierpka 2005). The structured programs depicted below have evolved from many of the empirical findings above; they have purposely been designed to support the most possible mental health development of the unborn during pregnancy, and of the newborn. The programs are not supposed to be therapy for pregnant women, though.

5.1.1. "Mutter-Kind-Bindungsanalyse" (Mother-Infant Bonding Analysis)

Mother-infant bonding analysis (Hidas & Raffai 2006) is a procedure of accompanying women in pregnancy enabling them to get in contact with their unborn; an approach for which Phyllis Klaus's work paved the way (Klaus 2014). It is not a structured program in the narrow sense of the word but a fairly structured interventional sequence of individual sessions. By these, early before delivery first steps of building a relation between mothers-to-be and their unborn are encouraged. Through relaxation on a couch, women focus on their perception of signals from the unborn. These will show in the shape of emotions, images, thoughts, and fantasies on a so-called 'inner screen' which both unborn and mother are related to. This communicative channel can be seen as 'umbilical cord' of psyche, enabling a dialog which is supposed to promote the intrauterine development of the unborn. The bonding analyst will support mothers-to-be get in contact with the unborn by encouraging them, by interpreting, and by helping to overcome blockades if necessary. Twenty to thirty sessions during the second half of pregnancy are usually taken, that is from twentieth to fortieth gestational week. Exactly this time frame is known as the unborn's highest brain sensitivity, and vulnerability, period (cp. Djordjevic, Linderkamp, Bruessau & Cierpka 2007). The history of mother-infant bonding analysis started in the early 1990s when Budapest-based Jeno Raffai recognized in his work with patients the importance of the prenatal mother-unborn-relation for the infant's and the adult's further development. Together with the Hungarian psychoanalyst Gyorgy Hidas, he conceptualized a research and treatment method that developed into bonding analysis. In around 2200 treatment analyses by Raffai and 800 analyses by Hidas (plus some of their followers) impressive effects were reported (Raffai 1997). Especially the focus on children's personality development through the well-being of mothers in pregnancy and birth-giving might serve as the prenatal reference to autobiographical memory (cp. Nelson & Fivush 2004).

5.1.2. "SAFE"

The structured program "SAFE" – Sichere Ausbildung fuer Eltern (Secure Education for Parents) (Brisch 2010) aims at what is best for mothers in pregnancy, during delivery, and in parenting issues. The main issue of the program is to avoid transferring of traumatic childhood experiences toward the baby. "SAFE" helps parents-to-be develop confidence in dealings with their baby. As early as in pregnancy they learn to recognize and react appropriately to the signals the baby shows. This is helpful in developing a secure mode of attachment in infants since securely-attached infants show more capability of empathy, are more creative, and are more capable of cognitive processing, as well as they search easier for help when needed. The well-examined program also addresses real-life issues like, e.g., 'do parents have to be always present?' or, 'what to do when parents are having different needs from those the baby does,' and 'when does pampering start, and which limits does an infant need, and when?' The program is for parents-to-be up to the seventh month of pregnancy, and it is continued after delivery until baby's first birthday. Parents may continue up to the second or third birthday of their baby. There is a training of sensitivity toward the baby within a group in ten days of class. Groups are run by two mentors in whole day seminars, four days during pregnancy, six after delivery. Stabilization and imagination exercises in stressful situations are conducted, especially in adaptation phase after delivery. A parental sensitivity training video supports the reading of signals and needs of the baby. There is an attachment interview with parents, and diagnostic questionnaires (Erhardt & Brisch 2010).

5.1.3. "Skin-to-skin care"/"Kangaroo Care"

An early experience of the infant's positive feedback cues is very important not only for intuitive parenting regulation but also for parental attachment behavior. The mother's feeling of self-efficacy evoked by positive feedback cues encourages her to rely on her intuitive competencies more and more since the mother herself is not an inexhaustible source of rich stimulation (Klaus & Kennell 1976). One of the very successful methods to moderate early and unexpected separation of an infant from the mother's body, which makes both the child and the parents (even more) insecure (Klaus et al. 1972), is "skin-to-skin care", or "kangaroo care". Kangaroo care originally comes from Colombia; it was introduced by Edgar Rey Sanabria in 1978 in a children's clinic in Bogotá that was overcrowded with premature born infants but not able to offer intensive care treatment or take adequate care of all of them. Mothers were advised to take their babies home and carry them on their breasts for days and weeks. Through this intervention babies were supplied with warmth and fed with milk (Doyle 1997). Imported from Colombia, adapted to newborn intensive care unit (NICU) application, and incorporated in the NICU setting, "kangaroo care" became one of the most important care standards in developed countries nowadays.

The mother/father of a premature infant is advised to lay down on a bed or a deckchair near the incubator or the infant's bed, to open their blouse or shirt, while the staff puts the premature infant between the mother's breasts or in the middle of the father's chest. The infant is covered with a piece of artificial fleece and with the parent's clothes. The naked infant experiences skin-to-skin contact; parent and infant rest together for several hours.

5.1.4. "NIDCAP®"

"NIDCAP®", i.e., Newborn Individualized Developmental Care and Assessment Program has been developed by Heidelise Als and her team members at Boston Children's Hospital. Distinguishing normal from abnormal neonatal behavior and trying to obtain some prognostic conclusions about long-term development from the behavior in the newborn period, Als became aware of the enormous influence that intensive care does have on the behavior of full-term and preterm newborn babies. Starting with these observations, the entire concept that should enable optimal development of each premature infant through individual care, and in spite of interfering intensive care treatment influences, was developed and patented (Als, Lester, Tronick & Brazelton 1982; Als, Duffy & McAnulty 1988a, 1988b; Als & McAnulty 2011). Neonatal care according to "NIDCAP®"principles has become more and more popular all over the world; it has been imported and implemented in Europe and is applied in the NICU at Neonatology Clinic at University Hospital of Heidelberg, Germany.

It has been designed for professionals that deal with premature infants and their parents; its main issue is 'reading the premature infant' (Als 1999). The individual intervention consists of daily (seven days a week) observation and evaluation of infant's behavior, of support for care-givers in understanding the infant's stress and comfort signals, and of suggestions for parents and staff in terms of ways to support infant's development, i.e., adjust their care according to these signals. The concept treats infants as active participants in the care provided.

5.1.5. "Das Baby verstehen" (Understanding Your Baby)

"Das Baby verstehen" (Gregor & Cierpka 2004) is a structured program for expectant mothers and their partners. Couples are supported through a midwife who will focus on the overall life situation of the family-to-be. Everyday communication between parents and their babies is illustrated in the instructions. The 'reading' of the baby is at the center of most of the course lessons. Live video tapes support the instructions. Playful exercises will focus on the personal well-being of parents-to-be as well as on how to remain a couple when there will be three of them. In 2003 and 2004 the program was developed at the University of Heidelberg, followed by a revision in 2005, with accompanying evaluation in a German county district. The strengths and shortcomings of the expert trainings as well as of the courses for parents were explored, aiming at an integrative package of counseling for parents with infants up to the age of three. In this way, potential development of dysfunctional interaction in families is avoided early in order to prevent bodily and mental disorders in infants.

5.2. An Intervention Concept for Pre-Schoolers: "Faustlos"

In a recently published textbook on educational science, an overview is given of programs directly supporting the development of emotional competencies in children (Seel & Hanke 2015, 408). In their chapter on personalization and individuation it becomes evident how demanding such a process is. In order to increase the support of the process, some concepts' approaches can be useful to parents reaching out to improve dealings with their children, be they infants, toddlers, or pre-schoolers.

Suggestions for socio-emotional education can be derived from programs for pre-schoolers like the following, "Faustlos" (meaning, without fists) for kindergarten age (Cierpka 2002). It has been designed for the development of socio-emotional skills and competencies as early as in kindergarten children four to six years of age, if not even earlier. It is an adaptation of Seattle-based program, "Second Step" (Beland 1988). The program has been developed at the University of Heidelberg and has continually been modified for German elementary school and middle school. Especially self-regulation has been proven to be difficult in traumatized and insecurely attached children. Poor modulation of emotions seems to be pivotal to violent acting; again, subjective aggression and violence obviously largely emerge out of complex trauma (Vance 2014). Though not replacing trauma therapy, "Faustlos" offers a wide variety of techniques and strategies for pre-schoolers in order to learn how to cope with inner impulses. Also, the program is conducted by constant relational persons in a closed group cycle of one pre-school year. This gives children a secure realm of learning and transfer. No-one is excluded from the group; stigmatization is avoided. Instead, children learn from one another how to apply “Faustlos” in everyday surroundings.

Socio-emotional learning aims at skills and competencies to be learned within an interactional framework. At the heart of “Faustlos” there are three issues to be transferred to children, a) getting to know empathy and the training to be empathic, b) learning to be capable of controlling one’s impulses, and c) dealing with emotions of anger and rage. These issues are playfully dealt with by way of twenty-eight continuous lessons. Each lesson contains a story that is told by the educator and is illustrated by an accompanying picture. Each lesson is structured the same way: at first, the topic of the lesson is outlined by playfully fantasizing what the lesson will bring. Moreover, hand puppets (a toy dog and a toy snail) open up getting in contact with each other, further illustrating the issue of the lesson to come. This is followed by the actual lesson in which the story is told, is shown in the picture, and is discussed with the group. Role-playing, or alternative exercises at the end of the lesson will make sure the transfer to everyday life of children is initiated. Additionally, the educator is advised to return to the contents of the lesson during the following week. Ideally, one lesson per week is conducted.

Strengthening parental competencies in general (Janus 2008a), and introducing the do’s and dont’s to parents either, is pivotal to emotional education. That is why parental involvement is a part of “Faustlos,” too. By way of continuous parental meetings, parents are grown accustomed to dealing with one another in rather empathic and non-violent terms. Ideally, a new culture of intra- and interpersonal conflict solutions is developed with parents. Additional literature is offered. Since the children learn how to cope with inner impulses, the range of possible reactions in stressful and conflict situations is broadened. Parents can learn from that. To some extent, the idea that within a secure realm of learning and transfer children learn from one another how to apply empathy, impulse control, and coping with anger and rage in everyday surroundings, can quite easily be instilled in parents.

Especially a change of perspective through stories seen from different personal viewpoints is strongly supported; something which has regularly been experienced revelatory (Egloff & Cierpka 2002; cp. Cierpka 2005) as it calls attention to divergent experiencing. In traumatized children not only changing of perspectives is difficult, but essentially persisting stress disorders from complex trauma can compromise their biographies severely and add to lifelong trauma-associated conditions like dissociation (Schindler 2006; Knoch, Kurth, Reiss & Egloff 2012; Vance 2014). Presently, a phenotypical similarity in dissociation and severe psychopathology like schizophrenia is being discussed (Pena Salazar et al. 2016). At any rate, for parents, deriving of educational objectives from socio-emotionally oriented programs should have some pro-social effect.

5.3. Aspects of Evaluation

The pre- and postnatal concepts introduced above approach parents-to-be relatively early. The two programs, "SAFE" and "Das Baby verstehen", are well-structured, are designed for parents, and tend to address important everyday dealings with the infant, such as the reading of signals, in a closed or half-open group setting. Different from these, "Mutter-Kind-Bindungsanalyse" has been conceptualized as an individually-shaped setting in which the emotionality of mothers-to-be and their empathic dealing with the unborn are in focus. Regarding this concept, only case studies, but these with promising results (Raffai 1997; Schroth 2009), were reported. More studies are needed here; it would also be interesting to study the combination of any structured approach with bonding analysis. However, there are recommendations for the application of bonding analysis in particular from neonatology experts that have intensely applied and examined bonding-/attachment-oriented concepts like "kangaroo care" or "NIDCAP®" (e.g., Linderkamp 2014).

The most important benefit from "skin-to-skin/kangaroo care", as studies have shown, is the change in the mother's perception of her child, attributable to the skin-to-skin contact ('bonding effect') which supports and promotes attachment of infant to mother. Mothers practicing "kangaroo care" blame themselves less for premature delivery, and they feel more competent ('resilience effect') in stressful situations in the NICU (Fischer, Sontheimer, Bauer & Linderkamp 1997; Fischer et al. 1998; Tessier et al. 1998). The mother-infant relationship is better; less interaction disorders and even less crying at the age of six months have been observed.

"NIDCAP®" has shown to have numerous positive effects on both the somatic and the neurological short-term development as well as on long-term developmental outcome of premature infants: better motor and mental development, better development of intelligence, better behavior and mother-child interaction have been observed (Als et al. 1994; Als, Duffy & McAnulty 1996; Westrup et al. 1997, 2000, 2002; Westrup, Boehm, Lagercrantz & Stjernqvist 2004; Westrup 2007; Kleberg, Westrup & Stjernqvist 2000; Kleberg, Westrup, Stjernqvist & Lagercrantz 2002). The "NIDCAP®" concept was also tested in terms of neurodevelopmental outcome in a randomized clinical trial – it was shown that early experience alters (also human) brain function and structure (Als et al. 2004). This was the first in-vivo-evidence of positive effects of early (postnatal) experience on brain development, i.e., of enhanced brain function and structure due to "NIDCAP®". This study demonstrated that the quality of the experience one has before term may influence brain development significantly. Care according to "NIDCAP®" has shown to be supportive also to the development of the infant's self-regulation capacities.

Apart from "NIDCAP®" the "Faustlos" kindergarten program for children has probably been evaluated the most. Beginning in 2001 at the University of Heidelberg a process evaluation (Cierpka, Egloff, Schick & Ott 2001) was followed by a pre/post randomized control trial study which proved the program to be effective especially as to a decrease of verbal aggression in children (Cierpka, Schick & Egloff 2004; Cierpka & Schick 2006). Shortly, identifying emotions turned out to be easier for children who took part in the program than for those who did not; the same for pro-social dealings with conflicts. Generally, a specific anxiety-reducing effect supporting the transfer of competencies to everyday life has been proven in the program (Schick & Cierpka 2003b) which is highly important since effects on the level of intrapsychic emotion entail even more appropriate interpersonal pro-social behavior (Cierpka 2005). Further evaluation of the "Faustlos" approach has been conducted in elementary education starting in 1999, as has in secondary education from 2005 on (Schick & Ott 2002; Schick & Cierpka 2003a, 2004, 2010, 2013; cp. Egloff, Djordjevic & Cierpka 2015). Moreover, it has widely been well-accepted and therefore has been implemented at many kindergartens in Germany. The well-received response is due to the special relational approach to early childhood learning, something that is more and more difficult the older they grow. Conversely, apt development of children through even earlier intervention in pre- and postnatal phases becomes ever so important.

CONCLUSION

Infants' mental health and the developing of parent-infant relationships are at risk all the time and even more affected the more the parents' resources are strained by other factors. Regarding preterm infants, in order to promote premature infant mental health and the developing parent-infant relationship, the family of the premature born infant should not only receive very careful care and support but also be identified as a family in need of specialized interventions and be offered some form of interaction-centered infant-parent care, counseling, and psychotherapy. Well-supported parents can substantially support and promote their infants in practicing self-soothing capacities and in developing self-regulation mechanisms.

Generally, the interpersonal competencies often emerging within the course of mental health intervention programs indicate a requirement of taking socio-emotional learning much more seriously. A closer look at empathy as an important personal competence and maybe as the pivotal substrate against destructive aggression (cp. Lacy 2014) provides options of prevention of bullying in school and of violence in general. Thus, a key to issues of psychopathology certainly is in empathy, in emotional reactivity, and in reflective functioning. Moreover, there are consequential limitations of individual psychopathology concepts since they cannot make up for societal depravation effects on the individual. By given socio-political structures psychic functioning may be compromised no matter what. Accordingly, the tendency in many people to silently accept and justify too much of economic rationale is not surprising. Still, it is to be faced and overcome. This can only be achieved by bridging, like Wright Mills (1959) suggested, the gap between mindless empiricism and great theory. Pragmatically, this would basically require connecting worldly life and individual experiencing with societal structure, with a moderate empirical approach. Such a task psychopathology research must be, and is, able to carry out.

Mental health intervention concepts are an option since they also strike out in a new direction of educational tasks. Room for extending to further surroundings might especially be in teenagers in secondary school education who would benefit from introductory classes in pre- and postnatal psychology. Not only in females there is usually high interest in these issues.

The knowledge of psychopathology development and of personality with their social implications in a globalized world is to be taken seriously. Contemporary societies may offer great opportunities on the one hand, yet on the other, they inherently seem to be on the brink of collapsing, tending to produce anomie – which is a catalyst for psychopathology. On a micro level, Papoušek (2011) has described the significance of communicative acting for early emotional relatedness; on a macro level, deMause's concept of societal development provides significant insight from a transnational perspective (cp. Janus 2015b). In clinics and in culture, realizing of such concepts sometimes may contra-direct the common sense; on the other hand many people, asked for their intuition, have quite an idea of what is the issue at stake.

REFERENCES

Als H (1999). Reading the premature infant. In: Goldson E (ed.). Nurturing the Premature Infant – Developmental Interventions in the Neonatal Intensive Care Nursery. New York: Oxford University Press, pp. 18-85.

Als H, Lester BM, Tronick EZ, Brazelton TB (1982). Manual for the assessment of preterm infants' behavior (APIB). In: Fitzgerald HE, Lester BM, Yogman MW (eds.). Theory and Research in Behavioral Pediatrics, vol. 1. New York: Plenum Press, pp. 65-132.

Als H, Duffy FH, McAnulty GB (1988a). Behavioral differences between preterm and full-term newborns as measured with the APIB system scores: I. *Infant Behavior and Development* 11:305-318.

Als H, Duffy FH, McAnulty GB (1988b). The APIB, an assessment of functional competence in preterm and full-term newborns regardless of gestational age at birth: II. *Infant Behavior and Development* 11:319-331.

Als H, Lawhon G, Duffy FH, McAnulty GB, Gibes Grossman R, Blickman JG (1994). Individualized developmental care for the very-low-birth-weight preterm infant. Medical and neurofunctional effects. *J Am Med Ass* 272:853-858.

Als H, Duffy FH, McAnulty GB (1996). Effectiveness of individualized neurodevelopmental care in the newborn intensive care unit (NICU). *Acta Pediatr Suppl* 416:21-30.

Als H, Duffy FH, McAnulty GB, Rivkin MJ, Vajapeyam S, Mulkern RV, Warfield SK, Huppi PS, Butler SC, Conneman N, Fischer C, Eichenwald EC (2004). Early experience alters brain function and structure. *Pediatrics* 113:846-857.

Als H, McAnulty GB (2011). The Newborn Individualized Developmental Care and Assessment Program (NIDCAP) with Kangaroo Mother Care (KMC): Comprehensive Care for Preterm Infants. *Curr Women's Health Rev* 7(3):288–301.

Ambrosini A, Stanghellini G (2013). The concepts of 'Depressive Pathogenetic Situation' and 'Melancholic Type of Personality' as applied in the case of postpartum depression. In: Stoyanov D (ed.). Psychopathology: Theory, Perspectives, and Future Approaches. New York: Nova Science, pp. 23-50.

Andresen S (2014). Just wait and don't upset yourself: when children are exposed to poverty in their daily lives. In: Emde RN & Leuzinger Bohleber M (eds.). Early parenting and prevention of disorder. Psychoanalytic research at interdisciplinary frontiers. London: Karnac, pp. 297-306.

Ballestrem CL von, Strauss M, Haefner S, Kaechele H (2001). Screening and utilization of treatment in mothers with postnatal depression in Germany. *Int J Prenat Perinat Psychol Medicine* 13(3/4):247-256.

Bandura A (1973). Aggression: a social learning analysis. Englewood Cliffs NJ: Prentice Hall.

Beland K (1988). Second Step: a violence prevention curriculum. Seattle: Committee for Children.

Benz M, Sidor A (2013). Early intervention in Germany and in the USA: a comparison of supporting health services. An overview article. *Mental Health & Prevention* 1(1):44-50.

Birkenbeil EJ (1987). Bezogenheit des Menschen als fundamentale Voraussetzung fuer Erziehung und Bildung [Human relatedness as fundamental precondition of education]. *Publication of the International Erich Fromm Society*, 1-9.

Bolten M (2013). Diagnostik von Regulationsstoerungen im Saeuglings- und Kleinkindalter [Diagnostics of regulatory disorders in infants and toddlers]. In: Tschudin S, Maier B, Bitzer J, Ditz S, Rauchfuss M (eds). Grenzen wahrnehmen – respektieren – ueberwinden. Beitraege der 2. Drei-Laender-Tagung fuer Psychosomatische Gynaekologie und Geburtshilfe 2012. Frankfurt: Mabuse, pp. 177-199.

Bornstein MH (2007). The nature and structure of human parenting: cultural universals and cultural specifics. Book of Abstracts, International Society for Theoretical Psychology (ISTP) Conference, Toronto, June 18-22, pp. 13-14.

Brisch KH (2010). SAFE – Sichere Ausbildung fuer Eltern [Secure education for parents]. Stuttgart: Klett-Cotta.

Brisch KH (2014). Praevention durch prae- und postnatale Psychotherapie [Prevention through pre- and postnatal psychotherapy]. In: Evertz K,

Janus L, Linder R (eds). Lehrbuch der Praenatalen Psychologie [Textbook prenatal psychology]. Heidelberg: Mattes, pp. 571-596.

Cierpka M (1999). Kinder mit aggressivem Verhalten. Ein Praxismanual fuer Schulen, Kindergaerten und Beratungsstellen [Aggressive behavior in children]. Goettingen: Hogrefe.

Cierpka M (2002). Faustlos. Ein Curriculum zur Foerderung sozial-emotionaler Kompetenzen und zur Gewaltpraevention fuer den Kindergarten [Faustlos. A curriculum for kindergarten supporting social-emotional competencies and preventing violence] (Co-authored by Schick A, Ott I, Egloff G). Heidelberg: University of Heidelberg.

Cierpka M (2005). Faustlos – wie Kinder Konflikte gewaltfrei loesen lernen [Faustlos: how children learn to solve conflicts non-violently]. Freiburg: Herder.

Cierpka M (2007). Moeglichkeiten der Praevention in der fruehen Kindheit [Prevention options in early childhood]. In: Lang H, Faller H, Schowalter M (eds.). Struktur – Persoenlichkeit – Persoenlichkeitsstoerung. Wuerzburg: Koenigshausen & Neumann, pp. 49-60.

Cierpka M (ed.) (2012). Fruehe Kindheit: 0-3 Jahre [Early childhood: zero to three]. Heidelberg: Springer.

Cierpka M, Cierpka A (1997). Die Identifikationen eines missbrauchten Kindes [Identifications of an abused child]. *Psychotherapeut* 42:98-105.

Cierpka M, Egloff G, Schick A, Ott I (2001). Pilotprojekt Faustlos Kindergarten. Heidelberg: University of Heidelberg.

Cierpka M, Schick A, Egloff G (2004). Evaluation des Faustlos-Curriculums fuer den Kindergarten. Heidelberg: University of Heidelberg.

Cierpka M, Schick A (2006). Die Evaluation des Faustlos-Curriculums fuer den Kindergarten. *Prax Kinderpsychol Kinderpsychiat* 55:459-474.

Cierpka M, Gross S, Egle UT, Stasch M (2006). Praevention seelischer Stoerungen bei Kindern [Prevention of psychic disturbances in children]. *Psychotherapeut* 51:433-439.

Cierpka M, Windaus E (eds.) (2007). Psychoanalytische Saeuglings-Kleinkind-Eltern-Psychotherapie, Konzepte – Leitlinien – Manual [Psychoanalytic therapy of infants, toddlers, and parents]. Frankfurt: Brandes & Apsel.

DeMause L (2000). Was ist Psychohistorie? Eine Grundlegung [Foundations of psychohistory]. Giessen: Psychosozial.

Djordjevic D (2010). Premature born infant's reaction to the mother's voice in comparison to their reaction to music: effects on heart rate and heart rate variability. Heidelberg: University of Heidelberg.

Djordjevic D (2015). Minimizing prenatal and perinatal psychic trauma in premature newborns – current interventions in Germany. Lecture at the 1st Intl. Congress on Psychic Trauma PTPPPA. Belgrade May 15-16.

Djordjevic D, Linderkamp O, Bruessau J, Cierpka M (2007). Zusammenhaenge zwischen dem Wohlbefinden der Mutter und der Herzfrequenzvariabilitaet von Fruehgeborenen [Interrelation between well-being of the mother and heart rate variability of the preterm newborn]. *Prax Kinderpsychol Kinderpsychiat* 56:852-869.

Djordjevic D, Egloff G (2011). Zur Bedeutung intuitiver Elternkompetenzen für die Entstehung von Bezogenheit [On the pertinence of intuitive parental competencies in creating human relatedness]. In: Langendorf U, Kurth W, Reiss HJ, Egloff G (eds.). Wurzeln und Barrieren von Bezogenheit [Roots and barriers of human relatedness]. Heidelberg: Mattes, pp. 117-123.

Djordjevic D, Egloff G (2016). Fruehe Kindheit: Intuitive Elternkompetenzen foerdern [Early childhood: supporting parental competencies]. *Dtsch Aerztebl PP* 14(2):68-69.

Doyle LW (1997). Kangaroo mother care. *Lancet* 350:1721-1722.

Egloff G (2012a). Objektbeziehung und Performanz – zur relationalen Dynamik der Libido [Object relations and performance – on the relational dynamics of the libido]. *Prax Kinderpsychol Kinderpsychiat* 61:497-511.

Egloff G (2012b). Die Irrationalitaet durchdringen. Zwischen der Operationalisierung psychodynamischer Diagnostik, Lacan und Jaspers – zum psychodynamischen Verstehen in der Postmoderne [Permeating Irrationality: on the operationalization of psychodynamic diagnostics, Lacan, and Jaspers – psychodynamic reasoning in postmodernity]. *Dtsch Aerztebl PP* 10(8):358-360.

Egloff G (2013). Otto Rank Revisited. Rueckblick auf die Otto Rank Tagung der ISPPM und der Deutschen Otto Rank Gesellschaft am 1. und 2.11.1997 in Heidelberg. In: Janus L (ed.). Die praenatale Dimension in der Psychotherapie [The prenatal dimension in psychotherapy]. Heidelberg: Mattes, pp. 308-310.

Egloff G (2015). Integrative Psychoanalyse. In: Janus L, Kurth W, Reiss HJ, Egloff G (eds.). Verantwortung fuer unsere Gefuehle [Responsibility for our emotions]. Jahrbuch fuer psychohistorische Forschung 16. Mattes, Heidelberg, pp. 303-331.

Egloff G, Cierpka M (2002). Faustlos – Curriculum zur Gewaltpraevention. Conference Presentation/Workshop at the Congress ‘Adoleszenz –

Bindung – Destruktivitaet' of the International Society for Adolescent Psychiatry (ISAP), chair: Streeck Fischer A, Goettingen, June 14-16.

Egloff G, Becker B (2011). Defizit- und Loesungsorientierung in der systemischen Psychotherapie. Chancen und Gefahren am Beispiel der Einzeltherapie eines 32-jaehrigen Patienten mit depressiven und aggressiven Tendenzen [Deficit orientation and solution orientation in systemic psychotherapy]. *CoMed* 17(3):66-69.

Egloff G, Djordjevic D, Cierpka M (2015). Socio-emotional learning through Faustlos in Germany. In: Brekhman G, Sovilj M, Rakovic D (eds). Proceedings of the 1st Intl. Congress on Psychic Trauma PTPPPA. Belgrade May 15-16, pp. 340-345.

Ehrenberg A (2004). Das erschoepfte Selbst. Depression und Gesellschaft in der Gegenwart [The exhausted self]. Frankfurt: Campus.

Erb L, Thiel Bonney C, Cierpka M (2014). Zum Zusammenhang von Fruehgeburtlichkeit und fruehkindlichen Fuetterstoerungen [Preterm delivery and early infant feeding disorders]. *Aerztl Psychother Psychosom Med* 9(1):19-25.

Erhardt I, Brisch KH (2010). SAFE – Sichere Ausbildung fuer Eltern. Ein bindungstheoretisch basiertes Praeventionsprogramm fuer werdende Eltern [Secure education for parents: an attachment-based prevention program for parents-to-be]. *Familiendynamik* 35(1):84-85.

Fernald A, Taeschner T, Dunn J, Papoušek M, Boysson Bardies B, Fukui I (1989). A cross-language study of prosodic modifications in mothers' and fathers' speech to preverbal infants. *J Child Lang* 16:477-501.

Fischer CB, Sontheimer D, Bauer J, Linderkamp O (1997). Die Kaenguruh-Pflege Fruehgeborener. Stand der Forschung und Erfahrungen in Heidelberg [Kangaroo care of pre-term infants: research findings and experiences in Heidelberg]. *Paediatr Praxis* 52:609-618.

Fischer CB, Sontheimer D, Scheffer F, Bauer J, Linderkamp O (1998). Cardiorespiratory stability of premature boys and girls during kangaroo care. *Early Hum Dev* 52:145-153.

Flechner S (2005). On aggressiveness and violence in adolescence. *Int J Psychoanal* 86(5):1391-1403.

Freud S (1900). Die Traumdeutung. GW, Vol. 2/3. Frankfurt: S. Fischer, p. 543.

Fuchs T (2007). Gibt es eine leibliche Persoenlichkeitsstruktur? Ein phaenomenologisch-psychodynamischer Ansatz [Is there a bodily personality structure? A phenomenological-psychodynamic approach]. In: Lang H, Faller H, Schowalter M (eds.). Struktur – Persoenlichkeit –

Persoenlichkeitsstoerung. Wuerzburg: Koenigshausen & Neumann, pp. 75-86.

Fuchs T (2014). The Virtual Other: empathy in the age of virtuality. *J Consciousness Studies* 21(5/6):152-173.

Fuerstenau P (2002). Psychoanalytisch verstehen, systemisch denken, suggestiv intervenieren [Understanding psychoanalytically, thinking systemically, intervening suggestively]. Stuttgart: Pfeiffer.

Graybow S, Eighmey J, Fader S (2015). Privatization and psychoanalysis: the impact of neo-liberalism on Freud's tool of social justice. *J Psychohistory* 42(4):280-294.

Gregor A, Cierpka M (2004). Das Baby verstehen [Understanding your baby]. Bensheim.

Grossmann KE, Fremmer-Bombik E, Friedl A, Grossmann K, Spangler G, Suess G (1989). Die Ontogenese emotionaler Integritaet und Kohaerenz [Ontogenesis of emotional integrity and coherence]. In: Roth E (ed.). Denken und Fuehlen. Aspekte kognitiv-emotionaler Wechselwirkung [Thinking and feeling. Aspects of cognitive-emotional interaction]. Berlin: Springer, pp. 36-55.

Grossmann KE (2003). Die Bedeutung der ersten Lebensjahre fuer die Organisation der Gefuehle [The pertinence of first childhood years for the organization of emotions]. In: Doerr M & Goeppel R (eds.). Bildung der Gefuehle. Innovation? Illusion? Intrusion? [Education of Emotions]. Giessen: Psychosozial, pp. 123-145.

Grossmann KE, Grossmann K (2007). Die Entwicklung psychischer Sicherheit in Bindungen [Development of psychic security through attachment]. *Z Psychosom Med Psychother* 53(1):9-28.

Habermas J (1981). Theorie des kommunikativen Handelns [The theory of communicative actions]. Vol.1&2. Frankfurt: Suhrkamp.

Heitmeyer W (1994). Gewalt [Violence]. Weinheim: Juventa.

Hellbruegge T (1966). Zur Problematik der Saeuglings- und Kleinkinderfuersorge in Anstalten – Hospitalismus und Deprivation [On problems of infant and toddler care in institutions – hospitalism and deprivation]. In: Optiz H & Schmid F (eds.). Handbuch der Kinderheilkunde [Textbook pediatrics]. Berlin: Springer, pp. 384-404.

Hellbruegge T, Becker Freyseng I, Menara D, Schamberger R (1973). Deprivations-Syndrome im Saeuglingsheim [Deprivation syndromes in infant institutions]. *Muench Med Wochenschr* 115:1753-1760.

Hertel S, Eickhorst A, Kachler M, Zeidler N, Wolf K, Abrie Kuhn M, Cierpka M (2014). Cognitive stimulation and parental sensitivity in toddlers' homes: how do children and parents interact and how effective are trainings for parents? In: Emde RN & Leuzinger Bohleber M (eds.). Early parenting and prevention of disorder. Psychoanalytic research at interdisciplinary frontiers. London: Karnac, pp. 283-296.

Hidas G, Raffai J (2006). Nabelschnur der Seele [Umbilical cord of the soul]. Giessen.

Hurrelmann K (1992). Aggression und Gewalt in der Schule – Ursachen, Erscheinungsformen und Gegenmassnahmen [Aggression and violence at school – origins, phenomena, interventions]. *Paedagogisches Forum* (5)2:65-74.

Janus L (2008a). Ueber Grundlagen und Notwendigkeiten der Foerderung der Elternkompetenz [On basics and necessities of supporting parental competencies]. *Psychoanalyse im Widerspruch* 20(40):25-38.

Janus L (2008b). Menschheitsgeschichte als psychologischer Entwicklungsprozess [The history of mankind as psychological developmental process]. Heidelberg: Mattes.

Janus L (ed.) (2013). Die praenatale Dimension in der Psychotherapie [The prenatal dimension in psychotherapy]. Heidelberg: Mattes.

Janus L (2015a). Die emotionale Dimension der Aufklaerung [The emotional dimension in enlightenment]. In: Janus L, Kurth W, Reiss HJ, Egloff, G (eds.). Verantwortung fuer unsere Gefuehle. Jahrbuch fuer psychohistorische Forschung 16. Heidelberg: Mattes, pp. 13-47.

Janus L (2015b). Lloyd deMause: Das emotionale Leben der Nationen (review). In: Janus L, Kurth W, Reiss HJ, Egloff G (eds.). Verantwortung fuer unsere Gefuehle. Jahrbuch fuer psychohistorische Forschung 16. Heidelberg: Mattes, pp. 405-411.

Janus L (2016). Transformations in emotional structures throughout history. *J Psychohistory* 43(3):187-199.

Jotzo M, Poets CF (2005). Helping parents cope with the trauma of premature birth: an evaluation of a trauma-preventive psychological intervention. *Pediatrics* 115(4):915-919.

Jovanovich G (2008). Bindung zwischen “Gemeinschaft” und “Gesellschaft”. Wandlungen der sozialen Konstruktionen [Bonding between “community” and “society”:“ transformations in social constructions]. In: Ottmueller U, Kurth W, Reiss HJ (eds.). Psychohistorie und Globalisierung. Jahrbuch fuer psychohistorische Forschung 9. Heidelberg: Mattes, pp. 193-211.

Juan S, Pescio N, Roussos AJ (2014). Diagnostico Psicodinamico Operacionalizado 2 (OPD-2): Una revision bibliografica sobre su en investigacion empirica psicoanalitica. In: Memorias VI Congreso

Internacional de Investigacion y Practica Profesional en Psicologia. Buenos Aires Nov. 26-29, pp. 187-188.

Juengst P (2004). "Raubtierkapitalismus"? Globalisierung, psychosoziale Destabilisierung und territoriale Konflikte ["Predatory capitalism?"]. Giessen: Psychosozial.

Kilgus MD, Rea WS (eds.) (2014). Essential Psychopathology Casebook. New York/London: Norton.

Kirshner LA (2003). The Man Who Didn't Exist: The case of Louis Althusser. *American Imago* 60:211-239.

Kirshner LA (2010). Intersubjektive Transmission in Familie, Gruppe und Kultur. Die Arbeiten von Rene Kaes [Intersubjective transmission in family, group, and culture. The writings of Rene Kaes]. In: Nielsen B, Kurth W, Reiss HJ, Egloff G (eds.). Psychohistorie der Krise [The psychohistory of crises]. Jahrbuch fuer psychohistorische Forschung 11. Heidelberg: Mattes, pp. 129-138.

Klaus MH, Kennell JH (1976). Maternal-infant bonding. St. Louis, MO: C.V. Mosby.

Klaus MH, Jerauld R, Kreger NC, McAlpine W, Steffa M, Kennell JH (1972). Maternal attachment. Importance of the first post-partum days. *N Engl J Medicine* 286:460-463.

Klaus P (2014). Kurzzeitpsychotherapie in der perinatalen Zeit zur Verringerung von psychischen und koerperlichen Symptomen und zur Erleichterung der Entwicklung der Eltern-Kind-Bindung [Perinatal short term psychotherapy for a decrease of psychic and bodily symptoms and for a support of parent-infant bonding development]. In: Brisch KH & Hellbruegge T (eds.). Die Anfaenge der Eltern-Kind-Bindung [The beginnings of parent-infant bonding]. Stuttgart: Klett-Cotta, pp. 237-252.

Kleberg A, Westrup B, Stjernqvist K (2000). Developmental outcome, child behavior and mother-child interaction at 3 years of age following Newborn Individualized Developmental Care and Assessment Program (NIDCAP®) intervention. *Early Hum Dev* 60:123-135.

Kleberg A, Westrup B, Stjernqvist K, Lagercrantz H (2002). Indications of improved cognitive development at one year among infants born prematurely who received care based on Newborn Individualized Developmental Care and Assessment Program (NIDCAP®). *Early Hum Dev* 68:83-91.

Klinger C (2015). The Selfie, das Subjekt, das Selbst in seinem Welt-Bild [Selfie, subject, self in their images on the world]. Lecture, Congress of Deutsche Gesellschaft für phaenomenologische Anthropologie,

Psychiatrie und Psychotherapie (DGAP): 'Das ueberforderte Subjekt – Psychopathologie und beschleunigte Lebensformen.' University of Heidelberg, Oct. 2.

Knoch H, Kurth W, Reiss HJ, Egloff G (eds.) (2012). Die Kinder der Kriegskinder [Children of war children]. Jahrbuch fuer psychohistorische Forschung 13. Heidelberg: Mattes.

Kurth W (2003). Schule und politische Sozialisation: Der heimliche Lehrplan [School and political socialization: the hidden curriculum]. In: Ottmueller U, Kurth W (eds.). Trauma, gesellschaftliche Unbewusstheit und Friedenskompetenz [Trauma, societal unconsciousness, and competence for peace]. Jahrbuch fuer psychohistorische Forschung 3. Heidelberg: Mattes, pp. 183-214.

Kurth W (2005). Terrorismus, Krieg und soziale Degradierung als Ausagierung destruktiver Wuensche, die von vielen Menschen des Westens geteilt werden [Terrorism, war, and social degradation as an enactment of wishes of destruction that are shared by many people in the West]. In: Janus L, Galler F, Kurth W (eds.). Symbolik, gesellschaftliche Irrationalitaet und Psychohistorie [Symbolics, societal irrationality, and psychohistory]. Jahrbuch fuer psychohistorische Forschung 5. Heidelberg: Mattes, pp. 65-96, pp.73ff.

LaChance Adams S (2007). Loneliness in the Glare of the Gaze: A Challenge to Sartre's Ontology. Book of Abstracts, International Society for Theoretical Psychology (ISTP) Conference, Toronto, June 18-22, p. 74.

Lacy HR (2014). Lack of empathy. In: Kilgus MD & Rea WS (eds.). Essential Psychopathology Casebook. New York/London: Norton, pp. 579-603.

Layton L (2014). Some psychic effects of neoliberalism: narcissism, disavowal, perversion. *Psychoanalysis Culture & Society* 19(2):161-178.

Levold T, Wedekind E, Georgi H (1993). Gewalt in Familien. Systemdynamik und therapeutische Perspektiven [Violence in families: system dynamics and therapeutic perspectives]. *Familiendynamik* 3:287-311.

Linderkamp O (2014). Gehirnentwicklung und fruehe Foerderung [Brain development and its early support]. In: Evertz K, Janus L, Linder R (eds). Lehrbuch der Praenatalen Psychologie. Heidelberg: Mattes, pp. 19-33.

Lorenz JM (2000). Survival of the extremely preterm infant in North America in the 1990s. *Clinical Perinatology* 27:255-262.

Maier B (2014). Is the narrow concept of individual autonomy compatible with or in conflict with Evidence-based Medicine in obstetric practice? A philosophical critique on the misapplication of the value concept "autonomy". *Woman – Psychosomatic Gynaecology and Obstetrics* 1(1):40-49.

Maiso J (2010). Elementos para la reapropiacion de la Teoria Critica de Theodor W. Adorno. Salamanca: Ediciones Universidad de Salamanca.

Maiso J (2013). La subjetividad danada. Teoria Critica y Psicoanalisis [Damaged subjectivity]. *Constelaciones – Revista de Teoria Critica* 5:132-150.

Marlow N, Wolke D, Bracewell MA, Samara M (2005). Neurologic and developmental disability at six years of age after extremely preterm birth. *N Engl J Medicine* 352:9-19.

Marneros A (2012). Persistent Delusional Disorders – myths and realities. New York: Nova Science.

Mead GH (1973). Geist, Identitaet und Gesellschaft [Mind, self, and society]. Frankfurt: Suhrkamp.

Moeller Leimkuehler AM, Bogerts B (2013). Kollektive Gewalt. Neurobiologische, psychosoziale und gesellschaftliche Bedingungen [Collective violence: neurobiological, psychosocial, and societal factors]. *Nervenarzt* 84:1345-1358.

Nelson K, Fivush R (2004). The emergence of autobiographical memory: a social cultural developmental theory. *Psychological Review* 111(2):486-511.

Notman MT (2012). The Female Body: integrating psychoanalytic and biological concepts. *The American Psychoanalyst* 46(2):15.

Nyssen F, Janus L (eds.) (1997). Psychogenetische Geschichte der Kindheit. Beitraege zur Psychohistorie der Eltern-Kind-Beziehung [Psychogenetic history of childhood]. Giessen: Psychosozial.

Papoušek M (2000). Persistent crying, parenting and infant mental health. In: Fitzgerald HE & Osofsky JO (eds.). WAIMH handbook of infant mental health. New York: Wiley, pp. 415-453.

Papoušek M (2011). Verwundbar, aber unbesiegbar – Ressourcen der fruehen Kommunikation in Eltern-Saeuglings-Beratung und –Psychotherapie [Vulnerable but invincible – resources of early communication in infant parent counseling and psychotherapy]. In: Hellbruegge T & Schneeweiss B (eds.). Fruehe Stoerungen behandeln – Elternkompetenz staerken [Treatment of early disorders and the support of parental competencies]. Stuttgart: Klett-Cotta, pp. 69-92.

Papoušek H, Papoušek M (1983). Biological basis of social interactions: implications of research for an understanding of behavioural deviance. *J Child Psychol Psychiat* 24:117-129.

Papoušek H, Papoušek M (1987). Intuitive parenting: a didactic to the infant's integrative competence. In: Osofsky JO (ed.). Handbook of infant development, 2nd ed. New York: Wiley, pp. 669-720.

Papoušek M, von Hofacker N (1998). Disorders of excessive crying, feeding, and sleeping. The Munich interdisciplinary research and intervention program. *Infant Mental Health J* 19:180-201.

Papoušek M, Schieche M, Wurmser H (eds.) (2004). Regulationsstoerungen der fruehen Kindheit [Regulatory disorders in early childhood]. Bern/Goettingen: Hans Huber.

Papoušek M, Rothenburg S, von Hofacker N, Cierpka M (2005). Regulationsstoerungen der fruehen Kindheit [Regulatory disorders in early childhood]. CD-basierte Fortbildung, Munich.

Papoušek M, Cierpka M (2012). Der klinische Blick: Grundlagen und Gefaehrdungen der intuitiven elterlichen Kompetenzen [The clinical view: basics and endangerings of intuitive parental competencies]. Presentation at the 62. Lindauer Psychotherapiewochen Congress, April 19.

Pena Salazar C, Arrufat Nebot FX, Alvarez MJ, Masramon Fontsere H, Coll Negre M, Roura Poch P, Valdes Stauber J (2016). Do concepts of childhood trauma and dissociation provide an epistemological linkage between schizophrenia and PTSD? *Nervenheilkunde* 35:242-251.

Petschauer PW (2015). Amerika damals und heute. Alleinwerden in einer komplexen Gesellschaft [America then and now: on your own in a complex society]. In: Janus L, Kurth W, Reiss HJ, Egloff G (eds.). Verantwortung fuer unsere Gefuehle. Jahrbuch fuer psychohistorische Forschung 16. Heidelberg: Mattes, pp. 287-292.

Raffai J (1997). Mutter-Kind-Bindungsanalyse im praenatalen Bereich [Prenatal bonding analysis of mother and child]. *Int J Prenat Perinat Psychol Medicine* 9:457-466.

Rakonjac M, Dobrijevic L (2013). The influence of early communication on child development and learning. In: Sovilj M & Subotic M (eds). Proceedings of the 4th International Conference on Fundamental and Applied Aspects of Speech and Language. Belgrade Oct 25-26, pp. 368-371.

Rank O (1998). Das Trauma der Geburt und die Bedeutung für die Psychoanalyse [The trauma of birth and its meaning for psychoanalysis]. Giessen: Psychosozial [first publ. 1924].

Ratzke K, Sanders M, Diepold B, Krannich S, Cierpka M (1997). Ueber Aggression und Gewalt bei Kindern in unterschiedlichen Kontexten

[On aggression and violence in children in different contexts]. *Prax Kinderpsychol Kinderpsychiat* 46:153-168.

Reck C, Hunt A, Fuchs T, Weiss R, Noon A, Moehler E, Downing G, Tronick EZ, Mundt C (2004). Interactive regulation of affect in postpartum depressed mothers and their infants: an overview. *Psychopathology* 37: 272-280.

Richter HE, Strotzka H, Willi J (1976). Familie und seelische Krankheit. Neue Perspektiven für die psychologische Medizin und Sozialtherapie [Family and psychic disorder]. Reinbek: Rowohlt.

Rochford L (2014). Panic in childhood. In: Kilgus MD & Rea WS (eds.). Essential Psychopathology Casebook. New York/London: Norton, pp. 425-447.

Roth G (2011). Bildung braucht Persoenlichkeit [Education wants personality]. Stuttgart: Klett-Cotta.

Roth G (2016). Wirkung vorgeburtlicher und frueh-nachgeburtlicher Umwelteinfluesse auf Gehirn und Psyche [Effects of prenatal and early postnatal environmental influences on brain and psyche]. *Psychotherapeut* 61(2):118-123.

Samardzic L, Nikolic G (2014). Transference patterns and working alliance during the early phase of psychodynamic psychotherapy. *Vojnosanitetski Pregled* 71(2):175-182.

Schick A, Ott I (2002). Gewaltpraevention an Schulen – Ansaetze und Ergebnisse [Violence prevention at school – approaches and results]. *Prax Kinderpsychol Kinderpsychiat* 51:766-791.

Schick A, Cierpka M (2003a). Faustlos: Aufbau und Evaluation eines Curriculums zur Foerderung sozialer und emotionaler Kompetenzen in der Grundschule. [Faustlos: structure and evaluation of a curriculum for social and emotional competencies in elementary school]. In: Doerr M & Goeppel R (eds.). Bildung der Gefuehle. Innovation? Illusion? Intrusion? [Education of emotions]. Giessen: Psychosozial, pp. 146-162.

Schick A, Cierpka M (2003b). Faustlos: Evaluation eines Curriculums zur Foerderung sozial-emotionaler Kompetenzen und zur Gewaltpraevention in der Grundschule. [Faustlos: evaluation of a curriculum for social-emotional competencies and preventing violence for elementary school]. *Kindheit und Entwicklung* 12:100-110.

Schick A, Cierpka M (2004). Faustlos: Ein Gewaltpraeventions-Curriculum für Grundschulen und Kindergaerten [Faustlos: a curriculum for elementary school and kindergarten preventing violence]. In: Melzer

W & Schwind HD (eds.). Gewaltpraevention in der Schule [Violence prevention at school]. Baden-Baden: Nomos, pp. 54-66.

Schick A, Cierpka M (2010). Foerderung sozial-emotionaler Kompetenzen mit Faustlos: Konzeption und Evaluation der Faustlos-Curricula. [Promoting social-emotional competencies through Faustlos: concept and evaluation of Faustlos curricula]. *Bildung und Erziehung* 63(3):277-292.

Schick A, Cierpka M (2013). International evaluation studies of Second Step, a primary prevention programme: a review. *Emotional and Behavioral Difficulties* 18(3):241-247.

Schindler S (2006). Entwicklung im Krieg. Empirische Daten zu Einfluessen auf die Kindheitsentwicklung [Development and war: empirical data of influences on children's development]. In: Janus L (ed.). Geboren im Krieg. Kindheitserfahrungen im 2. Weltkrieg und ihre Auswirkungen [Born in war: childhood experiences in World War II and their consequences]. Giessen: Psychosozial, pp. 104-122.

Schroth G (2009). Die Bindungsanalyse nach Raffai und Hidas – eine Einfuehrung [Introduction to prenatal bonding analysis according to Raffai and Hidas]. *Int J Prenat Perinat Psychol Medicine* 21(3/4):343-347.

Seel NM, Hanke U (2015). Erziehungswissenschaft [Textbook Educational Science]. Heidelberg: Springer.

Sennett R (1998). The Corrosion of Character: The Personal Consequences of Work in the New Capitalism. New York: Norton.

Sidor A, Fischer C, Eickhorst A, Cierpka M (2013). Influence of early regulatory problems in infants on their development at 12 months: a longitudinal study in a high-risk sample. *Child Adolesc Psychiat Ment Health* 7(1):35.

Sidor A, Fischer C, Cierpka M (2013). Early regulatory problems in infancy and psychopathological symptoms at 24 months: a longitudinal study in a high-risk sample. *J Child Adolesc Behav* 1(3):10.

Spitz RA (1967). Vom Saeugling zum Kleinkind [From infant to toddler]. Stuttgart: Klett-Cotta.

Spitz RA (1976). Vom Dialog [On dialog]. Stuttgart: Klett Cotta.

Stierlin H (1994). Ich und die Anderen. Psychotherapie in einer sich wandelnden Gesellschaft [I and the others.]. Stuttgart: Klett-Cotta.

Stierlin H, Ruecker Embden I, Wetzel N, Wirsching M (1977). Das erste Familiengespraech [The first family interview]. Stuttgart: Klett-Cotta.

Taubner S (2008a). Gewalt als Symptom? Antisoziales Verhalten in der Adoleszenz zwischen Normalitaet und Pathologie [Violence as a symptom? Antisocial behavior in adolescence between normalcy and pathology]. *psychosozial* 31(3):101-117.

Taubner S (2008b). Einsicht in Gewalt [Insight into violence]. Giessen: Psychosozial.

Taubner S, Juen F (2010). Gewalt in der Spaetadoleszenz. Perspektiven der Bindungsforschung [Violence in late adolescence: perspectives of attachment research]. *Psychotherapie & Sozialwissenschaft* 12(2):59-77.

Taubner S, Curth C (2013). Mentalization mediates the relation between early traumatic experiences and aggressive behavior in adolescence. *Psihologija* 46(2):177-192.

Taubner S, Wolter S, Rabung S (2015). Effectiveness of early-intervention programs in German-speaking countries – a meta-analysis. *Mental Health & Prevention* 3(3):69-78.

Tessier R, Cristo M, Valez S, Giron M, Figueroa de Calume Z, Ruiz Palaez JG, Charpak Y, Charpak N (1998). Kangaroo mother care and the bonding hypothesis. *Pediatrics* 102:17.

Thiel Bonney C, Cierpka M (2004). Die Geburt als Belastungserfahrung bei Eltern von Saeuglingen mit Selbstregulationsstoerungen [Childbirth as stressful experience in parents with infants with regulatory disorders]. *Prax Kinderpsychol Kinderpsychiat* 53:601-622.

Valtin R (1995). Was ist Gewalt? Definitionen von Kindern und Erwachsenen [What is violence? Definitions from children and adults]. In: Valtin R & Portmann R (eds.). Gewalt und Aggression. Herausforderungen fuer die Grundschule [Violence and aggression. Challenges for elementary school]. Frankfurt: AK Grundschule, pp. 22-25.

Vance JE (2014). Complex trauma. In: Kilgus MD & Rea WS (eds.). Essential Psychopathology Casebook. New York/London: Norton, pp. 448-474.

Westrup B, Kleberg A, Wallin L, Lagercrantz H, Wikblad K, Stjernqvist K (1997). Evaluation of the Newborn Individualized Developmental Care and Assessment Program (NIDCAP®) in a Swedish setting. *Prenat Neonat Medicine* 2:366-375.

Westrup B, Kleberg A, von Eichwald K, Stjernqvist K, Lagercrantz H (2000). A randomized controlled trial to evaluate the effects of the newborn individualized developmental care and assessment program in a Swedish setting. *Pediatrics* 105:66-72.

Westrup B, Stjernqvist K, Kleberg A, Hellstroem Westas L, Lagercrantz H (2002). Neonatal individualized care in practise: a Swedish experience. *Semin Neonatol* 7:447-457.

Westrup B, Boehm B, Lagercrantz H, Stjernqvist K (2004). Preschool outcome in children born very prematurely and cared for according to the Newborn Individualized Developmental Care and Assessment Program (NIDCAP®). *Acta Pediatr* 93:498-507.

Westrup B (2007). Newborn Individualized Developmental Care and Assessment Program (NIDCAP) – family-centered developmentally supportive care. *Early Hum Dev* 83:443-449.

Wiefel A, Titze K, Kuntze L, Winter M, Seither C, Witte B, Lenz K, Grueters A, Lehmkuhl U (2007). Diagnostik und Klassifikation von Verhaltensauffaelligkeiten bei Saeuglingen und Kleinkindern von 0-5 Jahren. [Diagnostic classification of mental disorders in infants and toddlers age 0 to 5]. *Prax Kinderpsychol Kinderpychiat* 56:59-81.

Wolke D, Ratschinski G, Ohrt B, Riegel K (1994). The cognitive outcome of very preterm infants may be poorer than often reported: an empirical investigation of how methodological issues make a big difference. *Eur J Pediatr* 153:906-915.

Wolke D, Meyer R (1999). Cognitive status, language attainment, and prereading skills of 6-year-old very preterm children and their peers: the Bavarian Longitudinal Study. *Developmental Medicine & Child Neurology* 41:94-109.

Wright Mills C (1959). The Sociological Imagination. New York: Oxford University Press.

Ziegenhain U, Kuenster AK (2012). Fruehe elterliche Bindungsfoerderung in der interdisziplinaeren Zusammenarbeit [Support of early parental bonding in interdisciplinary cooperation contexts]. *Familiendynamik* 37(2):84-93.

Žižek S (2008). Violence: six sideways reflections. London: Profile.

BIOGRAPHICAL SKETCHES

Goetz Egloff, MA, ECP, BCIM, is a psychoanalyst and a child psychotherapist and has been a research assistant at the Psychosomatic Hospital at the University of Heidelberg. He has a private practice in Mannheim, Germany, and is a member of the German Association for Psychiatry (DGPPN), the German Association for Psychosomatic Ob/Gyn (DGPFG), the German Association for Phenomenological Anthropology, Psychiatry and Psychotherapy (DGAP), and an associate member of the American Psychoanalytic Association (APSAA). In his research and practice he focuses on bio-psycho-social perspectives in psychiatry of adolescence, on gynecological psychosomatics of eating disorders, and on prenatal psychology. As a long time co-editor of the German Yearbook of Psychohistorical Research, he has pursued an integrative approach of merging sociology and psychology. Apart from several articles on mental health, psychoanalysis, and literary criticism, his latest book editions are:

Verantwortung fuer unsere Gefuehle - die emotionale Dimension der Aufklaerung (Responsibility for our emotions: the emotional dimension in enlightenment), with L. Janus, W. Kurth, and H.J. Reiss (2015);

Gespaltene Gesellschaft und die Zukunft von Kindheit (Disrupted society and the future of childhood), with U. Langendorf, W. Kurth, and H.J. Reiss (2013);

Die Kinder der Kriegskinder (Children of war children), with H. Knoch, W. Kurth, and H.J. Reiss (2012).

E-Mail: goetz.egloff@alumni.uni-heidelberg.de; g.egloff.medpsych.ma@ email.de

Dragana Djordjevic, MD (University of Niš, Serbia), pediatrician (University of Niš), with special interests in neonatology, developmental pediatrics and psychosomatics in (premature born) infants, PhD Magna cum Laude in Psychosomatics by Prof. M. Cierpka (University of Heidelberg), dissertation "Premature Born Infant's Reaction to the Mother's Voice in Comparison to their Reaction to Music – Effect on Heart Rate and Heart Rate Variability" as a cooperation project between the Clinic for Neonatology and the Institute for Psychosomatic Cooperation Research and Family Therapy, Heidelberg. Guest pediatrician and researcher at the Institute for Psychosomatic Cooperation Research and Family Therapy (today Institute for Psychosocial Prevention) in Heidelberg. Scholarship holder of DAAD – German Academic Exchange Service as well as fellowship holder of HWK – Hanse-Institute for Advanced Studies in Delmenhorst, Germany. Implementation and establishment of an outpatient clinic service for developmental pediatrics and psychosomatics in infants and toddlers at the University Children's Clinic Niš in Serbia. Reviewer for the University of Niš journal "Facta Universitatis". Serbian expert group member for perinatal and neonatal accreditation standards development. Member of GAIMH. Latest publications:

Djordjevic D., Egloff G. (2016): Fruehe Kindheit: Intuitive Elternkompetenzen foerdern [Early childhood: supporting parental competencies]. *Deutsches Aerzteblatt PP* 14(2):68-69;

Egloff G., Djordjevic D. (2015): Schwangerschaftshypertonie – eine psychosomatische Kasuistik [Gestational hypertension]. *gyn – Prakt Gynaekol* 20(6):455-458;

Egloff G., Djordjevic D., Cierpka M. (2015): Socio-emotional learning through Faustlos in Germany. In: Brekhman G., Sovilj M., Rakovic D. (eds.): Proceedings of the 1st Intl. Congress on Psychic Trauma PTPPPA, pp. 340-345;

Djordjevic D. (2015): Minimising Prenatal and Perinatal Psychic Trauma in Pemature Newborns – Current Interventions in Germany. Book of Abstracts, 1st Intl. Congress on Psychic Trauma PTPPPA, Belgrade, May 15-16;

Djordjevic D., Egloff G. (2011): Zur Bedeutung intuitiver Elternkompetenzen für die Entstehung von Bezogenheit (On the importance of intuitive parental competencies for creating human relatedness). In: Langendorf U., Kurth W., Reiss H.J., Egloff G. (eds.). Wurzeln und Barrieren von Bezogenheit (Roots and barriers of human relatedness). Jahrbuch fuer psychohistorische Forschung 12. Heidelberg: Mattes, pp. 117-123.

E-Mail: dragana.djordjevic@alumni.uni-heidelberg.de

In: Psychopathology
Editor: Jeremy Williams
ISBN: 978-1-63485-745-1

Chapter 7

ADVANCES IN THE STUDY OF MALE PSYCHOPATHY

Robert Eme, PhD
Illinois School of Professional Psychology at Argosy University, Schaumburg Campus, Schaumburg, IL, US

ABSTRACT

This article reviewed three of most important advances that have been made in the understanding of psychopathy in the past half century since the landmark 1966 study of Lee Robins. This study had a major influence on the subsequent study of psychopathy which is arguably the most important construct in the study of violence. The advances occurred in identifying the basic personality traits of psychopathy, its earlier developmental manifestations, and its neural underpinnings. The review concluded with a recommendation that next 50 years of research on psychopathy should have prevention as its paramount focus.

INTRODUCTION

A half a century ago Lee Robins (1966) published her landmark study *Deviant Children Grown Up: A Sociological and Psychiatric Study of Sociopathic Personality*. This research, which presented the findings of a 30-year follow-up of 524 white juveniles (73% male) most of whom were referred for antisocial behavior to a child guidance clinic in the 1920's, proved to be of paramount importance for the succeeding 50 years of the study of psychopathy for two main reasons. First, it was a major influence on the American Psychiatric Association's (APA) diagnosis of psychopathy. Although this diagnosis traces its history back to Cleckley's 1941 classic *Mask of Sanity*, it does so primarily via the work of Robins (Hare, Neuman, & Widiger, 2012). Robins developed a list of diagnostic criteria for "sociopathic personality disturbance" derived in large part on the work of Cleckley. As a member of the *Diagnostic and Statistical Manual of Mental Disorders-III* (American Psychiatric Association, APA, 1980) personality disorders work group, she was very influential in constructing the criteria for Antisocial Personality Disorder (ASPD). Second, her seminal finding that severe adult antisocial behavior virtually requires childhood antisocial behavior, which she subsequently confirmed in three other studies (Robins, 1966, 1978), helped launch the study of the developmental origins of antisocial behavior (Beauchaine & Hinshaw, 2016). Hence, a half a century after her ground-breaking publication seems a fitting time to review some of the major advances that have been made in the study of psychopathy. After providing a definition of psychopathy and the association of psychopathy with violence, the article will briefly review the critical importance of the construct of psychopathy for understanding violence. It will then provide a concise summary of an emerging consensus on three of the most important advances that have been made in the understanding of psychopathy over the past half century as identified in Miller and Lynam's (2015) review of this literature. Specifically, a general agreement has been reached on the core personality traits constitutive of psychopathy, its earlier developmental manifestations, and its basic neural underpinnings.[1] Parenthetically it should be noted that some might wonder why the most widely used measure of psychopathy in both research and practice, the *Psychopathy Checklist-Revised* and its progeny, has not been included as an important advance. The reason for the omission is despite its well documented predictive validity, its construct validity remains debatable (Boduszek & Debowska, 2016).

[1] As this review is meant to selectively focus on the emerging consensus of some of the most important advances that have been made in the study of psychopathy over the past 50 years relevant some of Robin's findings (as identified in Miller & Lynam's 2015 literature review), the reader who is interested in reviews of other aspects of psychopathy can consult the following: For an overall review, see Hare and colleagues (2012). For etiology, see Hamilton, Racer, & Newman, (2015); Smith & Lilienfeld, (2015). For assessment and treatment of psychopathy, see Moreira, Almeda, Pinto, and Favero (2014).

Lastly, since most research on psychopathy has focused largely or exclusively on males (DeLisi & Piquero, 2011; Dhingra & Boduszek, 2013), the following discussion of "advances" should be interpreted as applying primarily to male psychopathy.

DEFINITION OF PSYCHOPATHY

Psychopathic personality, or psychopathy, is a condition characterized by several features such an ability to charm, manipulate, and ruthlessly exploit other persons. Psychopathic persons are "lacking in conscience and feeling for others; they selfishly take what they want and do as they please without the slightest sense of guilt or regret" (Hare, Neuman, & Widiger, 2012, p. 478). Psychopathy's "presumed" counterpart in the *Diagnostic and Statistical Manual of Mental Disorders-5* (DSM-5) (APA, 2013) is Antisocial Personality Disorder (ASPD). The designation "presumed" underlines the erroneous belief, perpetuated by the DSM-5 itself, that the two disorders are synonymous (Smith & Lilienfeld, 2015). However, although the two disorders are moderately correlated, there are some important differences (Smith & Lilienfeld, 2015). For example, psychopathy differs from ASPD in being characterized by more pronounced affective and interpersonal traits, especially *meanness* and *boldness* (Smith & Lilienfeld, 2015) which subsequently will be discussed. There is also growing support for two subtypes of psychopathy, primary versus secondary (Smith & Lilienfeld, 2015). Primary psychopathy is marked by traits of meanness, low fear, and emotional attachment that are presumed to be largely genetic in nature. In contrast, secondary psychopathy is characterized by an emotional disturbance that is the consequence of environmental factors such as childhood maltreatment and manifested in traits such as anxiety and impulsivity (Smith & Lilienfeld, 2015).

PSYCHOPATHY AND VIOLENCE

Three current reviews of psychopathy and criminality have concisely summarized the association between psychopathy and violent crime (DeLisi & Vaughn, 2015; Dhingra & Boduszek, 2013; Fox, Jennings, & Farrington, 2015). Psychopathy is one of the strongest individual-level risk factors for both general and criminal offending. For example, although the community prevalence of psychopathy is only 1% (Hare et al., 2012), psychopaths are likely responsible for up to 50% of all violent crime in the United States and approximately one in four prisoners in the United States is a psychopath (Fox et al., 2015). The violence perpetrated by psychopaths is more instrumental i.e., purposeful and predatory, than the violence committed by other offenders which tends to be more reactive, i.e., impulsive and emotion driven in response to a perceived threat or provocation (Dhingra & Boduszek, 2013). Psychopathy is also one of the strongest individual-level predictors of age of criminal onset, offending frequency, severity, recidivism, and criminal career length. Indeed, psychopathy is arguably "the most important construct in the criminal justice system" (Fox et al., 2015, p. 275). Its value in understanding and predicting criminal behaviors is now widely recognized both by forensic clinicians and the courts (Hare et al., 2012).

ADVANCE #1: CONVERGENCE ON THE BASIC PERSONALITY TRAITS OF PSYCHOPATHY

In reviewing the voluminous research on psychopathy and personality, Miller and Lynam (2015) have concluded that there is a convergence in positing three basic personality traits that characterize psychopathy. Although described somewhat differently by different theorists, the four traits of *meanness, disinhibition, boldness,* and *antisociality* adequately captures this convergence. *Meanness* is described as involving characteristics such as "deficient empathy, contempt for others, and predatory exploitativeness." *Inhibition* entails characteristics such as "impulsiveness, hostility and mistrust, difficulty in regulating emotion." *Boldness* involves "confidence, social assertiveness, and venturesomeness." Lastly, the final trait of *antisociality* requires somewhat more discussion, as the reader may be surprised to learn that there has been significant debate regarding whether or not psychopathy can be conceptualized without reference to antisociality (Hare et al., 2012; Miller & Lynam, 2015). This debate is often framed as to whether antisocial behavior represents an "inherent part of the construct or instead a nonessential correlate or consequence of it" (Miller & Lynam, 2015, p. 8). However, whatever the cogency of the nuances of such a debate, virtually all the experts would agree that antisocial behavior, in some form or other, is intimately related to psychopathy (Miller & Lynam, 2015), and, "if there is an essential behavioral feature in common across the conceptualizations of psychopathy, it is the presence of antisocial behavior" (Hare et al., 2012, p. 7).

In short, the "psychopathic syndrome is probably the most dangerous and virulent constellation of personality traits that one can imagine" (Crego & Widiger, 2015, p. 10).

ADVANCE #2: PSYCHOPATHY HAS A DEVELOPMENTALLY EARLIER MANIFESTATION

DSM-5 requires that for a diagnosis of ASPD (i.e., psychopathy) a pervasive pattern of disregard for and violation of the rights of others must begin in childhood or early adolescence. This requirement reflects a major advance in the understanding of psychopathy in that there is now a general recognition that certain psychopathic traits can be reliably identified and assessed in juveniles, even as early as 4-6 years (Assary, Salekin, & Barker, 2015; Frick & Ray, 2015; Frick, Ray, Thornton, & Kahn, 2014; Golmaryami & Frick, 2016; Miller & Lynam, 2015). Frick and colleagues (Frick & Ray, 2015; Frick, Ray, Thornton, & Kahn, 2014; Golmanyami & Frick, 2015) have focused on the trait of *meanness* which they designate as a cluster of callous-unemotional (CU) personality traits. The reason for this focus is that in contrast to other traits (e.g., *disinhibition, boldness*), CU traits designate a unique and important subgroup of antisocial youth that differ on important social, biological, cognitive, and emotional characteristics from other antisocial youth. Based upon the findings of Frick and colleagues, CU traits are now included as a DSM-5 conduct specifier titled "with limited prosocial emotions." This specifier involves traits related to lack of remorse or guilt, callous-lack of empathy, unconcerned about performance, and shallow or deficient affect. CU traits occur in 21 to 50% of clinic referred youth (Frick et al., 2014), and approximately 10% of boys with conduct problems have an early onset (age 7) of such traits which continue into adolescence (Byrd, Hawes, Loeber, & Pardini, (2016). These traits characterize an especially severe, pernicious form of antisocial youth as such youth have an earlier onset of antisocial behavior, are more likely to persist on an antisocial trajectory and to engage in more serious and destructive forms of antisocial behavior such as severe, premeditated instrumental aggression (Blair, Leibenluft, & Pine, 2014). Furthermore, even after controlling for severity and age of onset of conduct problems, juveniles with CU traits have more antisocial outcomes in adulthood when compared to other children with conduct problems without CU traits.

Lastly, it is also important to note that the sex difference in CU traits parallels the sex difference in violent psychopathy. Thus, boys score higher than girls on various CU measures from preschool to adolescence (Essau, Sasagawa, & Frick, 2006; Ezpeleta, Osa, Granero, Penelo, & Domenech, 2013; Frick, Bodin, & Barry, 2000; Humayun, Kahn, Frick, & Viding, 2014; Rowe et al., 2010) and are also four times more likely than girls to be on a stable-high trajectory for the development of CU traits in middle childhood (Fontaine, Rijskijk, McCrory, & Viding, 2010).

ADVANCE #3: THE NEURAL UNDERPINNINGS OF PSYCHOPATHY

There has been a major advance in understanding the neurobiology of the three core psychopathic traits of *meanness, inhibition,* and *boldness* based upon findings from functional neuroimaging studies which have examined the differences in neural activation in response to a variety of emotional cognitive tasks between individuals with high and low levels of these traits (Miller & Lynam, 2015). Briefly, the neurobiological findings of individuals with a high level of these traits are as follows.[2]

The neurobiology of *meanness* involves a reduced empathic response to the distress (e.g., fear, sadness, pain) of other individuals and primarily reflects reduced amygdala responsiveness to distress cues. The amygdala is a subcortical structure that can be described as the "neural seat of emotion" (Raine, 2013, p. 97). This abnormal neurobiological response can be expected to result in a reduced aversion for actions that harm others and thereby increase the likelihood that such harmful actions will occur. The neurobiology of *inhibition* involves reduced physiological arousal when punished (i.e., hyposensitivity to punishment), which primarily reflects low activity in the behavioral inhibition system (BIS) (Core & McNaughton, 2016). The BIS functions to inhibit activity so as to avoid negative or painful outcomes in the presence of aversive stimuli or punishment. The BIS contains complex

[2] For more comprehensive discussions the reader can consult several current reviews: Blair, (2013); Byrd, Loeber, & Pardini, (2014); Corr & McNaughton, (2016); Patrick, (2015); Raine, (2013); Seara-Cardoso & Viding, (2015); Zisner & Beauchaine, (2016). Also note that there is no specific discussion of the neurobiology of *antisociality* as this trait arises from a confluence of the other traits as well as other factors.

elements that are hierarchically structured involving the prefrontal cortex with connections to the hypothalamus and other subcortical components (Core & McNaughton, 2016). This abnormal neurobiological response is theorized to result in reduced responsiveness to cues signaling impending punishment and thus increases the likelihood that antisocial behavior will occur. The neurobiology of *boldness* involves a *hyposensitivity* to typical rewards (Matthys, Vanderschuren, & Schutter, 2013; Zisner & Beauchaine, 2016), which reflects a compromised mesolimbic function mediated by chronically low tonic dopamine levels and blunted phasic dopamine response to rewards (Zisner & Beauchaine, 2016). This abnormal neurobiological response is theorized to result in sensation-seeking antisocial behavior to alleviate the aversive mood state generated by this hyposensitivity.

Lastly, although it is not a *neurobiological* difference, it would be exceedingly remiss not to mention that the most well validated biological risk factor for violence (and thus by inference, psychopathy) is low resting heart rate (RHR) (Raine, 2013, 2015). For example, in a recent longitudinal study of 700,000 men, there was the remarkable finding that RHR (measured in late adolescence) was found to be a risk factor for violence more than 30 years later (Latvala, Kuja-Halkola, Almqvist, Larsson, & Lichtenstein, 2015). Furthermore, the two main theories that have been advanced to explain how low RHR increase risks for violence, fearlessness theory and impulsive stimulating seeking theory (Raine, 2013, 2015), closely correspond to two of the core traits of psychopathy - *inhibition* (i.e., relative fearless to punishment) and *boldness* (i.e., sensation seeking).

CONCLUSION

The field of psychopathy research although not without continuing controversies (see Miller & Lynam, 2015), has made several important advances over the past half century since Lee Robins monumental seminal research. This chapter provided a concise summary of three such advances (with references to other resources for more in depth discussion) for which there is robust agreement among leading researchers and theoreticians in the field. And, although other putative advances might also have a similar level of robust agreement, it would be difficult to deny the important status of these three advances. Finally, whatever advances may be made in the next half century, none is more vital than those that will hopefully be made in interventions to prevent the development in psychopathy. However, such interventions are still in their "infancy" (Ozonoff, 2016, p. 933) for two major reasons. First, the early detection of mental health disorders in general, including antisocial behaviors that are the antecedents for the development of psychopathy, poses a high risk for false-positive diagnoses (Ozonoff, 2015). For example, it is estimated that about one-half of 5-year-olds with conduct problems usually desist (Brent & Loeber, 2015) and it is currently not possible to determine which 50% do not remit and therefore should be the target of preventative efforts (Russell & Odgers, 2016).

Second, despite however many prevention programs may be deemed "promising" (De Lisi, 2015), robust evidence for the efficacy of preventative interventions for juvenile mental disorders in general (Polanczyk, 2015), including interventions for antisocial behavior, is scant. For example, Dekovic and colleagues (2011, p. 532) in a meta-analysis of early prevention programs on adult offending concluded that "there is still no convincing evidence that they can prevent adult crime." Sandler and colleagues (2014) in a meta-analysis of programs to prevent the development of conduct problems found only a small effect. Lastly, and perhaps most discouraging, are the findings from the *Fast Track* prevention program (Brent & Loeber, 2015; Dodge et al., 2015). *Fast Track* is the most comprehensive, intensive program to date involving 891 children with early onset of aggressive and disruptive behavior (age 5) who were randomly assigned to a 10-year intervention or control. The intervention was high intensity involving multimodal components that simultaneously addressed multiple risk and protective factors. However, the program had almost no effect on convictions for property crime (the most common form of delinquency) or on educational or occupational outcomes (Brent & Loeber, 2015). The lack of an effect on delinquency is perhaps the most disappointing since most criminal and anti-social behaviors are mainly perpetrated by adults with a history of delinquency, thus making the prevention of delinquency the most important intervention for preventing adult criminality (Basto-Pereira, Comecanha, Ribeiro, Maia, 2015).

REFERENCES

American Psychiatric Association (1980) *Diagnostic and statistical manual of mental disorders-III*. Washington, DC: Author.

American Psychiatric Association (2013) *Diagnostic and statistical manual of mental disorders*-5. Washington, DC: Author.

Assary, E., Salekin, R., & Barker, E. (2015). Big-five and callous-unemotional traits in preschoolers. *Journal of Psychopathology and Behavioral Assessment, 37,* 371-379.

Basto-Pereira, M., Comecanha, R., Ribeiro, S., & Maia, A. Long-term predictions of crime desistence in juvenile delinquents: a systematic review of longitudinal studies. *Aggression and Violent Behavior, 25,* 332-342.

Beauchaine, T., & Hinshaw, S. (2016). Preface. *The Oxford handbook of externalizing spectrum disorders* (xvii-xx). New York: Oxford University Press.

Blair, J. (2013). The neurobiology of psychopathic traits in youth. *Nature Reviews: Neuroscience, 14,* 786-797.

Blair, R., Leibenluft, E., & Pine, D. (2014). Conduct disorder and callous-unemotional traits in youth. *New England Journal of Medicine, 371,* 2207-2216.

Boduszek, D., & Debowska, A. (2016). Critical evaluation of psychopathy measurement (PCL-R) and SRP-III/SF) and recommendations for future research. *Journal of Criminal Justice, 44,* 1-12.

Brent, D., & Loeber, R. (2015). The prevention of detention. *American Journal of Psychiatry, 172,* 6-8.

Byrd, A., Loeber, R., & Pardini, D. (2014). Antisocial behavior, psychopathic features and abnormalities in reward and punishment processing in youth. *Clinical Child and Family Psychology Review, 17,* 125-156.

Byrd, A., Hawes, S., Loeber, R., & Pardini, D. (2016). Interpersonal callousness from childhood to adolescence: developmental trajectories and early risk factors. *Journal of Clinical Child and Adolescent Psychology.* Advanced on line publication, 4/21/16.

Corr, P., & McNaughton, N. (2015). In T. Beauchaine & S. Hinshaw (Eds.), *The Oxford handbook of externalizing spectrum disorders* (pp. 220-238). New York: Oxford University Press.

Crego, C., & Widiger, T. (2015). Psychopathy and the DSM. *Journal of Personality, 83*, 665-677.

Dekovic, M., Slagt, M., Asscher, J., Boendermaker, L., Eichelsheim, V., & Preinzie, P. (2011). Effects of early prevention programs on adult criminal offending: a meta-analysis. *Clinical Psychology Review, 31,* 532-544.

DeLisi, M. (2015). Career criminals and the antisocial life course. *Child Development Perspectives, 10,* 53-58.

DeLisi, M., & Piquero, A. (2011). New frontiers in criminal careers research, 2000-2011: A state-of-the-art review. *Journal of Criminal Justice, 39,* 289-301.

DeLisi, M., & Vaughn, M. (2015). Ingredients for criminality require genes, temperament, and psychopathic personality. *Journal of Criminal Justice, 43,* 290-294.

Dhingra, K. & Boduszek, D. (2013). Psychopathy and criminal behavior: a psychosocial research perspective. *Journal of Criminal Psychology, 3,* 83-100.

Dodge, K., Bierman, K., Coie, J., Greenberg, M., Lochman, J., McMahon, R., & Pinderhughes, E. (2015). Impact of early intervention on psychopathology, crime, and well being. *American Journal of Psychiatry, 172,* 59-70.

Essau, C., Sasagawa, S., & Frick, P. (2006). Callous-unemotional traits in a community sample of adolescents. *Assessment, 13*, 354-369.

Ezpeleta, L., De laosa, N., Granero, R., Penelo, E., & Domenech, J. (2013). Inventory of callous-unemotional traits in a community sample of preschoolers. *Journal of Clinical Child and Adolescent Psychology, 42,* 91-105.

Fontaine, N., Rijsdijk, F., McCrory, E., & Viding, E. (2010). Etiology of different developmental trajectories of callous-unemotional traits. *Journal of the American Academy of Child and Adolescent Psychiatry, 49,* 656-664.

Fox, B., Jennings, W., & Farrington, D. (2015). Bringing psychopathy into developmental and life-course criminology theories and research. *Journal of Criminal Justice, 43,* 274-289.

Frick, P., Bodin, S., & Barry, C. (2000). Psychopathic traits and conduct problems in community and clinic-referred samples of children: Further development of the psychopathy screening device. *Psychological Assessment*, *12*, 382-393.

Frick, P., & Ray, J. (2015). Evaluating callous-unemotional traits as a personality construct. *Journal of Personality, 83,* 710-722.

Frick, P., Ray, J., Thornton, L., & Kahn, R. (2014). Can callous-unemotional traits enhance understanding, diagnosis, and treatment of serious conduct problems in children and adolescents? A comprehensive review. *Psychological Bulletin, 140,* 1-57.

Golmaryami, F., & Frick, P. (2016). *Callous-unemotional traits and the development of externalizing spectrum disorders*. In T. Beauchaine & S.

Hinshaw (Eds.), The Oxford handbook of externalizing spectrum disorders (pp. 360-374). New York: Oxford University Press.

Hamilton, R., Racer, K., & Newman, J. (2015). Impaired integration in psychopathy: A unified theory of psychopathic dysfunction. *Psychological Review 122,* 770-791.

Hare, R., Neumann, C., & Widiger, T. (2012). *Psychopathy*. In T. Widiger (Ed.), The Oxford handbook of personality disorders (pp. 478-504). New York: Oxford University Press.

Humayun, S., Kahn, R., Frick, P., & Viding, E. (2014). Callous-unemotional traits and anxiety in a community sample of 7-year-olds. *Journal of Clinical Child and Adolescent Psychology*, *43*, 36-42.

Latvala, A., Kuja-Halkola, R., Almqvist, C., Larsson, H., & Lichtenstein, P. (2015). A longitudinal study of resting heart rate and violent criminality in more than 700,000 men. *JAMA Psychiatry, 72,* 971-978.

Matthys, W., Vanderschuren, L., & Schutter, L. (2013). The neurobiology of oppositional defiant disorder and conduct disorder: Altered functioning in three mental domains. *Development and Psychopathology, 25,* 193-207.

Miller, J., & Lyman, D. (2015). Psychopathy and personality: Advances and debates. *Journal of Personality, 83,* 585-592.

Moreira, D., Almeida, F., Pinto, M., & Favero, M. (2014). Psychopathy: A comprehensive review of its assessment and intervention. *Aggression and Violence, 19,* 1911-195.

Ozonoff, S. (2015). Early detection of mental health and neurodevelopmental disorders. *Journal of Child Psychology and Psychiatry, 56,* 933-935.

Patrick, C. (2015). Physiological correlates of psychopathy, antisocial personality, habitual aggression and violence. *Current Topics in Behavioral Neuroscience, 21,* 197-227.

Polonczyk, G. (2015). Addressing the evidence gap on preventative interventions. *Journal of the American Academy of Child and Adolescent Psychiatry, 54,* 793-794.

Raine, A. (2013). *The anatomy of violence*. New York: Pantheon Books.

Raine, A. (2015). Low resting heart rate as an unequivocal risk factor for both the perpetration and exposure to violence. *JAMA Psychiatry, 72,* 962-964.

Robins, L. (1966). *Deviant children grown up: A sociological and psychiatric study of sociopathic personality*. Huntington New York: Robert E. Krieger Publishing Company.

Robins, L. (1978). Sturdy childhood predictors of adult antisocial behavior: replications from longitudinal studies. *Psychological Medicine, 8,* 611-622.

Rowe, R., Maughan, B., Moran, P., Ford, T., Briskman, J., & Goodman, R. (2010). The role of callous and unemotional traits in the diagnosis of conduct disorder. *Journal of Child Psychology and Psychiatry*, *51*, 688-695.

Russell, M. & Odgers, C. (2016). Desistance and life-course persistence: Findings from longitudinal studies using group-based trajectory modeling of antisocial behavior. In K. Heilbrum (Ed.), *APA handbook of psychology and juvenile justice* (pp. 159-175). Washington DC: APA Press.

Sandler, I., Wolchik, S., Cruden, G., Mahrer, M., Ahn, S., Brincks, A., & Brown, C. (2014). Overview of meta-analyses of the prevention of mental health, substance use, and conduct problems. *Annual review of clinical psychology, 10,* 243-273.

Seara-Cardoso, A., & Viding, E. (2015). Functional neuroscience of psychopathic personality in adults. *Journal of Personality, 83,* 723-737.

Smith, S., & Lilienfeld, S. (2015). The response modulation hypothesis of psychopathy: A meta-analysis and narrative analysis. *Psychological Bulletin, 41,* 1145-1177.

Zisner, A., & Beauchaine, T. (2015). *Midbrain neural mechanisms of trait impulsivity*. In T. Beauchaine & S. Hinshaw (Eds.), The Oxford handbook of externalizing spectrum disorders (pp. 184-200). New York: Oxford University Press.

In: Psychopathology
Editor: Jeremy Williams
ISBN: 978-1-63485-745-1

Chapter 8

BIOFEEDBACK. AN EVIDENCE-BASED APPROACH TO THE MANAGEMENT OF TWO MAJOR HEALTH DISEASES: OBESITY AND PERINATAL MOOD DISORDERS

Gaia de Campora[1,*], PhD, Luciano Giromini[2], PhD, and Richard Gevirtz[3], PhD

[1]Department of Dynamic and Clinical Psychology, Sapienza, University of Rome, Italy
[2]Department of Psychology, University of Turin, Italy
[3]Department of Clinical Psychology, California School of Professional Psychology, Alliant International University, San Diego, California, US

ABSTRACT

Biofeedback application is an evidence-based technique to induce relaxation. Literature highlighted the efficacy of this technique in helping selected patients modify specific responses or response patterns associated with a mental disorder. For example, a ''*relaxed*'' Autonomic Nervous System (ANS) pattern include slow, regular heart rate, increased heart rate variability, dominance of EEG frequencies in the theta to low alpha bandwidth range, and warm skin temperature due to increased vasodilatation. Vice versa, an "*hyperactivation*" is reflected by increased

* Address correspondence to: gaiadecampora@gmail.com.

heart rate and decreased heart rate variability, high electrodermal activity, along with higher frequency EEG bandwidth ranges in high-alpha or beta, often reflecting anxiety and/or panic states (Putman 2000). Thus, biofeedback which targets maladaptive physiology may help enable patients to recognize and change problematic physical symptoms (Pal Singh and Kaur 2007) that may be promoting and/or perpetuating the associated psychological problem.

The clinical efficacy of biofeedback has been investigated in a range of psychiatric disorders, such as anxiety and depressive disorders, and through different approaches such as the EEG neurofeedback and the heart rate variability biofeedback (HRVB).

Aim of the current review is to report the state of the art of the literature about the use of the biofeedback as a tool to reduce psychopathological symptoms, and to improve mental health condition. In detail, our goal is to describe the efficacy of biofeedback on two major health diseases, namely perinatal mood disorders and eating disorders.

1. Biofeedback Background

Nowadays, it is well known that stress is critical to both physical and mental health. Stressful situations decrease the likelihood of cancer survival tumors (Conti, Angelucci, Ferri, Maccauro, Caraffa, Doyle, Fulcheri and Cianchetti 2011), threaten quality of life for those facing chronic health problems, increase the risk of worsening symptoms of various medical conditions such as psoriasis or inflammatory bowel syndrome (Mayer, Naliboff, Chang and Coutinho 2001), and may possibly even cause – or contribute to causing – psychological and physical health conditions, such as depression (Hammen 2005), anxiety (Robinson 1990), and headache (Nash and Thebarge 2006).

The current chapter presents a relatively recent approach to help individuals deal with stress and achieve relaxation, and describes its application on two specific clinical conditions, i.e., perinatal mood disorders and eating disorders.

The main idea beyond this method is that the Autonomic Nervous System (ANS) plays a key role in the management of stress, and that therefore learning how to influence ANS activity may affect our ability to react to stressful situations in a more flexible and adaptive manner. Indeed, while the sympathetic nervous system predominantly responds to stressful situations and the parasympathetic typically intervenes afterwards to restore calm and relaxation, continuous withdrawal of parasympathetic activity may lead to a persistent, sympathetic-predominant autonomic balance style, which reduces psychophysiological flexibility and weakens stress-regulation (Porges 1995; McEwen 2004; Thayer and Sternberg 2006). As such, by actively strengthening ANS flexibility, one may interrupt a vicious circle in which exposure to stress impoverishes the individual's abilities to adaptively cope with stress, thus exposing him- or her-self to additional, potentially threatening sources of stress.

This approach is referred to as "biofeedback," and may be adopted with several, clinical conditions. Below we briefly review its application on two specific, mental health disorders that, in our view, could largely benefit from biofeedback techniques.

2. Biofeedback as a Self-Regulatory Technique: Application on Obese Individuals

Biofeedback (BFB) application is an evidence-based technique to induce relaxation. Essentially, BFB helps individuals to modify their typical responses or response patterns, thereby producing major changes in their habitual ANS activity and improving autonomic flexibility. BFB techniques have been used since their introduction (Miller 1973) in various contexts of clinical practice and rehabilitation (Giggins et al. 2013). Fundamentally, the main goal of BFB techniques is to promote self-regulation.

It has been suggested that obese patients may benefit from BFB in several ways. Among them, using BFB to enhance self-control and self-efficacy seems to be particularly promising.

Indeed, individuals affected by obesity often feel frustrated and stressed out by their repetitive, unsuccessful weight loss attempts, and by their persistent exposure to stigmatization. Consciously or not, they regularly attempt to control these negative emotions by using food as a consolation mean (de Campora et al. 2016). However, this behavior puts them in a dangerous vicious cycle (Teufel et al. 2011), in which dysfunctional eating generates a sense of poor self-control and self-efficacy, thus in turn further increasing their risk for additional dysfunctional eating and weight problems (Laugero et al. 2011).

Additionally, many obese people report having "forbidden food" that they need to avoid, as they cannot control their behavior whenever they are exposed to it. Yet, when they do find that food or somehow get exposed to it, they tend to be subject to impulsive eating (Schlundt et al. 1990), which also associates with senses of poor self-control and self-efficacy. As such, BFB techniques may be used with obese patients so as to reduce stress, act on self-control and self-efficacy, and thus break the dangerous loop leading from stress to dysfunctional eating and vice versa.

According to Bozinovska's (2013) conceptualization, the hypothalamus plays a key role in influencing self-efficacy, confidence, willpower, and self-control. Indeed, it is implicated in several functional loops that are important to motivation and, therefore, also action. Accordingly, the idea beyond the use of BFB to help obese patients enhance their sense of self-control and self-efficacy is that certain hypothalamic-related, physiological parameters are below the threshold of conscious awareness, and that therefore by seeing them on a computer screen, one may learn how to influence them, along with their achievement motivation system (Mahoney 1976; Miller 1980).

Another interesting application of BFB related to obesity has been discussed by Ciampolini (2006), who introduced the *hunger biofeedback technique* based on the assumption that Blood Glucose (BG) levels and physical hunger fluctuate together. In this approach, also called "hunger recognition," participants are given a portable BG self-monitoring device and instructed to eat only when this BG device confirms the presence of physical hunger (i.e., BG in the target range of 60 - 85 mg/dl). Some research findings show that adults of varying weight statuses learned to accurately recognize physical hunger, achieved significant weight loss, and improved their insulin resistance.

The strength of this technique is that it teaches people to identify physical hunger sensations in a short time, such as less than 14 days. Potential limits to disseminate the use of hunger biofeedback are related to BG self-monitoring, which can be experienced as uncomfortable. However, vicarious learning is a powerful tool for learning new behaviors. Observing those who determine what, when, and how much to eat based on internal hunger/satiety cues may help disinhibited eaters learn internal dietary control.

Another application of BFB is called BELI (Biofeedback Enhanced Lifestyle Intervention), which has been developed with the goal to modify and reduce patterns of dysregulated eating, so as to achieve weight loss. It is based on the behavior change theory and it stresses the importance of strategies like internal dietary control, discouraging rigid dietary restraints, and addressing emotional and external overeating. BELI also includes unconventional techniques like hunger biofeedback, but this approach needs a deepen attention for the high risk of dropout.

It is important to conduct small-scale studies to determine acceptability and feasibility of interventions in an effort to conserve resources for larger randomized controlled pilot studies.

3. The Use of BFB for the Treatment of Perinatal Depression

Biofeedback may have a promising role as a complementary treatment for perinatal depression. Indeed, while BFB may be effective in treating all forms of major depression, it may be particularly useful among women going through the postpartum stage, as their sympathovagal balance needs to be re-adjusted after delivery. Probably because of a need to adapt to hemodynamic changes and aortocaval compression associated with enlarged uterus, during the late stages of pregnancy the autonomic balance of the woman shifts toward a sympathetic-predominant style, characterized by parasympathetic withdrawal (Walther et al. 2005; Matsuo et al. 2007). Immediately after the delivery, the ANS tends to return to a pre-pregnancy state, via parasympathetic activation. This process, however, is not risk-free: if it does not occur smoothly, it may put postpartum women at a higher risk for physical and mental disorders, due to their vulnerability to external stressors being increased.

For this reason, and because at this stage of the life, beginning psychotherapy may be difficult (if not undesirable), BFB might potentially be a very effective tool to promote a positive change and prevent postpartum depression. In fact, the application of BFB on the Heart Rate Variability (HRV), also referred to as "heart rate variability biofeedback" (HRVB), has already shown its efficacy on depressive and anxious symptoms (Karavidas et al. 2007; Christopher et al. 2012; George et al. 2000; Gevirtz, 2013; Lagos et al. 2008; Rene et al. 2011). It also has demonstrated efficacy in the treatment of attention-deficit disorder, headaches, hypertension, temporomandibular disorders, urinary incontinence, and fibromyalgia (Hassett et al. 2007; Horowitz 2006). Thus, one may speculate that HRVB will likely be efficacious also in the treatment of postpartum depression.

Technically, HRVB techniques utilize instruments that measure and "feed back" information about cardio-respiratory activity, therefore enabling an individual to interpret and respond to these signals for the purposes of improving their own health and well-being (Association for Applied

Psychophysiology and Biofeedback Inc. 2011; Barragan Loayza et al. 2011). The reason why HRVB may be a powerful tool in the treatment of depressive states is that depression is associated with alterations in autonomic function, such as impaired baroreflex sensitivity, changes in heart rate, and reduced heart rate variability (HRV) (Karavidas et al. 2007). Also, increases in heart rate variability have been demonstrated to occur in patients successfully treated with antidepressants (Balogh et al. 1993). Furthermore, a review of over 20 studies has recently revealed an association between abnormalities of HRV and the presence of anxiety (Cohen and Benjamin 2006).

Depression during pregnancy – among other risks - was found associated with an increased risk of preterm birth, defined as giving birth at less than 37 completed weeks of gestation (Shea et al. 2008; Misra et al. 2010). The pathogenetic link between stress and preterm birth has been suggested to be mediated by autonomic dysfunction including vasomotor disturbances (Gennaro and Hennessy 2003; Field et al. 2008). Autonomic dysfunction in patients with anxiety and depression was recently shown to be mediated by a reduced parasympathetic and/or increased sympathetic tone (Kemp et al. 2012). HRV-biofeedback has been shown to lower levels of depression when administered to patients with depressive disorders but not in healthy controls (Karavidas et al. 2007; Siepmann et al. 2008). Siepmann et al. (2014), in their study, provided the HRVB to women addressing preterm labour. Their findings showed a significant reduction of chronic stress, and a trend toward less preterm birth, even if this finding was not statistically significant. Taken together, these findings suggest that using HRVB to prevent or treat depression may be particularly useful during the first stages of postpartum.

CONCLUSION

Biofeedback opens a new channel of communication for the perception of our own body and emotions. Becoming aware of our physiological states can lead to a more functional way of being. Bringing awareness to hand temperature, respiration, blood pressure or heart beat can lead to the improvement in our attention to body activity that is usually self-regulated automatically. Nowadays, many of the symptoms individuals report can be seen as a breakdown of this self-regulation mechanism, in that we all tend to face the multiple challenges and tasks of our lives as if we were going on autopilot. This is the main reason why recovery of the capacity to pay attention to our mind-body functioning can effectively improve our health. And this is also the reason why BFB may effectively help us move toward better-controlled function, thus improving self-regulation. Indeed, the mind-body system has internal pathways to keep itself updated about various physical states, and via BFB, this mechanism is supported by external sources that, in a nutshell, provide information on how to re-normalize regulatory function.

REFERENCES

Association for Applied Psychophysiology and Biofeedback Inc. (2011) About Biofeedback. http://www.aapb.org/i4a/pages/index.cfm?pageid03463.

Barragan Loayza I. M., Sola I., Juando Prats C. (2011) Biofeedback for pain management during labour. *Cochrane Database Syst. Rev.*, 6: CD006168.

Balogh S., Fitzpatrick D. F., Hendricks S. E., Paige S. R. (1993) Increases in heart rate variability with successful treatment in patients with major depressive disorder. *Psychopharmacol. Bull.*, 29:201–206.

Bozinovska, L. (2013). Physiology, Medical Physiology and Engineered Physiology of Obesity., Paper presented at Biological Research Training Care for Minority Summer Seminar, South Carolina State University, Orangeburg, SC.

Ciampolini, M. and Bianchi, R. (2006) Training to Estimate Blood Glucose and to Form Associations with Initial Hunger. *Nutrition and Metabolism,* 3, 42.

Christopher, P. P., Leykin, Y., Appelbaum, P. S., Holtzheimer, P. E., III, Mayberg, H. S., and Dunn, L. B. (2012). Enrolling in deep brain stimulation research for depression: Influences on potential subjects' decision making. *Depression and Anxiety*, 29(2), 139–146.

Cohen H., Benjamin J. (2006) Power spectrum analysis and cardiovascular morbidity in anxiety disorders. *Auton. Neurosci.*, 128:1–8.

Conti C. M., Angelucci D., Ferri M., Maccauro G., Caraffa A., Doyle R., Fulcheri M., Cianchetti E. Relationship between cancer and psychology: an updated history.

de Campora, G., Giromini, L., Larciprete, G., Li Volsi, V., and Zavattini, G. C. (2014). The impact of maternal overweight and emotion regulation on early eating behaviors. *Eating behaviors*, 15(3), 403-409. doi:10.1016/j.eatceh.2014.04.013.

de Campora, G., and Meldolesi, C. (2014). Indexes of psychopathology risk in gestational overweight. *Giornale italiano di psicologia*, 41(3), 601-610.

de Campora G., Larciprete G., Delogu A. M., Meldolesi C., Giromini L. (2016). A longitudinal study on emotional dysregulation and obesity risk: From pregnancy to 3 years of age of the baby. *Appetite*, 96, 95-111.

Emeran A. Mayer, Bruce D. Naliboff, Lin Chang, Santosh V. Coutinho (2001) Stress and irritable bowel syndrome. *American Journal of Physiology - Gastrointestinal and Liver Physiology,* **Vol.** 280 **no.** 4, G519-G524.

Gennaro, S., and Hennessy, M. D. (2003). Psychological and physiological stress: Impact on preterm birth. *Journal of Obstetric, Gynecologic, and Neonatal Nursing,* 32(5), 668–675.

Giggins O., U. Persson, and B. Caulfield. (2013). Biofeedback in Rehabilitation. *Journal of Neuroengineering and Rehabilitation*, 10: 60.

Gevirtz R. (2013) The Promise of Heart Rate Variability Biofeedback: Evidence-Based Applications. *Biofeedback*, Volume 41, Issue 3, pp. 110–120.

George, M. S., Sackeim, H. A., Marangell, L. B., Husain, M. M., Nahas, Z., Lisanby, S. H., Ballenger, J. C. et al. (2000). Vagus nerve stimulation. A potential therapy for resistant depression? *Psychiatric Clinics of North America,* 23(4), 757–783.

Gnazzo, A., Guerriero, V., Di Folco, S., Zavattini, G. C., and de Campora, G. (2015). Skin to skin interactions. Does the infant massage improve the couple functioning?. *Frontiers in psychology,* 6:1468. doi:10.3389/fpsyg.2015.01468.

Hammen C. (1990) Stress and Depression. *Annual Review of Clinical Psychology,* Vol. 1: 293-319.

Hassett, A. L., Radvanski, D. C., Vaschillo, E. G., et al. (2007). A pilot study of the efficacy of heart rate variability (HRV) biofeedback in patients with fibromyalgia. *Applied Psychophysiology and Biofeedback*, 32(1), 1–10.

Horowitz S. (2006) Biofeedback applications. *Journal of Altern Complement,* 12:275–281.

Karavidas, M. K., Lehrer, P. M., Vaschillo, E., et al. (2007). Preliminary results of an open label study of heart rate variability biofeedback for the treatment of major depression. *Applied Psychophysiology and Biofeedback*, 32(1), 19–30.

Karavidas M. K., Lehrer P. M., Vaschillo E., Vaschillo B., Marin H., Buyske S., Malinovsky I., Radvanski D., Hassett A. (2007) Preliminary results of an open label study of heart rate variability biofeedback for the treatment of major depression. *Appl. Psychophysiol. Biofeedback*, 32:19–30.

Kemp, A. H., Quintana, D. S., Felmingham, K. L., Matthews, S., and Jelinek, H. F. (2012). Depression, comorbid anxiety disorders, and heart rate variability in physically healthy, unmedicated patients: implications for cardiovascular risk. *PLoS One*, 7(2), e30777.

Lagos, L., Vaschillo, B., Vaschillo, E., Lehrer, P. M., and Bates, M. (2008). Heart rate variability biofeedback as a strategy for dealing with competitive anxiety: A case study. *Biofeedback,* 36(3), 109–115.

Laghi, F., Baiocco, R., Ghezzi, E., Petrocchi, N., Pace, C. S. (2012). La fiducia nell'attaccamento ai genitori e ai pari e i disturbi del comportamento alimentare in adolescenza. Psicologia Clinica dello Sviluppo, XVI(3), 557-578. doi:10.1449/ 38839. ISSN: 1824078X (SCOPUS indexed).

Laugero, K. D., Falcon, L. M., and Tucker, K. L. (2011). Relationship between perceived stress and dietary and activity patterns in older adults participating in the Boston puerto rican health study. *Appetite,* 56(1), 194–204.

Mahoney, M. (1976). The Behavioral Treatment of Obesity: A Reconnaissance. *Biofeedback and Self Regulation 1*, (1): 127-133.

Matsuo, H., Inoue, K., Hapsari, E. D., Kitano, K., and Shiotani, H. (2007). Change of autonomic nervous activity during pregnancy and its modulation of labor assessed by spectral heart rate variability analysis. *Clinical and Experimental Obstetrics and Gynecology*, 34(2), 73–79.

McEwen B. S. (2004). Protection and Damage from Acute and Chronic Stress: Allostasis and Allostatic Overload and Relevance to the Pathophysiology of Psychiatric Disorders. *Annals of the New York Academy of Sciences,* 1–7.

Miller, N. E. (1973). "Biofeedback: Evaluation of a New Technique." (Invited editorial). *New England Journal of Medicine*, 290, 684-685.

Miller, N. E. (1980). Review of the "The Pain of Obesity" (1976) by A. J. Stunkard. In *Biofeedback and Self-Regulation*, 5: 347-349.

Misra, D., Strobino, D., and Trabert, B. (2010). Effects of social and psychosocial factors on risk of preterm birth in black women. *Paediatric and Perinatal Epidemiology,* 24(6), 546–554.

Nash J. M. Thebarge R. W. (2006) Understanding Psychological Stress, Its Biological Processes, and Impact on Primary Headache. *Headache: The Journal of Head and Face Pain*, 46(9):1377-86.

Pace C. S., Cavanna, D., Guiducci, V., and Bizzi, F. (2015). When parenting fails: alexithymia and attachment states of mind in mothers of female patients with eating disorders. *Frontiers in Psychology*, section Psychology for Clinical Settings, 6, Article 1145, 1-11. doi: 10.3389/fpsyg.2015.01145.

Porges S. W. (1995). Cardiac vagal tone: A physiological index of stress. *Neuroscience and Biobehavioral Reviews*, Volume 19, Issue 2, 225–233

Rene, R., Gevirtz, R., Muench, F., and Birkhead, E. (2011). The efficacy of a portable heart rate variability (HRV) feedback device in conjunction with mental health treatment of clients with major depressive disorder enrolled in a county welfare to work program. San Diego, CA: Alliant University.

Robinson (1990). Stress and anxiety. *The Nursing Clinics of North America,* 25(4):935-943.

Shea, A. K., Kamath, M. V., Fleming, A., Streiner, D. L., Redmond, K., and Steiner, M. (2008). The effect of depression on heart rate variability during pregnancy. *Clinical Autonomic Research*, 18(4), 203–212.

Siepmann, M., Aykac, V., Unterdo¨rfer, J., Petrowski, K., and Mueck-Weymann, M. (2008). A pilot study on the effects of heart rate variability biofeedback in patients with depression and in healthy subjects. *Applied Psychophysiology and Biofeedback,* 33(4), 195–201.

Siepmann M., Una-Dorothea Hennig U. D. Siepmann T., Nitzsche K., Mu¨ck-Weymann M., Petrowski K. Weidner K. The Effects of Heart Rate Variability Biofeedback in Patients with Preterm Labour *Appl. Psychophysiol. Biofeedback,* (2014) 39:27–35.

Schlundt, D. G., Hill, J. O., Sbrocco, T., Pope-Cordle, J., and Kasser, T. (1990). Obesity: A biogenetic or biobehavioral problem. *International Journal of Obesity,* 14(9), 815–828.

Thayer J. F., Sternberg E. (2006). Beyond Heart Rate Variability Vagal Regulation of Allostatic Systems. *Annals of the New York Academy of Sciences,* Volume 1088, 361–372.

Teufel M., Stephan K., Kowalski A., Ka¨sberger S., Enck P., Zipfel S., Giel K. E. (2013) Impact of Biofeedback on Self-efficacy and Stress Reduction in Obesity: A Randomized Controlled Pilot Study *Appl. Psychophysiol. Biofeedback,* 38(3):177-84.

Walther, T., Wessel, N., Baumert, M., Stepan, H., Voss, A., and Faber, R. (2005). Longitudinal analysis of heart rate variability in chronic hypertensive pregnancy. *Hypertension Research*, 28(2), 113–118.

Biographical Sketch

Name: **Gaia de Campora**

Affiliation: Department of Dynamic and Clinical Psychology, Sapienza, University of Rome, Rome, Italy

Education: Phd in Dynamic and Clinical Psychology, Perinatal Psychologist and Feeding Counsellor

Address: piazza maria teresa 6, Turin, Italy

Research and Professional Experience: My main interest is obesity and emotion regulation with a special attention to the early risk factors and to the intergenerational transmission processes. Also, my professional experience is on the field of perinatal stage and feeding disorders.

Honors:

Italian psychology association: Award for research abroad: "Socio-cultural factors and eating habits: a cross cultural investigation between Italy and US

Allan Rosenblatt Award 2012: *First Place Certificate for* Outstanding *Presentation*" in Psychodynamic Research. Conferito dalla San Diego Society and Psychoanalytic Institute

Reviewer for the following international Journals:

"Appetite"(IF 3.125)

"Eating Behaviors" (IF 1.796)

"BMC Pregnancy and Childbirth" (IF 2.15)

"Journal of Women's Health and Wellness".

"Global Journal of Health Science".

"Eating and Weight Disorders: Studies on Anorexia, Bulimia and Obesity" (IF 0.785)

Member of the 'Editorial Board:

"International Journal of Psychology and Psychoanalysis".

"Journal of Obesity and Weight Loss Medication".

"Obesity-Open Access".

"International Journal of Psychology and Behavioral Analysis"

Publications Last Three Years:

1) de Campora G., Giromini L., Larciprete G., Li Volsi V., Zavattini G. C. (2014). The impact of maternal overweight and emotion regulation

on early eating behaviors, *Eating Behaviors*, Volume 15, Issue 3, August, Pages 403–409, DOI: 10.1016/j.eatbeh.2014.04.013.

2) Giromini L., de Campora G., Brusadelli E., D'Onofrio E., Zennaro A., Zavattini G. C. and Lang M. (2015, July 7). Validity and Reliability of the Interpersonal Competence Questionnaire (ICQ): Empirical Evidence from an Italian Study Journal of Psychopathology and Behavioral Assessment. Advance Online Publication. DOI 10.1007/s10862-015-9499-5.
3) Gnazzo A., Guerriero V., Di Folco S., Zavattini G. C., de Campora G. Skin to skin interactions. Does the infant massage improve the couple functioning? *Frontiers in Psychology*, 6:1468. doi: 10.3389/fpsyg.2015.01468.
4) de Campora G., Larciprete G., Delogu A. M., Meldolesi C., Giromini L. (2016). A Longitudinal study on emotion dysregulation and obesity risk: from pregnancy to 3 years of age of the baby. *Appetite*, Volume 96, 95-101, doi:10.1016/j.appet.2015.09.012.
5) de Campora G., D'Onofrio E., Zavattini G. C. (2014) Fattori di rischio precoci nello sviluppo del sovrappeso in età pediatrica. Una rassegna della letteratura. *Giornale Italiano di Psicologia*, n.2, Maggio, pp.265-294, DOI: 10.1421/77906.
6) de Campora G., Meldolesi C. (2014) Indicatori di rischio psicopatologico nel rischio di sovrappeso gestazionale. *Giornale Italiano di Psicologia*, n.3, Settembre, pp. 601-610, DOI: 10.1421/78505.
7) Guerriero V., Gnazzo A., Zavattini G. C., de Campora G. (2015) Quando la relazione non funziona: il maltrattamento su bambini con Disturbo dello Spettro Autistico. Una revisione della letteratura. Maltrattamento e Abuso all'Infanzia, n.3, pp. 55-83, DOI: 10.3280/MAL2015-003004.
8) Di Folco S., de Campora G., Zavattini G. C. (in press). Sintonie e dissintonie nei legami precoci: traiettorie di valutazione e considerazioni cliniche nei contesti ad alto rischio per lo sviluppo infantile. Maltrattamento e Abuso all'Infanzia.
9) de Campora G., Gnazzo A., Fragomeni P. R., Giromini L. (in press). Indicatori fisiologici della capacità di regolare le emozioni. Giornale Italiano di Psicologia.

INDEX

B

C

D

E

F

G

H

I

N

Q

R

S

T